The Railway Carriage Child

Wendy Fletcher

First published in England 2019
By
Whittlesey Wordsmiths

A CIP record of this book is available from the British Library

ISBN
978-1-9164817-3-2

DEDICATION

I would like to dedicate this book to

EDWARD STOREY

A fellow Whittlesey writer

who shared my passion for the fens

and gave me the courage and confidence

to tell my story

also to IAN BRIDGE

who met the ghost of Granny

ACKNOWLEDGEMENTS

I would like to acknowledge all those who have helped and supported me in the dual task of writing this book and renovating the carriages.

Whether you have yawned at the ninety-third reading of the same chapter, or lent me your tools, advised on the technical stuff, or been covered in paint and woodworm treatment, you know who you are.

Special thanks to my daughters, sons-in-law
and grandchildren. I couldn't have taken this journey without you.

I would also like to express my gratitude to:
- Whittlesey Wordsmiths
  https://whittleseywordsmiths.com
- Members of the local U3A
  https://u3asites.org.uk/whittlesey/welcome
- Waveney Valley & District Preservation Society
- The Whittlesey Mud Wall Group, for photograph
  whittleseymudwallsgroup@gmail.com
- North Norfolk Railway Society
- Gordon Maslim, Vintage Carriage Trust Surveyor
- Patrick Burnside, for photograph
- Whittlesey and March Museums

Foreword

Against a backdrop of the Cambridgeshire fens, lies the small market town of Whittlesey. Here are many features of historical and architectural interest, including two medieval churches, a 17th century Butter Cross and rare examples of 18th century mud boundary walls.

Less well known, but still quite remarkable, are the pair of Victorian railway carriages which stand just outside the town.

Originally built for Great Eastern Railways in 1887, they have been home to Wendy's family since 1935.

Now, for the first time, Wendy shares the fascinating story of her childhood, growing up as a Railway Carriage Child in the mid to late 20th century.

With a wonderful memory for detail, she paints a picture so vivid that we are there with her.

Through the eyes of an exuberant child, whose imagination outpaced her years, we meet the characters central to her life: an ancient Granny, still governed by the old fen traditions of an earlier era, a domineering Mother, a long-suffering Father, and Grandfather who died before her birth but still inspires her dreams.

With the humour of hindsight, Wendy brings alive a time when life moved at a gentler pace.

The final chapter follows Wendy as she returns to live in the carriages as an adult, continuing the renovation and preservation, to ensure that they survive for another generation of her family.

Philip Cumberland, Whittlesey Wordsmith

The Carriages in 1953

Granny and her sister with the carriages decorated for
the Queen's Coronation

Disclaimer

The reader is advised that the Recipes and Remedies
may not have been tested to meet today's
Health and Safety regulations,
But rest assured that no mice or moles suffered in the
compilation of this book

CONTENTS

1 Listening to the Dawn

 I look back on a child's lifetime of listening to the gentle sounds of dawn through the changing seasons. Each morning as I woke, I was bathed in the early light, spreading from the blurred patches that were the windows above my bed. From the time of my birth, until I married, I slept in that same room.

I felt the stillness all around me but my bedroom had not been designed to stay still. Those windows were meant to look out on ever-changing scenery and an outside door should have allowed me to jump down at a new destination but this only happened in my child-sized imagination.

For many years I assumed that my home had started its life here, in a field just outside the Fenland market town of Whittlesey, as had all the houses which slowly grew up along our road. I had no knowledge of the origin of the two carriages built in Stratford, East London, in 1887, nor any thought of the forty years they had spent carrying passengers through the countryside, bearing the livery of Great Eastern Railway. I lived for so long, surrounded by so much history, but with so little appreciation.

To older eyes, it must have been apparent that there was something unusual here. We didn't have bricks like other people's houses, nor square corners. There were no walls that disappeared underground to rest on solid foundations. We had wooden panels that gently curved at the edges and we sat on dark railway sleepers. Underneath, was a space where a small child could have crawled and hidden in the cool darkness but wire mesh secured all the way round, originally to keep out small creatures such as chickens and rats, made that impossible. I remained largely unaware of these different features because we do not notice the familiar, nor question the commonplace.

In the 1920s, when old carriages were taken off the rails, they were often bought by local families as living accommodation. The new occupants converted them so successfully that their earlier purpose was all but lost. Many were incorporated into bungalows with an outer layer of bricks. Chimneys, washhouses and lavatories were built on. Interior walls were lined with boards to provide insulation and a flat surface which could be wallpapered. Ours remained in largely original condition on the outside, but homely features had been added inside, including three fireplaces and false ceilings. The doors were panelled with hardboard and each room was papered. There was little indication of a previous life.

If I could have peeled back the layers of wallpaper to reveal the sign above my bed, warning, 'It is dangerous for passengers to put their heads out of the carriage windows', I would surely have asked questions. If I had pulled the hardboard from the doors and seen the bold number threes, declaring that these were third class compartments, my curiosity might have been stirred. The first sign that did catch my eye was 'smoking', etched into the glass of my grandmother's bedroom window and that just seemed silly as Granny had never smoked in her life.

It would be many years before I saw the tie-rods which hold together the underframe members, or the casting in the middle of the headstock for a draw-hook. These features were always just inches below the floorboards, but unseen and unknown.

Granny had her own room as head of the household. I shared my parents' bedroom. Their double bed was just a foot from mine, but they were always up by the time I woke in the morning and I felt pleasantly alone before the bustle of the day.

I had learned to greet winter mornings with caution. The pale light could be deceptive: sometimes struggling through a sky of heavy cloud, sometimes reflecting off a garden drenched by overnight rain, or even cloaked in a layer of snow which had crept down since my bedtime. In very cold winters, snow built up on the ledges outside and I had to kneel on my bed to see over it.

The windows, still with the original glass, were draughty and condensation built up inside. Frost dressed them in an amazing pattern of falling leaves and intricate swirls which I traced with a finger until my hand got too cold. Then I retreated to the warmth of my flannelette sheets and the extra blankets added for the season.

It wasn't unusual to snuggle back down until at least ten o'clock on such mornings. The clock on the dressing table ticked softly and slowly. It seemed that there was always plenty of time. I knew Mother wouldn't allow me out to play too early. She would say 'Wait 'til the day's got up proper,' as I pleaded to be released from the kitchen door.

If I did have to be up early for some reason, I huddled in my dressing gown as she hunched over the hearth, willing a few damp sticks to catch light, aided only by a scrunched up sheet of newspaper and a match. Sometimes, even the matches were too damp to strike. An age passed before a curl of smoke and the smell of smouldering gave hope that the fire would crackle into life. She blew steadily between pursed lips to encourage the tiny flames, the yellow and pale gold gradually turning to a reassuring orange. Some days she resorted to a spoonful of sugar sprinkled carefully onto the wood. Finally, the coal was added, very gingerly, one piece at a time, so as not to disturb the criss-crossed kindling. An occasional burst of gas hissed blue as the coal ignited. This time-consuming ritual must have been played out daily in that room, from a time when Mother would have watched Granny, as I watched now.

On these raw mornings, I curled up in the armchair, waiting for the kettle to boil for our first pot of tea. Occasionally, I was allowed to hold a round of bread on a long fork, giving it the unique flavour of toast made on an open fire. An enamel butter-dish was placed right on the edge of the stove, so just enough butter melted at one side. Often, brown butter sizzled in the bottom of the dish, the larger lump skidding around in it. Timing was crucial.

All through the winter months, buckets of coal and wood were carried in during the day and lined up in the veranda, which had been built to cover the space between the back door and the outside lavatory, so the lavatory was now not outside, although it was still not inside the carriages. This structure was completely enclosed, bearing no resemblance to the traditional veranda with open sides and railings: another anomaly which I never questioned.

It was just reassuring to know we had those reserve buckets in case the weather got worse later, and it seemed it always did. A bright, crisp start to the day, glistening sun on a white expanse of garden, calling me to don Wellingtons, scarf and bobble-hat, often turned into a dull afternoon with fen skies hanging low, heavy with unfallen snow. An occasional car passed the end of the front garden in a slow, slushy spray and the wind began to rise.

By teatime, it felt good to sit by the fire in the fading light, listening for the bus to pull up and draw away again, heralding Father's safe return from the city. His journey was not long but it was across open, windswept fen where drifts gathered. I had once seen a bus being hauled back by a tractor and, ever-after, I awaited his return with unease.

As soon as he was inside, Mother drew a thick curtain over the kitchen door. Brown paper blinds, still in place after the war, were pulled down at the windows. The night was shut out although it was only about half past six. As we pulled our chairs closer to the hearth, thankful that we had those extra buckets of coal and wood, we knew that the path to the coal place would need to be cleared with a shovel before the door could be opened again.

For a child who did not notice for a long time that she lived in a pair of railway carriages, I do have vivid memories of the cold, the damp, the dark, the constant need to be prepared for the worst.

Life was harder for most people in those days, but we had relations who lived in houses with lavatories that worked whatever the weather. They had hot water indoors when we had only just installed a cold tap in the kitchen. When we visited them, they would be wearing only one jumper. They came to see us and kept their coats on. I wonder now if there was ever a time when my parents questioned the wisdom of raising a child in such primitive conditions.

I always felt that I was born into a race quite separate from even our near-neighbours in the city of Peterborough, little more than six miles away. Friends who grew up there, seem to have lived in a more advanced era. Their fathers were driving family cars, passing my father as he stood resolutely at the bus stop. They were more mobile, moving in wider social circles.

Many people lived in small terraced houses at this time and had only two bedrooms, the same as us. Their living accommodation was cramped, usually with the same heavy, cumbersome furniture that filled the carriages but they enjoyed the luxury of a gas fire and walked to school on safe pavements.

They lived closer to their neighbours, sometimes sharing a passage to reach their back door and their gardens were much smaller than ours, but they had a shop and often a pub on the corner of many of the narrow streets.

Mother had two elderly aunts who kept a sweet shop in Woodston, where the city gives way to the fen, and it was a treat for me to stand behind the counter. I pretended that I was serving the customers, not that I could have reached any of the glass jars from the high shelf, or read the handwritten labels.

One day a lady asked me, 'Where do you come from, then?'

I replied 'Whittlesey', and she enquired, 'Oh, where's that then?'

I think she really had no idea that our little market town existed.

Those who have spent their whole lives in the city, do not recall memories of the fens which lay within sight if they had looked. Safe in their towers of brick that did not creak in the wind, they had no knowledge of the origin of those bricks, nor the area in which they were made. They seem to have turned their backs against the ridge that marks the old edge of the water, from just a century earlier when Whittlesea Mere was the largest area of inland water in southern England.

They had never ventured down to England's lowest point, which is still only habitable because of the hundreds of pumps: first wind driven, then steam, diesel and now electric, labouring continuously to keep the water from five counties moving upwards towards the sea.

Stretching across most of Cambridgeshire and much of Lincolnshire and Norfolk, the broad expanse of fens, with their historical reputation for inhospitable conditions, lie in the shadows of the once great abbeys.

As early as Saxon and Norman times, monks were beginning to find solace and solitude on the remote islands that rose from the water in this sparsely populated area.

Often well bred and educated, they were equipped to give an account of life at this time as their religious communities grew.

From Ely, with its octagonal tower casting a guiding light across the wildness of its surroundings, to Crowland, with its danger bell, tolling to warn that floods were approaching, and last rung less than ten years before my birth, this is a landscape of ethereal mist.

2 Across the Fens

Many of my childhood memories are shrouded in this mist of whispering voices and fragmented scenes, but I have clear recollections of the contrasts between those who welcomed any sort of progress, and those of us who lived in railway carriages.

Mother still padded the kitchen table with a blanket and heated the flat-iron on top of the stove, waiting patiently until it was hot enough to hiss when she spat on it. She was eventually persuaded to buy a new one but soon gave up on it, chuntering that she couldn't 'git on wi' tha' new-fangled thing 'cus the flex gits in th' way'.

'I like t' see as me clo'se are clean, not all shoved in together,' was her response to the idea of a washing machine.

Televisions were appearing in many living rooms by this time, but we were years away from replacing the big old Bakerlite wireless. Granny would have described 'broadcasting' as the spreading of seeds from a basket, as a man walked up and down the furrows of the field, casting seed to both sides. The 'Web' was where the spiders lived. 'Broadband' was something that kept your hair tidy, and I assumed that telegraph poles carried wires right past our front gate just to provide a launching stage for the hundreds of birds that congregated there at dusk.

A gas-pipe was laid in the road, eventually supplying properties on both sides of us. I watched with interest as the workmen dug trenches but it never occurred to me that they might have brought a new way of life into the carriages. Only the postman, in his smart uniform, doing his rounds twice daily on a red bike, provided us with a life-line to the outside world.

Arrangements were much more formal at this time. A letter might arrive on a Tuesday, announcing that an aunt and uncle would be coming to tea at three in the afternoon on the following Sunday. Once such plans had been made, they would only be amended in dire circumstances so, if those relations were to not arrive by ten past three, Mother made reassuring noises but kept at least one eye on the clock. It might be considered that a serious illness or accident must have befallen them.

Granny's last job before she changed into a clean pinny to greet the visitors, was to sweep the front. This was the area outside the gate which, strictly speaking, wasn't ours to sweep, but it was a matter of pride that each house-hold kept its own length of path tidy, and she would have considered it most dilatory to let visitors arrive to the sight of straw, blown from the passing lorries, caught in the bottom of the fence. We might not have had a real house but we had our standards.

I took up the post of look-out, kneeling on a chair so that I could see over the half-door, always raising the first cry of 'the're 'ere, the're 'ere. I can see 'um'.

These Sunday visits followed a predictable pattern with hugs and handshakes, numerous cups of tea, and endless discussions on who had been took bad since the last visit. The most common maladies were those associated with damp in this area where water surrounded us. Rheumatism and arthritis were expected and even those not yet elderly, could be heard complaining of the 'screws' in their joints. Most men, and many women, worked outdoors in all weathers and bronchitis, pneumonia and diphtheria were common words in our vocabulary. Children suffered regular bouts of croup and mothers lived in fear of hearing the dreaded whooping cough. Stress was unheard of, although someone might be said to suffer with their nerves or 'woritt' too much. Remedies were being exchanged even over the first pot of tea.

Amongst all this gloom, one moment of humour I recall is Granny recounting her observation of a pregnant woman stretching to get her washing off the line.

'And 'er in the family way an' all.' She shook her head. 'I watched 'er reachin' an' I were thinkin' to mesen, if she stretch up there much more, she's gunna bust 'er fartin' clappers.'

Everyone nodded solemnly and I managed not to giggle.

At tea- time we shared plates of sandwiches, and tinned fruit topped with Nestle cream. My favourite was mandarin oranges because the acidity curdled the cream, so I could make swirly patterns with my spoon. The opened tin was left on the draining board to be used later. Buns were always homemade and the ones I remember best were those with caraway seeds: not because I particularly liked them but because the story was often retold of the first time I saw these and cried out, 'Oh, no, there's mouse poo in them buns'.

Only after all the plates were cleared away, was I allowed to eat any goodies that had been brought for me. Then we played card games at the kitchen table. Because I was an only child, I was always treated as a smaller version of the adults. Nothing was laid on for my entertainment so I just lurked, listening and learning. Hence, I could play a good hand of Rummy shortly after I learned to count.

These were evenings when I listened in awe to my softly spoken cousin as he described his job as night watchman at Ely cathedral. For eight years he patrolled the aisles, stoking the stoves which barely took the chill off the building. I'm sure the stories were enhanced for my benefit, making me shiver as he spoke of wind in the creaking trees outside and moonlight casting its silver beams across the marble of a sarcophagus, but I perceived it as the ultimate bravery to spend whole nights in that cavernous, towering house of God, alone but for the company of the long dead.

As the grown-ups frowned over the cards, the air filled with cigarette smoke, making it difficult to breathe, and I remember sore eyes by bedtime. About nine o'clock, someone would comment, 'Blimey, look at th' clock. It's nigh on nine. Ol' Father Time's run away wi' us ag'en,' and the visitors prepared to leave, starting with a trip to the lavatory, which Uncle referred to as 'the carsey' and Granny always called 'the closet'.

Having been out to warm up the car, Uncle often came back in with steamed up spectacles, muttering 'that ol' fog's gettin' wuss,' and 'we bett' be orf, don't want to be gettin' lorst t'night'.

They lived in Ely, only thirty or so miles away, but as I listened to Mother advising 'Mind 'ow y' gew by tha' river,' and 'Watch them ol' drains,' I shivered, imagining them driving away into the pitch black of the fens. The sound of the engine died in the distance and there was no certainty that they would ever be seen again.

Then the kitchen door was shut against the night and Mother stuffed strips of folded newspaper in the cracks where it never quite fitted tight. As she began to clear up, the overflowing ashtray was emptied into that fruit tin saved from earlier, and now filled with water. Her explanation for such diligence with anything fire-related, was 'Look what 'appened to Robert Sayles'.

This was in reference to a bulb which had been placed too close to material in a window display, igniting the fabric, starting a fire which spread unnoticed in the night to become an inferno, burning to the ground Robert

Sayles, Peterborough's largest department store, in the year that I was born.

The room felt cold now the door had been opened and I knew I would get away with a 'lick and a promise' with the face flannel tonight, instead of my usual strip-wash at the sink. As Mother waited for the kettle to get hot enough to do the last of the washing up and fill my hot water bottle, I sat on the edge of the hearth, close to the dying embers of the fire, wondering how long it took to get to Ely. I pictured stern faces pressed up against the inside of the car windows, vigilant to make sure they didn't stray from the course of the road into the dark water. I don't know if I consciously knew then that Ely had once been an island separate from our own, but I think I must have had some understanding because I pictured causeways and banks veiled by swirling mist. I am still unclear about the boundaries between what I heard, what I imagined and what I always instinctively knew.

Perhaps some of this awareness was genetic, along with the two webbed toes on each of my feet, which Mother delighted in showing to visitors, removing my socks for the umpteenth time, as she boasted, 'Ow 'arr. She's got 'em an' all, same as me and Mother'.

This was supposedly the mark of true fen-blood, but I just felt it unfair that it was always my socks that were pulled off, not her stockings nor her mother's.

As we survived to the end of each winter, the water levels across the fens dropped. Clay, peat and silt released the moisture. Fields which had become lakes, drained slowly into the dykes, winds dried up the surface mud and inaccessible places could be reached once more. The first signs of spring burst forth in the garden and it always felt as if the carriages took on a completely new character, once Mother announced 'I reckon we can do wi'out a fire now'.

The sun gathered strength, filling the rows of windows with shafts of dancing dust-motes, and the outside of the wooden bodies became warm to the touch. It was light early in the morning and gradually, as the days lengthened towards summer, it was still light at bedtime.

Mother came in quietly on fine mornings and drew back the cotton, flower-print curtains, lowering the window above my bed that was part of the outside door. The bottom half had been boarded up and papered, but the top half still dropped into it, just as it had when travellers reached over to turn the handle, opening this door at the end of their journey. Even as I roused, I was touched by a different world: the gentle flow of warm air on my face and the sound of birds drifting in from the garden. These were the days when I woke with a joyous spirit, sure that I could have jumped straight down to the platform of a strange station, but there was no platform here, just the sleepers that supported the ironwork that held us up. I had to leave by a more conventional route.

Barefoot, I padded through a door on the opposite side of the room, along the covered passage which ran between the two carriages, then into the kitchen at the far end of the same carriage, across that room and out again. This circuitous route brought me outside, about fifteen foot from my bedroom windows, on the same side of the same carriage. Is that conventional?

With hair flowing and nightie floating, I was free to run and grow. Feeling the dew still cool on the grass underfoot, inhaling the scents of the garden and enchanted by the colours of the fields beyond, I turned my face upwards as tiny puffballs of cloud drifted in the vast fen sky. It was the start of another wondrous day with all its possibilities and potential. Perhaps it was this promise of the glory of summer coming, that my parents saw when they chose to raise me as a railway carriage child.

3 Dreams of Freedom

In the late 1950s and through the 1960s, my father worked firstly at Woolworths and then at Marks and Spencer. This was a time when every town had half-day closing, so he only worked until dinnertime on Thursdays. I looked forward to Thursday afternoons and fine Sunday mornings, as a special time when we could leave the women to their daily tasks and spend a quiet hour or two away from the carriages. Neither of the women enjoyed walking for pleasure but I had inherited Father's love of fresh air and exercise. He and I regularly walked to the river, once known as Smith's Leam, but renamed The New Cut, when it had been widened and straightened to carry the water of the River Nene more efficiently to the coast.

We passed an ancient tree planted by the roadside to mark a mile from the town, rounded Mile Tree Corner and took a turning off our road onto Binder's lane. I don't know who Binder was but I assume he once lived on this lane, or perhaps the row of tiny cottages were once occupied by 'binders', who operated the binding machines at harvest time. The sign at each end reads Crossway Hand, some official title that was never adopted by the locals.

From the bottom of the lane a track, which we knew only as 'the back road', stretched before us. As we followed the dusty, well-trodden route, I watched the birds flitting around us, rising from the hedges on each side and swooping into a new hiding place. I had no idea that we were walking in the footsteps of Romans, along the old Causeway which spanned the fens. It had once reached from Water Newton, past the old Durobrivae, now Peterborough, through towns such as ours, and on to the Roman settlement of Caistor St Edmonds in Norfolk, linking a number of islands along its way.

On these walks, Father taught me to notice the changes in the year, drawing my attention to the signs of the passing seasons: the first leaves turning gold to herald autumn, the tiny shoots sprouting to signal that another spring was upon us. He never identified any but the most common plants or trees by name. I think perhaps a lot of them were unknown to him. Originating from a mining community in Nottinghamshire, he may have been drawn to this landscape where nature and industry vied for supremacy but he had not grown up in this area where our unusual geology hosts many unfamiliar species, and some that are found nowhere else in the British Isles.

Sometimes he placed a hand on my shoulder and crouched down at my side, silently pointing out a rabbit crossing the track ahead. Mostly, all I got to see was the flash of a white bob-tail as they jumped into the undergrowth, already alerted by our voices or perhaps even our footsteps. Despite the brevity of these encounters, we named them as we saw them and the following week we looked for the same ones again, sure that we had sighted Bertie or his sister, Beryl.

Occasionally there was a gap in the hedgerow, offering a tantalising glimpse of the knot-holes and knot-holes were my first love. Brazil has its rain-forests, Africa has its deserts, Holland has its tulip fields and we have our knot-holes. These are the excavations where knots of the self-burning Oxford clay are extracted to be used in the production of the world's finest bricks. Since the late

1800s, the workings have grown and evolved to meet the demands of the building industry. They have been described by outsiders as ugly scars but I marvelled at the patterns sculpted into the landscape, every crevice a shadow in the mid-day sun. I perched on a gate, supported by Father's safe grip, entranced by the colours that were exposed as the shale planer ate away at the edges, forming the first cliffs I ever saw.

The deepest channels lay below the old sea bed and some of the earliest seams, already abandoned as the clay was exhausted, were being reclaimed by undergrowth by the 1960s. From our vantage point at the summit, we looked down into valleys and across to a mountain range which peaked at ground level. Below us, tracks wove their way in and out of bushes. Rollers and cables clanked as trucks passed over them, disappearing and reappearing, each laden with wet clay. Winding houses at the top of the steep slopes, hauled their cargo upwards through a network of bridges and arches, all built with the bricks of an earlier time.

I listened to the reassuring sounds of the unseen machinery. I could not have named them nor recognised them by sight but I noticed if any stopped operating, just as a conductor would notice the absence of an instrument from his orchestra. I had fallen asleep and woken to that strange cacophony of sounds since my birth and been brought here on these paternal outings since I was in my pram. I felt at peace here, safe in a landscape that was ever changing yet timeless. I was completely unaware of just how much history was hidden here, never imagining that beneath our feet lay sharks' teeth and fossils that placed this area under a shallow sea in the Jurassic period, and woolly mammoth tusks which would later be dated as Pleistocene. We walked so close, so unknowingly, to the sunken boats and roundhouses which were to remain buried for almost another fifty years before leading archaeologists to life here in the Bronze Age.

I sat until Father's arms ached or a glance at his watch reminded him of the passing time. Then I pleaded to stay longer, basking in the warmth of summer and drawing breaths of the ever present, if not very healthy, essence of sulphur. The smell of the chimneys, smoking twenty-four hours a day as the raw clay was fired in kilns, pervaded our homes and gardens, part of the security of familiarity.

Every week, as we rambled along this same path, I put him in a difficult position, torn between two very strong females. On one hand he had Mother, who had dressed me in white, with a ribbon in my hair, since I was a toddler. She expected him to take me out in my frilly frock, ankle socks and sandals, returning me in pristine condition, in time for Sunday dinner. On the other hand he had me, with my total disregard for white socks and pretty bows, my lack of respect for boundaries and dinner times, always wanting to go nearer, stay longer, explore every detail and absorb the atmosphere. At this time when I was reliant on sensations, rather than knowledge, I needed to be right at the edge, feeling the clay squelch beneath my feet, dropping to my knees, collecting handfuls, stroking its grainy surface and squeezing it so tightly that the clammy, grey solid oozed like liquid between my fingers.

I never noticed the slight hesitance in his walk as we neared home. I just ran through the gate with wild hair and enthusiasm, up the kitchen step and through the open carriage door as steam filled the doorway and our dinners were cooling on the plates. Rushing to the table, I did notice the stern tone of Mother's voice as she grabbed me by the arm and pulled me to the sink, glowering at Father.

'Let's 'ave yer 'ere. Yer can't git up the table in this state. Look at yer 'ands. Look at yer nails. The gravy'll be cold. The Yorkshire'll be gone flat. Just look at yer.'

It was on one of these outings, perhaps as the foliage of summer started to die back, that I glimpsed for the first time, a blockhouse just off the track, overgrown by brambles. Hundreds, if not thousands, of these were scattered across the region, built during the Second World War as part of the strategy to defend East Anglia, should an invasion occur. We called them blockhouses because they were built of concrete blocks. Another name for them was 'pill boxes', because of their shape.

After much persuasion, which probably consisted of me tugging his hand or refusing to walk any further, Father agreed that we could go a little closer to look in the window. I'm sure he thought that if he lifted me high enough to see for a moment through the glassless hole, my curiosity would be satisfied and he could return me to Mother on time and unscathed by the brambles, but he was always the optimist.

From that first peep into the darkness, with my nose thrust as far as possible into the narrow space, I was captivated by the smell. It was like nothing I had ever smelled before: damp, dank, musty. I loved it. As he tried to prize away my hands and I clutched at the rough walls, my eyes adjusted to the darkness and I saw that there was a doorway on the far side. Now there was no chance of taking me home until he had pulled back the brambles, squeezing around the side of the building, making sure that it was safe for me to get a better look through the doorway.

I stood between two worlds. The sun was high in the sky and I could still feel its warmth on my back. The contrasting coldness inside chilled my face. The smell of lichen and fungus, untouched by sunlight, seeped into my nostrils, yet I sensed a welcome. I was rooted to that threshold. I had no idea of the structure's purpose but I felt as if I had stepped into the protection of those solid walls, built to withstand enemy attack, offering a sanctuary in a more troubled era.

I did love Father and I didn't like the sight of blood when I noticed where the brambles had torn the skin on his hands and scratched his arms. I held his hand very gently on the way home and tried to walk sensibly so as not to hurt him. I don't remember Mother's exact response to the state of my hair and clothes that day, but I do recall Father carefully washing, drying, and then applying soothing Germolene ointment to his injuries as she bustled about in the kitchen with no sympathy in her voice.

From then on, a lot of our walks to the river were curtailed, not by Mother who still thought the outings were good for me if only Father could be more diligent in my care, but by the fact that I no longer wanted to walk any further than the blockhouse. I pleaded to take my dolls and my food there so we could have picnics but parental approval could not be gained.

'Where d' yer think yer can wash yer 'ands?' was Mother's first objection.

In the face of this logic, I knew there was no point in voicing my next idea, that I could turn it into a house, where I could sleep as slivers of moonlight shone through the slit-windows, waking to rush out of the doorway in the morning, to find that the beautiful, magical knot-hole was now my garden.

Instead, as autumn passed and the evenings drew in, these ideas grew silently to take over my thoughts during the day and fill my dreams at night, until I convinced myself that this really was achievable, if only I could squeeze enough provisions for my survival into a case. Perhaps this fantasy was fuelled by memories of the previous summer when we had packed suitcases and moved to Skegness for a week in a relation's caravan. I don't recall being aware of any difference between going on holiday and leaving home. Nor did I consider that the limited facilities of the caravan were not even present in the blockhouse.

Father had once given me a very small case to play with, explaining that it was as an attaché's case. I loved it and carried it everywhere, calling it my 'tatcha-case'.

As I struggled to carry it around full of oddments, Granny laughed at the fact that, although it was so small, it was still big for my size and she teased me, ''ere she gew with 'er portmanteau'.

Now I packed it with digestive biscuits, a comic, a cup to catch rainwater and my nightie. I squeezed in the blanket from my doll's pram, as the ones from my bed were too bulky. I decided to take my teddy bear as he would be warm to snuggle up to, although he was too big for the case and would have to be carried. I had always believed him to be a boy with as much determination as I insisted that he was called Priscilla. My only misgiving that day was when I stood on tiptoe in the passage between the carriages but was still unable to reach the torch that lived on the pantry shelf. I had considered all the basic needs and I had never even heard of Maslow's Hierarchy.

I had heard talk of folk doing a moonlight flit and I understood that this meant leaving home in the night when the moon was out, but I wasn't that brave. I had never been out after dark without a grown-up hand to hold. So, while the women were busy preparing tea, I seized my chance and sidled out of the door, pelting to the gate, then adopting a slow, purposeful gait as I reached the path. I was conscious that it would be prudent not to draw the attention of nosy neighbours and passers-by. It didn't occur to me that a tiny child, still not old enough to start school, with no coat, carrying a 'tatcha-case' and a teddy bear, might be noticed anyway as I made my way carefully along the narrow path beside the main road into Peterborough. This was the route taken by the heavy lorries which serviced the brickyards, but I had no fear of these. I was used to their noise and the draft that threatened to pull you from your feet as they passed. This was my home and they were part of the familiar scene. My only niggling doubt was that I had not managed to secure that torch.

I needed no map as I knew exactly where I was heading and it was only a moment, once she noticed that I was missing, before Mother realised, too. By the time I reached the turning onto Binder's lane, it was already dusk. I noticed that the first headlamps were beginning to cast shafts of light on the road. I still remembered to walk purposefully but that torch on the top shelf kept creeping into my thoughts. The trees cast shadows now which hadn't been there before, and a rustling in the hedgerow didn't draw me to explore; rather it made me catch my breath. I had never walked this far on my own, or been out so late. It must have been at least five o'clock. I wondered whether I should have left earlier or waited until tomorrow when I could have had all day to settle in.

Of course, it was too late to turn back now. I had my pride and my dignity packed in that 'tatcha-case'. I just hugged Priscilla closer to my chest and stared straight ahead, to avoid catching sight of anything that might have been watching from the bushes.

When I heard the hum of bike tyres coming up behind me, I held my head high and quickened my step. Then there was the sound of brakes at my side and Mother loomed over me.

'Wha' d' yer think yer playin' at?' Her voice boomed in the fading light.

'I'm goin' a' live in th' blockhouse.'

I hoped she didn't hear the quiver in my voice.

'Yer, right y' are, now git 'um.'

She didn't even get off her bike and I had to trot to keep up with her on the way back, tightly clutching my 'tatcha-case' and poor Priscilla. As we rounded Mile Tree Corner, the carriages nestled in the darkness: just one light shining from the kitchen window, but I refused to notice the welcome glow. I stomped inside, petulant that my bid for freedom had been thwarted, lamenting life's unfairness. I don't think I ever did tell her how good those tyres and brakes had sounded.

It was the first of many occasions when she pedalled out to find me and haul me back, protesting. Throughout my childhood she appeared on that damned bike: at the rec where I was not allowed to play after tea, at the edge of the knot-holes where I was not allowed to play at any time of day, at a friend's house when we skived school and later, to my eternal embarrassment, at the side of an unsuitable boyfriend's car.

4 Friends in Fur

Another spectre which looms large in my early childhood memories, alongside Mother's bike, is my pram. On January 28th in the year of my birth, almost three months before the impending event, my parents went to Fairways Department Store in Peterborough, stockists of quality toys and baby paraphernalia. They bought the most impressive pram in the shop. It was a coach built Royale Windsor in navy blue, costing twenty-six pounds, seventeen shillings and sixpence. It was delivered to the carriages on January 30th and given pride of place just inside the front door. The chrome shone in the sunlight and it stood so high that Father could only see to push me when the hood was down, restricting our walks to fine days.

As the first child of a couple relatively old to be starting a family, I was paraded before our small community, like a princess in my sparkling carriage, but my life was already a paradox.

Within the dark confines of home, my sleeping-quarters were also extreme. Mother decided that a tiny baby like me, although I was born weighing a healthy nine pounds, ten ounces, might get an arm, a leg or even a head, stuck between the bars of a standard sized cot so Father acquired an 'orange box'. This was a wooden crate in which oranges arrived in this country. It was placed inside the cot with the dangerous gaps, ensuring that I slept safely. Consequently, there was no silk-lined bassinet for me. I spent my first weeks in a rough-hewn, extensively travelled, second-hand crate, when I wasn't being lauded as royalty in my magnificent pram.

I don't remember its arrival, of course, but I do remember how big it was because Mother kept it for years. She never intended to have more children, terrifying me with the nightmare tale of the three days' labour she had endured at the carriages before the planned home-birth was abandoned and an ambulance rushed us to Peterborough, where I had to be extricated by Caesarean section. Yet, still, she would not part with the pram. It stood at the end of the passage and, in fear of creases turning to cracks, she always kept the hood up, blocking any light from the narrow panes of glass in the front door. Post arrived through the letterbox and disappeared behind its huge body.

While Mother was irrevocably attached to it, I grew to loathe it. On wet days she hauled it out of the front door, down the two steep stone steps and onto the gravel path, with me bundled up inside. I was then pushed the mile into town and buried beneath an assortment of groceries for the return journey. It had a compartment for shopping within the well of the body, accessed by lifting my legs into the air. When loaded, it must have weighed at least a tonne but Mother strode forth in the bleakest of weather. I used to wonder how she saw over the hood as she was even shorter than Father but, with hindsight, I don't think she did. I believe she just set her course and followed the pram, confident that no-one would try to obstruct her path as we bore down on the flimsy pushchairs propelled by less determined parents. We were perhaps the first juggernaut in the area.

Even after I started school, I was subjected to these outings and I remember cowering under the hood with the storm-apron fastened as high as possible to ensure that I could not be seen, lest any of my new classmates might be out shopping too. I wanted to be their friend, not be teased as a five-year-old who still went out in a pram.

Although the first self-service store had opened in Croydon in 1952, technology took its time reaching the fens. One-stop shopping was unheard of here so I had to stay hidden as we toured the town, calling in shops owned by locals, often kept by second or third generations of the same family. Mothers chatted and exchanged gossip as the friendly shop-keepers bustled to get their orders, often reading from a hand-written note as they went. This could take a while if several women were waiting so chairs were kept close to the counter.

One item at a time was rung up and the number of pounds, shillings and pennies appeared in the glass window of the hand-operated till. The longest wait of all was usually at the Co-op where every transaction was dealt with by staff in an office overlooking the shop floor. A pulley system took money along a wire from each counter to the cashiers' window. Change was sent back down the wire in little screw-topped pots, a system very similar to the aerial ropeways that carried buckets of clay overhead from the knot-holes to the brickyards.

These nightmare excursions stopped eventually but the pram still stood silently in the passage, a hulking shape in the shadows. Its hood and apron were brushed regularly to prevent dust building up and its chrome was kept polished to deter any rust. The threat that it might be re-activated was ever present. I hated it more by the day.

Then fate intervened. One night, with the agility and timing of a gymnast, a beautiful brown mouse leapt from the pram before Mother's eyes and suddenly the precious pram was dirty, desecrated. It had to go. I loved that mouse and I glowed with self-righteousness. I knew that he had felt my anguish and was repaying me for the small ways in which I had tried to help him and his kin. I had always been the defender of all things small and furry, in a family where they were considered to be 'varmin'.

When the straight pieces of wood that formed the passage between the two carriages had been joined to the rounded carriage bodies, it had left small gaps in each corner. Granny stuffed these with old rags and newspaper in an annual attempt to thwart the efforts of the tiny creatures as the days shortened, the nights grew longer and they made their way in, looking for a little warmth and compassion. Each year I tried to be helpful by pulling out a bundle of her defence system and accidentally dropping a few crumbs nearby.

We didn't actually see them indoors very often. I think they felt it might be prudent to keep a low profile, but occasionally one made a dash across a room in daylight. I always marvelled at how sleek and well-groomed they looked, despite living in such adverse conditions, but I never really got time for a good look before Granny grabbed whatever was at hand and started a frenzied attack. I can still see clearly the frustration in her expression as she tried to wield a long-handled broom and I swung desperately on her arm, ensuring that she would miss her target. She would chunter crossly and turn the brush on me, calling me a 'little 'umbug'.

I think she genuinely believed that I was the villain. She would never have considered that a stout lady with a heavy brush, terrorising a body and tail totalling less than two inches, would appear to me as bullying of the worst degree.

As the nights drew in, Mother regularly carried home a can of paraffin in each hand. Two stoves were kept alight overnight: one in the passage and one in the lavatory, to protect us and the primitive pipework from frost. The lavatory had no electricity so it was always dark. It was at ground level, down two big stone steps. There were no windows, no sunlight, and it bore the brunt of the north wind, making it chilly even in summer. Only as the temperature dropped, was it redeemed by these stoves. The wicks burned slowly, an orange glow shining from the door, and the comforting smell drifted through the carriages: greeting me as I left my bedroom on icy mornings, welcoming me home every time I returned from the cold outside, but I was not the only one drawn by this homeliness.

I looked forward to the return of my little friends, who I thought of as Romany because they came and went. I was told that the word was 'rodent' but that never had the same resonance to it. My anticipation of a first sighting was marred only by the appearance of the traps, strategically placed in the darkest corners. In the winter months I never moved from one room to another without the stern warnings, 'Watch yer frock on the stove' and 'Don't touch them traps'.

They were cold, menacing metal, armed with deceitful bait that lured the unsuspecting and vulnerable. I was never allowed to see the gory remains of their victims but I knew there was much hand washing and I had overheard talk of splattered blood. I fought a long battle with my conscience. I knew in my heart that I should knock them off, perhaps with a stick or my shoe, but I feared them too much and fear overcame guilt. This instinct to protect, born of such troubled thoughts, stayed with me beyond my childhood, beyond the carriages of Cambridgeshire.

Moving from Norfolk to Suffolk a few years ago, I found that I had a new little lodger of the mouse species. He was in my flat and I didn't know how he had got there. He appeared late at night and only when it was very quiet. I wasn't sure if he had come in from outside or if he had stowed away in the furniture lorry and travelled with me.

This presented me with a dilemma. I was going away for Christmas and I worried that there would be no food for him. I knew I had to try to catch him in one of the friendly traps which would have made Granny laugh in derision, but I didn't know where to release him. If he had come with me, I couldn't turn him out in Suffolk where he would be lost and know no-one. On the other hand, if he had previously been resident here, I couldn't cart him to Norfolk and release him in a strange county. I had studied bird-song and knew that birds had regional accents but I had not studied mice. I wasn't even sure if Norfolk and Suffolk mice could communicate.

Christmas was getting closer and he resisted all my attempts to catch him. He had been quite happy to help himself to my Christmas chocolate balls, neatly extracting them from their foil wrappers, but he avoided the ones placed inside the friendly trap. I put all the others out of reach to tempt him into the trap but still no joy. The day before Christmas I gave up, carefully dismantled the trap, so he wouldn't get stuck in it while I wasn't there to release him, and I left.

On the journey home after the holiday I smiled to myself, imagining the heap of empty foil wrappers that would greet me. Then a horrible realisation clutched my heart. I had forgotten to put them back out. I searched the flat as soon as I arrived, imagining his hungry little face, button eyes watching me accusingly, but he wasn't there. Sadly, I had to accept that he must have been forced out by the need to find food. I just hoped that he was a Suffolk mouse and knew some nice sorts.

At the beginning of New Year, I gave my youngest daughter an armchair stuffed with horsehair. We tipped it up to put it in the car and his tiny, emancipated corpse dropped at our feet. She buried him in the garden and she made the little wooden cross because I was crying too much: shedding the same hopeless, guilt-ridden tears that I had wept all those years ago when I was too frightened to creep from my bed and kick the traps, so I'd just bury my head under the blankets because I couldn't bear to hear a metal snap in the silence of the night.

5 Tragedies and Triumphs

 During the 1950s, with the war not long over and rationing still fresh in everyone's mind, children did not have many toys. A boy might have a wooden truck in which he could cart tools to help with the gardening or odd bits of wood to build a den. A girl was more likely to have a pram in which to push a doll. Good toys were not thrown away to be replaced with something more fashionable. These basic but treasured possessions had to last for years. Even in the sixties, I recall my horror as I swung my doll by her arm and dislocated her shoulder. Well, actually, her arm had fallen off. I was very lucky that she wasn't assigned to the bin, as a replacement might have been a long time coming.

Perhaps because I was an only child and my parents could afford to indulge me, or perhaps because she was an expensive doll, with porcelain limbs and head, and hair that was glued to her scalp, she was packaged up and a grown-up cousin took her to the Dolls' Hospital. She made a marvellous recovery, although that left arm was paralysed in one position, and she spent the rest of her long life in a dress that covered her scarring and could not be removed, lest her arm fell off with it.

Christmas and birthdays were likely to bring practical gifts such as handkerchiefs and underwear, slippers and soaps. A parcel containing a new toy was a luxury, so old toys had greater value and were passed down the siblings. Having no older siblings put me at a disadvantage but a tattered suitcase behind Granny's bed-head held a few exciting oddments, the origin of which I never knew.

On a wet day, when I was confined to indoors and Mother was confined with me, she could occasionally be persuaded, by late afternoon, to help me heave this case out of its dark corner. I recall the fading light in that bedroom as we opened the rusty hinges and breathed in the smell of dust and damp leather. Inside was a box of wooden blocks, each side covered by paper that curled at the edges. These could be laid out to form six different pictures. Because there were so many permutations, I always got frustrated and whinged for assistance, hence Mother's reluctance to get them out except as a last resort.

Two clockwork figures resided in the case, too. One was Mary who had a little lamb, which hooked onto the back of her dress, following where-ever she should go, although the lamb had long since wandered off to follow his own destiny. The other was a pretty fairy with wings that glittered, her hand still raised, from a time when she had held a wand, also lost to time. These toys never came out of that bedroom and the tiny wheels under their dresses would not work on a rug, forcing me to sit on the lino with them, my legs getting colder by the minute. There was only one key which fitted both and I was never allowed to wind them up in case I lost or broke the key so, again, this required close supervision.

For the most part, it was preferred that I amused myself, but even the little wooden donkey with his elasticated joints could only amuse me briefly as I pressed his base and watched him writhe to a contorted heap, legs sagging beneath him. At times like this, I resented the fact that my parents had not had the forethought to provide me with a string of siblings to provide me with entertainment, but perhaps this isolation encouraged the development of my imagination as I improvised and embellished.

On days when I was not allowed access to the old case, I considered myself fortunate that Father worked in the stock-room at Woolworths and acquired an odd assortment of very small figures, which arrived one by one, each adding a new dimension to my imaginary world. I think they must have once been parts of sets which became separated or damaged in transit. I don't think he would have chosen them deliberately unless he had a very strange sense of the absurd.

A short, stout farmer in a battered hat, had to be leant against something so that he didn't topple over as he stood on his one leg, watching over his animals. He was the proud keeper of two sheep who had no legs at all; a cow whose side had been stoved in, leaving a gaping hole; a dog whose injuries suggested that he had been run over; and a battered kennel which looked like he might have been inside it at the time of the accident.

Outside this menagerie, I had one plastic character dressed as a parachutist. Everything he needed was attached to his body, except a parachute. I had the top half of a racing driver whose lower body had probably been lost at the same time as his car. Then there were families of sorts. My favourite was headed by a lead soldier, called Timothy, and his wife, a beautiful ballerina named Valerie, who had emerged from a Christmas cracker. Their children were twins, Ray and Mary, and baby Tommy, each made of white plastic and standing less than two inches tall. Next door to them lived another set of twins, Susan and Janet, who were made of the same plastic but pink. They had no parents as I had no more grown-up figures. Then there were five identical quintuplets, all girls and translucent, and five identical brothers who were yellow and wore peaked caps. I think they were originally dumper truck drivers but I never had the dumper trucks.

I played all sorts of games on the kitchen floor with these tiny people. Some days they went to school, sitting erect on their Domino seats. Other days they were doctors and nurses, and patients in Domino beds. I was never very good at playing Dominos but every child should have a set – they are so versatile.

My favourite game was when I was allowed water in the sink. Then I would load my troupe into a small plastic van which doubled as a school bus and take them to the swimming pool. Arriving at the base of the cupboard under the kitchen sink, they were hoisted like Borrowers to the enamel draining board. I had not read The Borrowers at that time but my little people led very similar lives.

On these excursions, I would kneel on a kitchen chair, push them headlong into the cold water and make them swim until my hands were red and numb, despite Mother urging, 'Ent yer done sossin' yet?'

Father had constructed a washboard: a length of plywood, with a thicker piece of wood attached beneath one end, so the water drained from the lower end, back into the sink. On washdays, it enabled Mother to scrub the collars that detached from his white shirts but on swimming days, it became an effective water-chute. I also invented an early wave-machine, my hand squiggling the water around so that the dolls bobbed up and down, just keeping their heads above water. They were all accomplished swimmers, except Timothy. He had never mastered the art, sinking unceremoniously to the bottom under the weight of his Napoleonic Guards Regiment uniform. On these outings, he opted to be a spectator, standing on the draining board, regal and forever presenting arms. He never sat down, even when he was off duty, as his legs were not bendable.

On one such day, however, disaster struck the pool. I was squiggling furiously when my hand caught in the chain and dislodged the plug. Instantly, I saw the image of the water gushing away and all my precious dolls, except Timothy, gasping their last breath as they were sucked to a watery grave beneath the carriages. I was too shocked to even place my hand over the hole, let alone try to replace the plug. I stood on the chair and screamed one long scream as Mother hurled herself across the kitchen to my side. I could do no more than wave my arms and point to the tragedy as it unfolded. I expect her first feeling was relief that I was not mortally wounded, but this came out as laughter.

I cried and she laughed. The more she laughed, the louder I cried because I thought she didn't care. She did scoop the tiny, distraught figures to safety but the enormity of the situation seemed to have eluded her. When the furore had died down, she managed to say at last, 'They wouldn't a' gone down 'cus th' 'oles 'ent big innuff'.

Through logical eyes, she saw the metal grid which prevented the loss of cutlery, while I recoiled in horror from a gaping chasm. Then she wanted to demonstrate her theory by refilling the sink, throwing my people back in and pulling the plug out again. Could she have been serious?

I gathered up the shivering, shocked little mites and carried them back to school without even waiting for the bus. From that day on, swimming lessons were removed from the curriculum and the water chute spent the rest of its life as a washboard for white collars.

During many long, hot summers, these same little people came out to play in the garden with me. I had discovered that, with the aid of a sea-side spade, I could dig knot-holes and every day I dug knot-holes. They were of varying sizes and depths, depending on how long I could dig before Mother hauled me back to the carriages to scrub my finger-nails or Granny chased me away with her hoe, scowling, 'Git out the road 'afore I git yer wi' this', because I was digging in the vegetable patch or under the washing line. Then it was time to abandon my tools and scarper. Left to my own task, I would have created the landscape seen more recently in the film 'Holes', but I was digging first.

Granny had been born a country girl but went into service straight from school, so she must have felt privileged to now have an expanse of garden to call her own. She tended it with utter devotion. Her tools were ancient even at that time, and very small compared to those available today. The wooden handles were shorter and the heads narrower. Even the lawn mower cut strips only about a foot wide. There was no petrol engine or electric start. It was propelled solely by muscle power and determination but this did not hamper her efforts. With just her hoe and rake, a fork and a spade, she grew potatoes, carrots, onions, cabbages, cauliflowers, swede, peas, runner beans, broad beans, leeks, Brussels and anything else that I might have forgotten. There were no chitting trays or even a greenhouse. Everything was planted straight into the ground and left to take its chance or, as she often asserted, 'left up to God now'.

Somehow, her faith seemed to be rewarded as we always had a plethora of vegetables and abundant fruit. There were bushes laden with red-currants, black-currants, elderberries and gooseberries. The apple trees that she had planted as pips in a tea-cup, grew sturdier each year and 'rubub' reliably turned red. It would be lovely to describe how the jams and chutneys bubbled on the Aga, how the pantry shelves were stocked with pretty, gingham covered jars. However, this was not the case. There was never a long-term plan to preserve a winter store. With the exception of a sack of potatoes and bunches of onions hanging in the wash-house, we just ate what was in season, picking it fresh, consuming it within an hour or two.

All year round, she weeded her way up and down the garden, sometimes spreading soot from a zinc bucket, claiming that it kept the worms down, and always working backwards along the rows like the old turf diggers in their turbaries. Often we couldn't even see her from the carriages but, despite her dogged efforts to feed us all well, it always seemed unfair to me that she reigned supreme over ninety-nine percent of the back garden.

In the mid-day sun, she was the typical mad dog or Englishman: always in a long dress, a pinafore and a woolly hat to protect her head. She wore the same heavy, lisle stockings all year round and slippers with zips and thick crepe soles, never shoes. She gardened in this odd garb until her ninetieth birthday, often working from breakfast until teatime, then doing a bit more in the evening, so perhaps there was some wisdom in her beliefs.

I never remember seeing her drink juice, squash or even cold water, which Mother always called Adam's ale. She had an unshakable belief in the refreshing properties of hot tea on a hot day and stopped for frequent tea-breaks, wiping her forehead with a crumpled handkerchief and declaring, 'I shall 'ave to gew an' wet m' whistle agen'.

I just took advantage of the absence of supervision during these tea breaks, to acquire water from the outside tank, in the small bucket that came with the spade, and pour it into the latest hole. The clay was only a few inches below the soil and it quickly formed a grey pudding. Then, in something resembling the local scenery, all my friends had a day out. The dumper drivers leapt from great heights into the newly excavated knot-hole in a show of bravado. Small girls with frocks and plaited hair, moulded in plastic, ran freely down the steep slopes. Even the baby called Tommy, bounced on his bottom over the sides where stones protruded like life-size rocks. These dolls were all me. They lived out my fantasies: going on adventures of which I could only dream. They courted danger, took risks, became exhilarated and had wild hair. They met life head-on.

Now, when I see my own daughters rush at life with single-minded determination, oblivious to caution, heedless of advice, I try to remind myself that I would not have wished them to inherit any other trait.

6 To Save a Lettuce

Mother always kept a well-stocked bird table and it was an early morning ritual that I climbed up to kneel on a chair at the kitchen window, watching as she emptied a bowl of the previous day's left-overs onto it, before returning indoors and joining me to wait for the first visitors of the day.

'They must a' bin watchin' fer me.'

She sounded content to have met their needs; perhaps because it was so soon after the end of rationing and a surplus of food was still a novelty.

Then we looked on as they crowded in: sparrows, blackbirds, starlings, all intent on getting a share. Much flapping of wings ensued and a barrage of squawking and pecking as the bigger birds bullied their way past the smaller ones.

'Gew on, shove 'im out the road, 'e 'ad 'is share.'

She encouraged the little ones to stand up for themselves and occasionally, if she thought the squabbling was getting too rough, she banged on the glass and waved her fist at them.

Sometimes we were graced with a visit from the colourful tits and finches. I liked to spot a robin and Mother's favourite was the water wagtail. Later in the day, swifts and swallows might be seen flitting in the sky but I don't remember them ever joining the breakfast party.

The only bird I ever saw her get really angry with, was a jackdaw who caught her attention by flying to the chimney top with a piece of twig in its beak. I might have expected an explanation that this was how they constructed their nests. Instead, I was pushed aside as she shrieked at Father, 'Git th' brum, quick, afore 'e puts that in th' chimney. 'e'll bun th' 'ole place down'.

This panic probably arose from her memories of a time when a chimney fire often burnt down a cottage, or sometimes a row of cottages and fire-fighting was less effective. Even our own town had nearly been destroyed by fire on at least two occasions, with the loss of lives and many homes. The dwellings had later been rebuilt and, with true fen spirit, the residents still considered themselves luckier than the inhabitants of Crowland, less than ten miles across the fields. They had suffered fires as well, but also claimed fame as one of very few fenland places to have been struck by an earthquake.

Later in the morning, after the birds had eaten their fill and our own breakfast table was cleared, the women started their next weekday morning routine: 'gittin' them jobs done'. They gathered up the lengths of coco-matting from the kitchen, squeezing past me as I sat on the kitchen doorstep, and shook them vigorously outside. A holey, ridged pattern of dust was revealed on the lino where they had lain. Before they were put back in place, the floor was swept and the crumbs, hair and debris of the previous day were collected in a dustpan. This was known as 'tekkin' the bits up'. A duster was flicked around and the sink and draining-board were scrubbed.

Once a week there was a more thorough clean. The corner of a rag was used to apply a coat of Mansion Polish to the sideboard. Fresh runners were laid out. Then the lino was mopped. The smell of disinfectant hitting hot water in the bucket was the cue for me to spring from my seat on the step, knowing it was the day when the kitchen chairs were lifted onto the table, becoming the top deck of a bus heading for an adventure. If I could clamber up before the floor was wet, I was allowed to sit there until the last damp patch on the lino had disappeared. If I was really quick, I grabbed a couple of dolls to accompany me on the journey. If I was too slow, and the first mop full of water had been spread, steaming across the floor, I wasn't allowed in - I had missed the bus that only ran once a week.

During my early summers I sat on this kitchen doorstep for much of the day, suspended between two worlds. In reality, I was a timid child who hung back in a crowd: lacking social graces and the confidence that comes from mixing with other children and finding a place in the pecking order of siblings. Yet I always lived on the edge of another fantasy, following pathways in my mind which led to worlds where I had never been but felt I belonged. Perhaps I was always destined to be a writer. Mother said I was destined to be a gypsy. She teased me, saying I had sat there long enough to have made a dozen clothes pegs.

Framed in this doorway, I was near enough to feel the security of the carriage behind me, to hear the women talking as they bustled about the housework, their wrap-around pinafores, pronounced 'pinifers', over their frocks. I carried Granny's genes, needing the comfort of that home within reach but, even as they teased me, they were aware of Grandfather's blood which flowed through my veins, carrying visions and impulses which drove me to feel the breeze in my hair, the warmth of the path that led to freedom beneath my bare feet.

Some days I balanced a bowl in my lap, prizing broad beans from their furry nests or popping peas into a pan on the step beside me, more content with the feel of the velvet-lined pods and more excited by the legumes making their very first appearance than I ever felt about any shop-bought toy. I loved the textures and the close-to-nature smells.

The garden which lay to the front of the carriages and extended round both sides was filled with colours and scents. I enjoyed the random, unsymmetrical borders, overflowing with an assortment of cottage-garden plants, often self-sown. This was not the home of the formal flower bed, but a haven of willowy hollyhocks, foxgloves and a profusion of lupins. On damp mornings, I could follow the sparkling silver trails of the snails and slugs that wandered in criss-cross patterns. I loved this early morning freshness, the dew poised in droplets on every stem and blade. I could roll around on the grass while it was still sodden and breathe in the scent of the wetness before I was hauled inside to the sound of Mother lecturing, 'What the blazes a' yer doin'? Look a' yer. Yer soppin'. Git them dry clo'se on. Folks'll think yer 'alf sharp'.

I had a swing at the front of the carriages and I spent hours, not really swinging, hardly moving, just listening. The whole garden was full of life. Bees hummed softly as they rummaged in the borders. An array of butterflies, with beautiful patterns on their wings, alighted on quivering stalks, seemingly too fragile to hold even their tiny weight. I searched the hedges for caterpillars, gently stroking their furry bodies, always amazed at how they could be covered with fine spikes yet so soft to touch. Some had stripes and some had spots and all had emerged from the sticky cocoons in the bushes. Ladybirds appeared in large numbers to have their spots counted, to crawl up and down an arm or leg, not objecting to being passed from one hand to another, just flying away when bored. I was intrigued by woodlice and turned over rocks and logs, hoping to find them, but always unsure if they welcomed my visits. Somehow, they never looked pleased to see me. I have never seen a smiling wood-louse. Occasionally, a grasshopper contributed his own unique sound as he passed through and birds were a constant presence, ranging in size from the tiny, timid wren to the confident, cooing doves. The sounds blended, each creature adding a new chord to the medley.

Baby spiders could be found in family groups, starting as tiny black specks in the webs that hung high inside the wash-house. Gradually they grew legs and took shape under the watchful eye of their mother who lurked in the shadows above the six-inch nails where the clothes-props rested. I wasn't that comfortable with the way she stood guard but I reasoned that if I didn't poke at them, or disturb the nursery, then she would have no need to suddenly jump out and frighten me to death. In this way we retained a mutual respect. She watched me and I watched the babies. It was an amazing sight when they finally left home, dropping from the web, one after another, like parachutists dropping from an aircraft. I had never seen parachutists dropping from aircraft but, later, they always reminded me of the baby spiders bailing to freedom.

With most of the nature that lived around my doorstep, I was happy to observe, not feeling the need to interfere. The exception to this were the ants. They lived mostly in the cracks of the rough concrete, coming out to play in the warmth and rushing about their business but, sometimes, as if driven to madness by a full moon, although the day was sunny, they set off on a suicide mission up the steps and into the carriages. In broad daylight they marched in columns, straight into the open doorway. Then I had to intervene, lest they reached the pantry. I don't know if they appreciated my efforts or if they were just annoyed by the lengths of wood I put across their path to divert them onto the gravel and back to safety, but at least I knew they were safe. The alternative would not have been good. I had seen Granny wield a kettle of boiling water. There was only one kind of ant in her pantry - a dead ant.

The lawn at the front was an irregular shape and changed size with the seasons, bigger in winter when the over-hanging foliage died back. On his Thursday half-days, Father ran with me holding his hand, doing figure-of-eights around the flower beds, a complete lap of the carriages and then another circuit of the lawn. Mother and Granny watched and called encouragement from the garden seat where they sat in the shade of a voluminous lilac bush which had its roots next door but overhung our garden. Its branches were laden with lilac blossoms, such a pretty pastel colour against the foliage, but not allowed indoors with the other cut-flowers as it was considered unlucky to take it inside.

As I puffed along, complaining of a stitch in my side, Father assured me that all this practising would ensure that by the time I started school I would be the fastest runner in the class. Later, I was just glad that sports day was always on a weekday when he was working, so that he was spared the disappointment of watching as I puffed up to the finishing line on my chubby little legs: always last.

During the warm weather we often ate tea outside, usually a picnic with an assortment of cakes and biscuits on tiny china plates with matching cups from my tea-set. I had a low, wooden table that Father had made for me. Around this I entertained a number of dolls and Granny, who could be quite civilized when she wasn't murderous.

The evenings seemed longer then and we regularly sat in the garden, watching the sun glow red in the west as Mother sighed, 'It's no good goin' t' bed while it's this 'ot'.

'It's still swelterin' in there.' She reported back after trips to the lavatory or to make fresh tea.

Sometimes we watched as the first stars appeared and I can recall the excitement of seeing the harvest moon rise, at first just a sliver of silver emerging from a bank of cloud, then riding on top like a jaunty beach-ball on waves of indigo and cream, before finally breaking free and soaring to new heights, a balloon with no string.

In early autumn I remember being startled by the snapping of dry twigs at the bottom of the hedge, my parents hushing me to stand still and watch. The rustling of dried leaves heralded the arrival of a hedgehog, to be treated to a bowl of food and feted like a celebrity on a brief visit.

As the night air grew cooler and a breeze began to stir, Mother would warn me, 'Time to git yer in now, afore th' owls git yer'.

Mosquitos which had plagued the fen-dwellers of the past were no longer considered to be an ague carrying threat. They were just annoying as they buzzed close to our ears, leaving an itchy bump if they got chance to land on an exposed inch of flesh, necessitating a good rub with calamine lotion. If any got indoors, and often they did, we sought them out and swotted them before bedtime with the rallying cry of 'There 't is!' as Father balanced on a bed with a folded newspaper. A miss might be greeted with an encouraging call of 'That were cluss', or a disparaging sigh of 'Ye missed be a mile'.

Behind the carriages, past the wash-house, the coal-place, the wood-shed, and through the garden gate, lay another acre or so: the back garden where Granny and I had a constant clash of interest. I loved the flowers there just as much as those in the front. I had no prejudice against the squat clumps of dandelions, the dainty little daisies or the blushing poppies. Each had their own elegance. I admired the tiny yellow flowers of the groundsel and enjoyed watching bees on the white clover. I even humoured the nettles as long as they left my legs alone. I found pleasure in the tiny mosses that spread over the cinder path and the ivy that clung to the fences and clambered up the hedge at the bottom of the garden but Granny saw with different eyes. She spied enemies to be extricated and forked onto the bonfire. Bindweed, known as twitch, and chickweed, with the tiny peck-eye flowers, were the bane of her days. A thistle in her neat row of cauliflowers was made as welcome as the ant in her pantry. She spent hours unravelling the weeds that climbed among the runner beans or threatened to choke her flowering potatoes. Even the kek that hid under the hedge could not escape.

At the end of a day's gardening the short-tined fork, used for turning the ground and breaking up the clods, was left by the garden gate ready to round up the bonfire at bedtime. Any stray greenery that had not yet been reached by the flames, was forked onto the top so that the fire smouldered through the night. Sometimes these bonfires burned for a week, emitting a slow curl of smoke, rising against the darkening sky. Even as she strode into the dusk to perform this last task of the day, she could be seen bending and straightening as she went, gathering another handful of hapless weeds who had thought they were safe for the night.

I became the protector of the small and vulnerable again, defying her efforts to move me away from a weed as precious to me as a rare orchid until she raised the hoe at me, the same scowl on her face as when she wielded the broom on a mouse-chase, muttering 'Yer'll cop it, time I git yer'.

This was another time that I felt helpless. I carried with me the image of tiny plants being torn from the succour of the earth: babies being ripped from the womb, roots like dangling limbs.

I only realised what a deep impression these scenes had made when, in the 1990s, as part of home-educating my own children, we grew organic vegetables. I was advised that we should pull out the weaker, smaller lettuces to give the bigger ones more space. I left the children indoors with another task so that they would not have to witness the horror that had lived with me for so long. Walking calmly to the row of plants with the self-assurance that accompanies adulthood, I bent over with serious intentions but I could not choose. I could not grasp any of them by the neck and destroy their chance of life, especially the limp ones which lagged behind. I might have felt it more justifiable to pull out the strident ones which had pushed themselves ahead, but I didn't do that either. I walked purposefully back indoors and explained that there was plenty of room. They could all expand - sideways.

If Wendy Thrower, the Local Education Authority's coordinator for Home Education in Norfolk, reads this, she will know it's a confession: the real reason why our crop of lettuces failed to thrive. I hope she will appreciate that relaying this story to the girls when they were older, taught them a valuable lesson about compassion, perhaps more important than good gardening techniques.

7 Couplings Reconnected

As an only child, I always had time to listen and look, to absorb what was going on around me. We never had windows that opened so Mother just dropped down the top part of the door in the kitchen to let in fresh air and let out the steam when she was cooking. On warmer days the whole door was opened and fastened back with a chain. I sat on my chair at the end of the kitchen table, opposite this door, and watched the world as it passed.

Sometimes I had sheets of paper and a box of paints, trying to recreate the transient scene but the vehicles moved too fast and my hand was too slow, so the activity outside was usually only captured in my mind.

I counted lorries. In earlier years those from the brickyards had hauled their loads of the renowned Flettons, the length and breadth of the country: meeting the need for air-bases, runways and military defences. Now, they made the same journeys with the bricks to be used in building houses, factories, hospitals, bridges and roads. The seasonal ones carted beet from local farms to the sugar factory, depositing a rutted layer of mud on the roads and dropping whole beets when they took the corners too fast. Nets were beginning to be used to secure the loads but enough escaped to feed the local rabbits. The low-loaders in Pickford's livery, came and went from their depot just six doors away. Every twenty minutes a bus passed on its way to the city, carrying workers and shoppers. I knew the sound of those engines and could identify them before they came into sight.

At Easter time I watched out for the pilgrims who passed on their way to Walsingham shrine, singing and carrying a cross: always cheerful at this point in their journey as they neared The Nag's Head in Eastrea, where they received food and took the opportunity to bathe sore feet.

In the summer months there seemed to be a steady flow of hawkers and men in suits: often young and disabled in some way, trying to make a living by selling items from a suitcase. They enthused about the virtues of a particular scrubbing brush with very good bristles, or the cleaning properties of a bar of carbolic soap.

Then came gypsies, with their homemade dolly-pegs and lengths of lace, and fortune-tellers, with golden ear-rings and gnarled hands that reached out to touch my hair, offering, 'I'll sell y' a bunch o' lucky 'eather to keep the child safe', before Mother hauled me to the security of her hip. There were scissor grinders, rag and bone men and tramps. I always thought they looked sad and bedraggled with their worn out shoes and ratted hair, but Mother, with her 'Cleanliness is next to Godliness' philosophy, didn't extend the Christian spirit this far and they always left empty handed.

Occasionally the road was closed and I could peer through the gate as a gang of workmen arrived to resurface the tarmac, towing their hut behind a huge steam-roller. The delicious aroma of hot tar drifted over the gate. On other days, the traffic was stopped as a massive Robert Wynn lorry with more wheels than I could count, heaved its enormous load to some unknown destination.

In all weathers, I watched the men on bikes. Sometimes

they were bent double in a struggle against the wind: neckerchiefs tucked tightly in their thick jackets, cloth caps pulled low to shelter their faces from the pelting rain, and sometimes those same caps shielded their eyes from the blistering sun. These were the drawers and burners, the diggers and fitters, the shunters and smudgers, the setters and stokers, keeping alive the tradition of their fathers and grandfathers, harvesting their crop of clay and firing it in kilns, producing the building blocks of this country. Riding at least two abreast and sometimes in groups of up to twelve, they could be heard shouting and laughing as they overtook each other, the last stragglers passing just as the buzzer wailed, heralding the change of shift. They worked long hours against the harsh clay face or in the heat and dust of the brickyards and pedalled slower on their way home.

I watched with envy when the Corona lorry started to do a round, delivering colourful bottles to the nearby houses but Mother wasn't to be moved from her belief that 'All them bubbles 'ent n' good fer yer innards'. The dream of cherryade and dandelion and burdock had to be put aside for another day as the lorry pulled away again.

Once or twice a year, an old traction engine trundled by. I could hear its approach even if I was indoors. Running to the gate, I looked in awe at the huge wheels, bigger even than those on the steam-roller. A plume of smoke belched from the funnel. It was the most majestic piece of machinery I had ever seen. Its name was painted on the side in ornate writing and Mother caught up with me in time to read the words, 'Pride of the Fens'. I could imagine no more fitting accolade.

One summer, when it was still light enough to play outside after tea, my attention was caught by an unfamiliar sound. Always curious, I stopped to listen, trying to establish the source, but the whirring noise seemed to build to a roar and then die away again as if coming closer and then fading into the distance. Afraid that it would stop before I could identify it, I ran indoors to summon a grown-up. Pulling Mother by the sleeve, I jumped out of the kitchen door, urging her to listen with me. At first I feared that we were too late. The air was silent. Then I heard it again, revving and receding.

'Oh, the show mus' be on,' Mother nodded her head. 'Them's the mo'orbikes.'

'What mo'orbikes? What show?'

She really should have anticipated my next questions.

'Can we gew see? Can we gew now?'

I should have anticipated her reply.

'No, yer don't wan' a gew see them. They're dirty, smelly, noisy, dang'rus'.

Of course, this sounded exactly like somewhere I would very much like to go, but it was still another couple of years before I managed to persuade her. Then she coerced a neighbour into keeping us company and we set off in summer frocks and sandals. The weather was very dry and dust swirled across the entrance to the field. Hay bales were arranged as seating around a central ring but I was instructed firmly not to sit on them as they were sure to be 'full o' fleas'.

I believe there were a few animals being exhibited, as this was the local agricultural show, but I don't recall what they were. I wouldn't have been allowed to get too close, as they would have had fleas, too. Anyway, I was just there to see the motorbikes.

'Oh, they won't be on till tonight.' Mother smiled. 'We'll 'ave t' be 'ome afore then t' git yer father 'is tea.'

I don't remember enjoying any of the show, just feeling cheated because I had waited so long to see the motorbikes and now I was hauled away, protesting, before they even warmed up their engines.

As the seasons passed, I continued to listen to the familiar sounds that surrounded me. Across the road, just one field away, ran the railway line. The sound I recall most vividly was the rattle of the trains carrying passengers and goods to the East Coast and Ely, Cambridge and Norwich. All day, the air was filled with their rhythmic passage. I could stand on tiptoes on the top step to the front door and watch them pass. There were wagons of various kinds: uncovered flats, tanks with names painted on the side, hoppers and passenger carriages not dissimilar to ours. By now I had some awareness that my home had once played a different role and trains had become rooted in my innocent perception of life, firing my imagination.

In the bright sun of summer afternoons, as I played in the garden, I paused to hear them pass. Some days, immersed in a game, I only hesitated momentarily to listen but, other days, I took off into another of my earliest fantasies. I pictured what it would be like if the engine came back for the carriages and there was a grand reunion, with lots of tears as the neighbours stood in their gardens and saw us off. Hanging out of the windows, we'd wave happily as our heroic engine towed us away, the second carriage waiting just a moment before falling into line behind the first. The fact that we had only a wooden frame under the floors, and were no longer on wheels, seems not to have occurred to me.

On such days I scrabbled inside, lugging my family of toys with me, slamming the heavy door behind us. I did my waving out of the window with great vigour, to neighbours who probably thought I should be put somewhere safe.

After a suitable interval of probably just a few seconds, because I was never a patient child, my ragged family of toys and I alighted again at a new destination. The gravel path was now a meandering stream, babbling coolly over my feet. The cluster of sheds beyond the carriages was an encampment of gaily painted wagons, inhabited by the colourful and intriguing gypsies, who I had heard lived on the edge of the Wash road but had never met. Now was the chance to pursue this dream and I splashed along the stream that led me to them. Beyond the camp were the lawns, now a beach. The expanse of vegetable garden, stretching as far as I could see, became the water and I ran with my legs and swam with my arms, so far out to sea that I could no longer see the carriages. When I tired of this, I would swim back to the lawns and stretch out to dry on an exotic beach.

A game like this could go on all day, weaving in the grown-ups as other characters. Going into the kitchen for my meals, I saw a café where Mother worked as a waitress. I could even come back later and find that it was now an inn, where I'd book a bed and stay overnight.

These were exciting adventures which could be conjured up at any time, unhindered by siblings who may have wanted to play different games, supported by my submissive toys and largely unnoticed by the busy grown-ups. Mother served food as normal and wasn't fazed if I pretended that we had not met before. Granny carried on with her planting or weeding and didn't even look up as I swam past. They wouldn't have wanted to ask questions which led to long and bizarre explanations. I think they were just happy that I was able to amuse myself in those days when children's entertainment was homemade, before television came into our lives.

I was happy, too, in this world which existed only in my imagination, although I did occasionally conjure up images that frightened me. The one I remember most clearly came to me on nights when the wind was from the south, carrying the sound of the overnight freight trains, bringing them nearer. On very windy nights, they were borne eerily close, and I clung onto the bed covers and held my breath until they were gone, wondering what would happen if the engine really did come back for the carriages. Would I hear the workmen chatting to the driver, see their shadowy figures and soot-blackened faces outside my window and smell the oil on their overalls, or would they sneak through the darkness so that I was unaware of their presence until I heard the clanging of the buffers and the couplings being reconnected and it was too late to call out to my sleeping parents?

My bedroom shuddered as it trundled through the garden, probably due to that lack of wheels, following the kitchen and leading the front room and Granny's bedroom into the darkness: into a world that was not mine. On these nights the grown-ups slept soundly but I felt uneasy. I didn't know the old saying, 'Be careful what you wish for', but I knew its meaning.

8 A Sunday Excursion

In the days of the Sunday Excursion, steam engines from all parts of the country hauled long trains of carriages to the sea every week of the summer. Each would carry a full load of passengers. We lived two miles from our local station and regularly walked there to board. Father carried our provisions for the day in Mother's shopping bag and she had our macs draped over her arm.

I skipped along between them, questioning my captive audience, often not even waiting for an answer as new ideas flitted through my mind.

'How come we 'ave a queen but no king?'

Why d' ladies wear bonnits at Easter?

What birds built them nests?'

As we neared the station buildings, a sign announced Whittlesea and I always felt that this was where our journey began: an adventure taking us out of our little town which had been known as Whittlesey for decades, back to the days when we were much nearer to the sea, back to the time before the spelling of our name had been corrupted.

We joined the throng of other families, queuing at the ticket office, before reaching the one platform for eastbound trains. This was curiously offset so that it wasn't quite opposite the platform for trains heading west. A waiting room with leather benches was always open, with windows looking out towards the track. An imposing fireplace suggested that travellers might huddle by a blazing fire on colder days. I don't remember ever seeing a fire; perhaps because we only ventured out in summer.

Outside, there were metal benches and red fire-buckets and the hanging baskets were always well tended. This was the era when the rural railways were a credit to those responsible for their upkeep. Uniformed staff were on hand, always looking efficient. They could be relied on for up to date information and an informal chat about the prospect of a hot day, sea breezes and tide times.

There were crowds on the short platform every week, all eagerly awaiting the same train. The conversation was animated. These were the people of the brickyard community and those who cultivated the land under the unpredictable fen skies, and they were going to savour every moment of this hard-earned day out.

The men were less likely to wear a suit than in the previous decade. Now it was more common to see them in light trousers and an open-necked shirt, sometimes sporting a blazer for the seaside. Both men and women wore open-toed sandals, the men with socks. The women had dresses, belted at the waist and buttoned right down to the hem, with a tendency to pop the lowest button if they stretched a leg too far. They all clutched shopping bags or covered baskets, often opened for the first helping of freshly made white-bread sandwiches, before the last of the carriages had clattered out of the station.

A cluster of children jigged around them as they waited: thin white legs beneath their shorts, each dangling a bucket and spade. Balls were carried in net bags. An early version of 'flat-pack' was the beach-ball, only inflated once it reached the beach where it was considered safe to play. This myth persisted despite the fact that they were regularly caught by the wind and whipped along the sand, outpacing both children and parents, usually finishing up in the surf and bobbing out to sea.

All around me, I saw relaxed faces and laughing children but the knot in my stomach would be getting uncomfortable now. Although I spent my entire childhood living in the familiar surroundings of railway carriages, I had an uneasy relationship with trains that moved.

The first sign of an imminent arrival was the gatekeeper strolling across the road, closing the gates in case an occasional car should come that way. Now all faces were turned west, necks craned to get the first glimpse of the puffing smoke in the distance. I held the hands of my parents, clinging tighter as it got nearer, lumbering into the station. The image in my memory is of screeching brakes and steam, hissing and swirling around us as it shuddered to a halt, the power temporarily reigned in, but poised to surge forward again, like a horse only half-tamed, and I was terrified of horses too.

Behind the engine were men with blackened faces, who stoked the boilers. Their smiles were probably genuine but I looked away, afraid that I might meet their eyes, white orbs against the soot-covered background. My clearest memories are not of the engine or the carriages, but of the spaces where the buffers met. On one occasion, when I had been brave enough to look down into this ravine, I had seen the sheer wall, dropping into darkness, a pit of hot vapour, reaching up to me with curling fingers. From then on, I didn't even look.

Just moments before, this had been an innocuous space beyond the platform, where rails glinted in the early morning sun, drawing the eye to the distance where the gap between them appeared to narrow. Now it became a dark chasm into which a small child might slip, impaling herself on the greasy, dripping metal, but not this child, who pulled her parents backwards, as they tried to move forward with the crowd.

At home, we had concrete steps to each door and I had clambered in and out ever since I learned to walk, suffering only a few minor scrapes when I lost my footing. Here, on these bright Sunday mornings, I faced the nightmare of climbing from the platform to the narrow step, hardly wider than a ledge, and up to the carriage. This was an ordeal to be overcome as quickly as possible if I wanted to see the sea. I just extended one leg and screwed up my eyes, as the parent behind steadied me from falling backwards and the parent in front hauled me to safety. I bet they thanked the Lord that they had only one child.

Once inside, I was fine. These carriages were designed for comfort. I perched on the edge of the long seats with my feet on the floor, or sat back against the upholstery, not able to do both at the same time. The antimacassars were starched white and armrests could be lowered or raised. If I kneeled on the seat, I could see my reflection in the bevelled mirrors. Pastel paintings showed relaxing scenes of the countryside and coast. Posters advertised boating holidays on the Norfolk Broads for four pounds. The woodwork had a high sheen, windows were clean, and blinds could be pulled down to give shade from the sunlight. Lamps were turned on with individual switches and a pull-cord, safely out of reach, bore the words 'in case of emergency'.

Bags were stowed on the luggage racks overhead and we settled down for the journey. The noise of the engine was muffled to a background sound. The smoke was just an occasional distraction as it wafted past the window and I enjoyed the rhythm and the rocking motion as we passed signal boxes clad in the traditional tar paper and clackety-clacked over the points. The vibration of the glass was soothing against my face as I watched the shifting scenery. Like a million other children, I was intrigued by the wires that stretched between the telegraph poles at the side of the track, seeming to rise and fall before my eyes.

I tried to spot rabbits as they scurried into their burrows in the banks that rose steeply on both sides. Often, long stretches of the grass were blackened, where it had been set on fire and left charred by sparks from the engine. We saw cows and sheep and horses, so used to the passing trains that they barely paused in their chewing to mark our passage. Men in fields of wheat, searching for tares, straightened their backs slowly, pained by lumbago, yet waving cheerfully. Later in summer, bales of hay stood in these same fields, awaiting collection. I always looked for windmills, mostly disused by this time, often abandoned and derelict, many without their sails.

Occasionally we ventured as far as Great Yarmouth, with its reputation as the finest seaside on the east coast, but Mother always thought that this was not such good value as the travelling time was longer, lessening the time spent there. Our normal destination was Hunstanton and we got to know this route well, always looking for the same landmarks. One of these was a church that had fallen into disrepair and become overgrown. As Father pointed it out to me, commenting on its neglected state, a fellow passenger volunteered the information that it had been abandoned following a tragic wedding when the bride had collapsed and died at the altar. I have no idea if this was true, or even where the church was but, from that day on, we never passed the spot without experiencing a moment's sadness for that poor woman.

Through the fens and into Norfolk, we crossed many level crossings, although they were never level, as shrinkage of the surrounding peat meant a raised hump where the track was higher than the farmland and roads up to the gates were more like hills. We tooted to warn tractors and walkers of our approach, then glided past as they waited below, their passage barred as we commanded right of way. Sometimes, there were children with bikes and I looked down at them, imagining how sad they must feel that they could only go for a bike ride while we sallied forth in a shining carriage.

As we passed through Wolferton, my parents always commented on the regal status of this station, with its coronets of wrought iron and leaded windows. They explained that this was where the royal train stopped to allow the Queen and her family to alight on their journeys to nearby Sandringham House. Now I understood the wistful look of those waiting children, who must surely have imagined that I was a princess, perhaps accompanied by my governess, at the beginning of a long summer retreat. I never once spoiled this vision by asking myself how much they would have laughed if they had seen me earlier, being wrestled into the carriage like an obstinate donkey.

At Snettisham we marvelled at the intricacy of the hedge which had been sculpted to include the name of the station and the letters GER. Approaching Heacham, we started to see the first signs of holiday accommodation: caravans and chalets, dotted across a wide, flat area reminiscent of the fens. Another structure that we always looked out for in the last minutes of the journey, was an old carriage at the far side of a field, squashed against a hedge. It appeared to have been lifted into the air and dropped there by the wind but Father claimed, and again I don't know if there is any evidence, that it was a relic of the 1953 floods, carried inland to its final resting place by the surge that had devastated this coastline, and left there where the hedge had caught it, stranded as the water receded.

Now we were getting nearer to the coast, the excitement grew and voices reached a higher pitch. Parents began to retrieve the remnants of picnics and round up their children. I seemed to have less trouble getting out of the train, being able to leap over the gap to whichever parent was waiting to catch me on the platform. Then it was just a matter of cramming as much as possible into the short hours before we had to leave again.

My parents hired stripy, canvas deckchairs by the hour and sat close to the water's edge while I splashed in the surf. They only moved to shuffle the chairs back if the tide threatened to reach their feet or the shopping bag. This was the time when I most envied those children who had come in a pack of siblings. Now they chased a ball or ran in and out of the water, kicking up a spray, splashing and squealing to each other. I watched but was always too shy to join them and eventually Father would be moved to stir from his chair and kick the ball around with me. I know he tried to compensate for my lack of company but it was never quite the same.

I watched the waves and he skimmed stones out to sea, a skill I never acquired despite his patient endeavours to teach me the wrist movement. He did build me some pretty impressive sand castles and at least I was spared the tears that came from further up the beach: a brother insisting it was an accident when he trod on someone's newly completed masterpiece; a sister protesting her innocence when sand was kicked into another child's eyes. By comparison my play was sedate and my ball never escaped to the freedom of the surf.

At this time there was still a pier strutting out to sea and a boating lake, as well as the skating rink, fairground rides and indoor amusements. We ate a packed lunch on the sand if it wasn't too windy. On rougher days we found a space in one of the concrete shelters built into the wall that enclosed the boating lake. Here, we unwrapped our food on the slatted benches, often fish paste or cheese sandwiches. It was not until much later that I realised that sandwiches could contain more than one filling. They did not have to be cheese or tomato, fish paste or cucumber. Some people combined these ingredients.

On one occasion, I had mouth ulcers and could only chew very slowly. A chilly wind was blowing into the shelter and Mother, having finished her own food and keen to move on, suggested that I finished eating mine as we walked. I struggled with that dry cheese sandwich all the way from the boating lake back to the pier, feeling too poorly to even appreciate the novelty of being allowed to eat as I walked, something that she would never have permitted if we had been in our own town where someone might have recognised me.

'Eatin' yer food in th' street. What 'ud folks think?' she would have scolded.

A band played on the Green and shops were always open on Sundays, selling trinkets and souvenirs. I loved the cheap jewellery, the garish ornaments. As I learned to read, I liked to join Father at the postcard stand, though I was often disappointed as he chivvied me on, drawing my attention elsewhere before I could ask any awkward questions about the meaning of the double-entendres. Kiosks on the front offered sticks of rock. Ice-cream could be bought from vendors who pedalled along the promenade on specially adapted bicycles. I don't ever remember having hot-dogs or burgers but we ate fish and chips out of newspaper in the late afternoon, or took them to share with Auntie and Uncle if they were at their summer residence, a caravan on a site at the end of the fair.

When a refreshing breeze came off the sea, we might walk along the sand as far as Old Hunstanton, famous for its russet and crimson striped cliffs: pleasant enough but I never found them as impressive as the knot-holes with their jagged, jutting faces. Paths with overhanging flowers led to the formal gardens at the top of these cliffs and, from this high vantage point, we could see right across the Wash to Skegness. On days that were clear of a sea mist, it was possible to discern the outline of the tower of St Botolph's church, known locally as 'Boston Stump', rising from the flat fens of Lincolnshire.

One Sunday, the breeze brought in a plague of ladybirds. The prom literally crawled with them. We sat at a table on the raised balcony outside the café, sweeping them aside before we could put down the cups. All around us people were brushing them out of their hair and picking them from their clothes. It was an amazing sight to see and even I gave up trying to count them.

My most vivid memory of these excursion days is of the train pulling out of the station on the return trip. We left behind the beautiful, orange glow of the sun setting over the sea: a sight not normally seen on the east coast, but possible at Hunstanton because the town actually faces west.

Then it was a sleepy journey home and a slow procession back from the station with parents carrying the smallest children, the slightly bigger ones straggling behind, their exuberance of the morning now spent. At each turning, families branched off to their own street until we walked alone again, back to the safety of our carriages that didn't move.

9 Let us Pray

In the fens, where generations have lived so close to nature, their very survival has been dependent on the vagaries of the weather. With the dangers of floods and tempests always present, great store has been placed on faith and belief. Within a number of denominations, prayers have been asked in desperation and answered with relief and thanksgiving. At one time, the importance of delivering the message was so great that when the people couldn't get to church because of the water, the same water was used to get the church to the people. The ingenious minister of the day reached outlying farms and hamlets, along rivers and dykes on a boat which became known as the Fenland Ark.

My spiritual grounding, at a time when church or chapel played such a central role in family life, was a little disjointed. I have a very early memory of a little cardboard house, standing on the tall-boy in Granny's bedroom. It had a slit in the roof, through which we poked coins. I was allowed to help with this task but when I wanted to tip it upside down, shake them out and start again, as I did with my money-box, I learned that these coins were irretrievable. The bottom was sealed with a label which Granny insisted could only be removed by 'The lady from the Home League'.

I was never totally convinced that it would take much strength to pull it aside but Granny had spoken. Her authority was not something to be questioned. When the lady arrived, I was anxious to see what made her special, but she didn't seem particularly muscular. She was just a normal size with a quiet voice, but I did like her hat. It had a ribbon under her chin and a decorative bow at the side. It was similar to the one worn by Granny in some of the old photos, showing people in tunics, carrying instruments. I finally realised that this was the uniform of the Salvation Army, to which Granny and both my parents belonged.

I listened to the stories of how my parents had met when Father came to town with the band from his native Nottingham. He had stayed on when the band left and lodged at the carriages, renting the room that was now our front-room. I loved to imagine him sitting quietly in his armchair next to the fire, dreaming of what his future held as he slowly fell in love with the daughter of the house. Around this image, I wove a fantasy of the dashing young bandsman who wooed Mother with his beautiful music. Only recently was this illusion shattered when I learned that he was a Colour Sergeant. He led the band, carried the flag, but never played an instrument. Finally, I know why I did not inherit any musical talent.

Despite my parents' mutual background in the Salvation Army, there seems to have been a shift in allegiance before they married because their wedding took place in the Church of England. Late on a winter's afternoon, with snow on the ground, they took their vows as dusk fell and St Andrew's church was lit with candles. I have always held this image as the pinnacle of romance. Four years later, it was to this same building that Mother returned to be churched on her first outing after my birth, as was the custom for women at that time. On Whit Monday of the same year, the family gathered there to witness my baptism.

There appears to have been another wind-change in my early childhood as I attended Sunday school in the Methodist chapel at King's Dyke, although this may have been an act of convenience rather than conversion. From the time I started school, I pleaded to be allowed to go to Sunday school because the other children went and I felt I was missing some important part of my social life. Mother held out for a long time, saying 'I tek yer to school five days a week, I ent goin' out on Sundys an' all'.

Eventually she relented and I was escorted to this nearest place of worship, opening up a whole new world for me. I wasn't particularly overcome by any religious fervour but I loved the smells. The chapel was closed after the service on a Sunday night and the heating turned off until we were due to arrive the following Sunday morning so we opened the heavy door to the scent of damp wood, damp walls and the dust of old books that were rarely used. I breathed in these smells that were reminiscent of the lichen and fungus in my beloved blockhouse and I was home.

I spent many happy hours in that room where the tall windows cast different lights according to the season and left the shadows in the cob-webbed corners untouched. In the tiny vestry, where we said prayers and read in small groups, we huddled around a heater as the whitewash peeled and flaked. We pored over old texts, searching for words and phrases relative to a particular theme. Only on special occasions were we paraded into the main body of the chapel where glorious, coloured light shone through the stained glass windows, giving a pale sheen to the oak pews and the organ as it sent its music soaring to the rafters.

Within the church calendar there were celebrations, rehearsals for celebrations and the celebration of every celebration that had gone well. We seemed to spend the whole year celebrating. Mother recalled that the only time I ever sleep-walked was one year on the eve of the Sunday School Anniversary, when she woke to find me standing beside her bed, eyes closed, hands together, chanting the ditty that I was to recite from the stage the next day.

Each year's Anniversary was a grand performance to entertain the adults: to show off our talents if we had any, or at least to be on stage providing backing for those who had. Prize-giving was part of this event. Prizes awarded by Sunday school were quite easily attained, sometimes just by turning up, but they were treasured possessions. I passed some of mine on to my children, with the date of the award and my name on a label pasted inside, signed with the authority of the minister, still in pristine condition because I never had a bookcase, so they lived in the protected environment of a cupboard.

One of my favourites was called 'The Harveys see it through'. This told the story of four motherless children, left by their father whilst he went to New York on business. They fended for themselves in the day and were loosely supervised at night by a woman they had never met, but she 'had good references'. As well as running the house, they sewed cushions and made friends with a strange man. This was not a time when fear of strangers was endemic and paedophiles haunted every nightmare. It all ended well with their father and the man chatting and smoking cigarettes together: an excellent illustration of what a different culture existed in the 1960s.

When the last of the prizes had been gratefully received, tea and squash were served and we all pranced around in our new rig-outs. To not have a new frock for Anniversary would have been unthinkable. Often this was accompanied by new patent shoes and, after all the jollities were over, it seemed a long walk home, with just the dim beam of Mother's torch in the dark: trying to avoid the puddles in the ruts on the path by the brickyards; trying not to splash the pale satin of the frock; fretting that the sash might come undone and drabble in the mud left by the lorries; anxious to get back to the light of the carriages to check that my new shoes had not been scuffed.

The main focus of autumn was the Harvest Festival, when an assortment of home-grown vegetables were carried to the chapel and laid at the altar. In this rural community, every family had a garden and even the poorest managed to contribute. The food was blessed during the service and then taken to the local elderly. Donations included sheaves of corn, sacks of potatoes and baskets of vegetables from nearby farms, as well as the produce children brought from their own gardens, still smelling of damp earth. To have arrived bearing a tin would have been greeted with much distain, so I was saddened recently to read the letter from my grandson's city school, inviting parents to partake in the Harvest Festival but asking 'No fresh produce, please'.

One of the highlights of my Sunday school days was when I won a competition for writing the best poem about Christmas. My entry was forwarded to the area heat in Peterborough and I had to go to a big city church in Wentworth Street and read it from the pulpit. It was the first time I ever spoke into a microphone and the church was packed. I can't remember the words of the poem, or even if I won a prize, but I do recall that Granny took me on a bus and it was winter. She wore her thick blue coat and a matching hat with a hat-pin, not her normal woolly one, so it must have been a real event.

The most eagerly awaited day in the chapel calendar was the Sunday school outing. Thankfully, the horrors of the steam train had now been superseded by a new generation of coaches as the favoured carrier of families bound for the sea. Gone were the hissing, the roaring, and the belching smoke. No more long walks to and from the station. These beauties arrived with a gentle purr: a sleek convoy in blue and cream livery that could have been chosen for the seaside, gliding to a halt right at the chapel's iron gates where we could all board elegantly through the door that slid easily on its runners. Everyone scrabbled for a place on the lead coach, eager to head this cavalcade towards the rising sun.

We rode on coaches built for the future, with names such as Panorama, Europa and Super Vega, which were to survive into the preservation era, noted for their shining chrome trims and maximum glass to give light, air and a magnificent view. We experienced the exhilaration of being part of the era that became known as the 'Golden Age of the Coach'.

As we bounced along the open fen roads and into Norfolk, we were the new kings of the road. Sections of the highway to the coast had been widened to three lanes to ease congestion. This overtaking lane, used by traffic heading in both directions, and later considered a dangerous configuration, was the most exciting place to be. It was also the most natural position for us fen-dwellers. We were at home in the middle of any road, used to tracks which rose to a central crest, crumbling and falling away at the sides, giving camber a whole new meaning.

Now that we could communicate with the driver, requesting lavatory stops or a pull-over in a layby so someone could retrieve a much needed item from the vast recesses of the boot, the whole scenario became much more personal.

Unrestrained by seatbelts, everyone was free to mingle, like guests at a cocktail party. Grown-ups stood in the gangway to chat and children moved up and down the coach to swap seats with friends. It was a huge step from the anonymity of the railway. No longer divided by the train compartments, we could see and hear everyone else: the raised voices and laughter as we sang 'If you're 'appy and you know it'.

The driver was often the instigator: encouraging everyone to join the singing, telling jokes, calling the men 'Sir', flattering the ladies, humouring the children. A good driver could have the whole coach in uproar and, at the end of the day, his passengers' appreciation could be measured by the number of coins thrown into the hat that was passed round.

At the seaside nothing much changed. The weary donkeys still trod the same stretch of beach. The same rides still waited in the fair that never travelled. The real novelty to be savoured was the journey itself. It took longer to travel by road than it had by rail but most considered this a small disadvantage. I don't ever recall thinking of it as a disadvantage at all. Surely a longer ride was an advantage. At night we could be dropped right outside the carriages but I begged to be allowed to stay on an extra five minutes to the chapel, although it meant a ten minute walk back.

Another time of year when we took part in a ritual celebration was Guy Fawkes Night, but I recall no mention of its religious connotation. To us, it was just bonfire night, and the excitement of being wrapped up warm and taken into a neighbour's garden after dark. Each November, we stood around the fire and watched the flames lick at the stuffed guy which the neighbour's children had carted around in an old push-chair during the preceding weeks.

It was a rare occasion when we socialised after dark. Mother prepared hot soup and jacket potatoes for supper, and Father annoyed everyone by letting off jumping-jacks just behind them. I recall this so clearly because it was so out of character. A quiet, timid man, more likely to nod or shake his head, than speak in a crowd for the rest of the year, suddenly became a rebel, darting around the garden with the grin of a demon in the dark. I don't know what words were exchanged privately, but Mother seemed resigned to this annual performance.

She just concentrated on not trying too hard to persuade me to hold a sparkler like the other children. I don't know which of us was more scared of me clutching the thin stick as sparks rained down on my woolly gloves but I remember never quite grasping it. I kept open the option of withdrawing my hand at any moment, happier just watching the Shower of Golden Rain or a spinning Catherine Wheel.

Each year, after all the other bonfires along the road had diminished to a curl of grey smoke, ours burnt bright against the night sky, the heat forcing us further and further back, our faces feeling as if they might scorch. Only when I was older and questioned the ferocity of these fires, was I told that the neighbour brought home the left over pieces of wood from work. As he worked for the local undertaker, I'm sure we had a good quality bonfire. Perhaps Father wasn't the only one there with a surprising sense of humour.

I had come to Sunday school late and I stayed late too, helping with the younger children as they came in and my age group dwindled. However, as High School took over my time, I didn't give much thought to any religion beyond what was taught in Christian Education, which was yet to be replaced by the broader Religious Education. The shadow of William Booth did not look over my shoulder in the way that he lingered beside Granny. In fact, my only visits to church during those years could perhaps be considered nefarious.

My last school was opposite St Wendreda's church in March, famous for its hammer beam ceiling and flying angels, but I never went inside to admire this medieval structure.

When the cross-country group loped out of the school grounds on damp days with heavy clouds threatening to soak us, my friend and I lagged behind. As those with enthusiasm jogged heartily round the churchyard, we were far enough behind that our absence would not be noticed. We took refuge in the church porch, sheltering where we could listen out for the pounding footsteps to return, tagging on again after the rest of the group passed, reaching the school in our same position right at the back. In some circumstances our gym mistress might have been pleased that we saw the church as a place of refuge, shelter and sanctuary, but on these occasions it seemed more prudent not to mention it.

10 Christmas is Coming

My first Christmas treat was the annual visit to Santa's grotto in Fairways store. Dressed in my best shoes and whitest socks, my hair would be brushed to a glowing sheen, before being hidden under my bonnet. This preparation was necessary as there was always a photographer in the grotto, capturing the moment every year when each child was encouraged to whisper her most secret wishes into the hairy ear of the bearded gentleman. He was actually very efficient at his job, delivering the goods in the early morning silence of Christmas morning. My expression in these photos, however, suggests that I was never quite at ease in his presence.

My parents believed strongly in the old adage that Christmas was a time for family and their interpretation of 'family' was those of us who lived within the carriages: Mother, Father, Granny and me.

Those outside, even if they were related, were not included. Cousins, once married, were described as 'having their own families now', so we would not visit them or expect them to call on us over the holiday. There were no parties, nor dancing, music nor drinking. We never socialised at this time of year. I didn't see rowdy behaviour or what Granny called 'gallivanting'. We didn't even see the neighbours. We simply retreated into our own safe, miniature world, remaining cocooned as the same rituals were played out each year, yet we had our own brand of magic.

By the middle of December cards were written and mostly hand-delivered. I remember just one or two parcels being prepared for posting and this was quite an event. Firstly, the kitchen table was cleared. This was unusual in itself because a residue of frequently used items was normally left on it from day to day: the biscuit tin, the teapot, the tea caddy, cups and saucers covered with a tea-cloth.

Once this space was clear, Mother produced the present; perhaps a knitted pull-over for a cousin or a knitted pair of mittens for an aunt. Most gifts at that time were handmade, and for 'handmade', read 'knitted'. She wrapped the item in the normal sheet of Christmas paper, patterned with bells or holly. Father then spread out a sheet of thick, brown paper and wrapped it again. This was a man's job, evidently. I just watched in silence, a stance not often seen, but quietly aware of the gravity of the situation.

The presents, which may have been weeks in the making, were being made safe for an epic journey. Some of them travelled miles across the fens on a train which kept going all through the night. Others went as far as Leicester, where there were hills to contend with. Each parcel was secured with ample lengths of string and I recall both parents checking and testing the bulky knots. Father wrote the address in bold print on both sides and added our address in smaller writing, so that it could be returned should some disaster befall it. It was finally handed back to Mother for dispatching at the post office.

The run-up to Christmas seemed to last for ever, with up to a week's wait between school breaking up and the dawn of Christmas morning. This was a period of hushed voices that died as I appeared from the shadows, silent looks exchanged, and the sleight of hand as objects were removed from Father's pockets when he thought I was busy. I don't know whether I was just a nosy child or if I lived with three extremely inept adults, but I do remember being very aware of all this subterfuge.

Another sign that the time was imminent was the symbolic arrival of the cake, from the bakery at the back of Miller's shop in High Causeway. It was carefully borne home in Mother's bike basket and placed on the sideboard in the front room. It could only be viewed by persuading a grown-up to lift the cloth, securely tucked in around the base to protect it from mice with sweet teeth. The mixture of rich fruit and cherries was topped by marzipan and a layer of perfect snow. At the moment that it was unveiled, a scene was captured, frozen in action. A tiny robin with unblinking eyes and a snowman in a scrumpled felt hat, looked on as small figures on skates and sledges went gliding past bushes sprinkled with frost. I could see their tracks etched behind them and the mound of crisp snow that had just fallen from the bushes. Many times a day I asked to peep, knowing that one day I would catch them moving, yet never quite quick enough. As in a game of musical statues, I knew the play would resume as soon as the cloth was replaced.

Relations and friends visited for the last time before the big day, leaving with a card, sometimes a parcel, and many good wishes. Tradition decreed that tradesfolk, who usually performed the same duties year after year, were recognised at this time. The ten shilling note or a few coins were thought to reward their diligence and ensure continued good service in the coming year. These tips went to the butcher when he delivered the Christmas meat; the baker when the last bread arrived; the coalman as he heaved extra sacks to the coal-place to last over the holiday; the dustmen who had emptied bins and closed the gate behind them for twelve months; and the postman who cheerfully delivered letters in all weathers. The money was counted out and left in a tin on the sideboard in the kitchen, handy as each person called. As the contents of the tin diminished it was like a countdown to the big day - the closest we ever got to an Advent calendar.

By now any nativity plays or Sunday school activities were behind us. We never attended church on Christmas Eve or Christmas Day. It was only much later that I was able to embrace that other magical moment: the thrill of stepping out of church to a sky full of stars and the ringing of bells after Midnight Mass.

As each day of the countdown passed we became more insular until, finally, Father arrived home after the last of the shoppers were served and the last pound sign clanged onto the till. By now the roads were growing quieter too. The lorries were parked up and their drivers home for the holiday. Even the buses were garaged until lunchtime on Boxing Day.

Now all we could do was wait, relaxed in the knowledge that fuel and food were plentiful. I never remember a time when I wasn't aware of the emphasis placed on these essentials. By today's standards the pantry was probably quite bare. There was nothing in the fridge or freezer because there was no fridge or freezer.

Home-grown vegetables might be not so plentiful at this time of year. The land might be frozen solid so we visited Andrews' little green-grocers on High Causeway, where everything was laid out on the counter except the dog biscuits, which were in open tubs. I don't know why I remember the dog biscuits - we never had a dog.

Carrots, swedes, leeks and Brussels were all weighed on scales with brass weights and a scoop which lifted off, sliding the produce straight into the right sized brown paper bag. There was no plastic packaging to turn vegetables into a sweating slush, not that anything had ever sweated in our pantry. It was further away from the warmth of the kitchen than anywhere else, except the lavatory. Even the milk froze in the bottles after it was brought indoors and now we could finally enjoy a jelly. This was the time of year when the red slosh set in the bowl.

The chicken for Christmas dinner and the joint, usually beef, for Boxing Day were in the meat-safe along with sausages and bacon and a pork pie for Christmas Day breakfast. A sack of potatoes, and another of onions, were stashed in the pantry. These were brought in the boot of Uncle's car because he was from Ely and knew a farmer out that way. Granny was always happy to accept these contributions, although she was regularly heard saying 'We've got short shrift 'ere. They allus think they can suck yer in at this time a' year. There's a bushel o' muck in the bottom'.

She still measured in bushels and gills, just as she added up her money in guineas and always paid in cash. A lot of shops offered the opportunity to put groceries 'on the slate', especially close to Christmas, to be paid in instalments after New Year, but neither her nor Mother would have considered such an option. They had been raised to pay on the nail and a familiar quote was 'If yer can't pay fer it, yer wait 'til yer can'.

Both were similarly critical of the new trend to buy larger items 'on the never-never'. They would have been so ashamed if the club-man had come knocking. Consequently, money was secreted throughout the year in various jars and envelopes. Lists were kept of every purchase and items needed in order of priority. If the roof had leaked in December of any year, I'm sure I would have been very short of presents as I slid rapidly down that list.

Fortunately that never happened and the thrill of novelty mingled with the security of predictability as a carrot was left on a plate for Rudolph, along with a mince pie and a glass of milk for Santa. There was no hope of a sherry here. Perhaps our Santa was in the Salvation Army.

Although a lot of the proceedings were set in stone, they were still exciting because of the long wait until they happened again next year. The nut-crackers only came out on Christmas Eve and the first slice of pork-pie was always cut on Christmas morning. I don't know if the choice of foods was still extraordinarily restricted into the 1960s or if rationing had instilled a frugal attitude in those that had learned to make do on very little. Perhaps we were just not very adventurous, but I only remember the choice of Brazil nuts or not, and for a long time I didn't even have that choice as Mother feared me choking, explaining 'Yer not big enough fer nuts 'case they gew down the wrong way'.

We had sugared sweets, orange and lemon coloured segments alternating around the box, and dates which came with their own fork. I urged Mother to buy figs as well but she assured me that I wouldn't like them, which meant that she didn't like them. This happened with a number of foods and it was years before I discovered that I actually did like liver and mushrooms, as well as figs and several types of nut that were not Brazil.

11 Christmas Past and Presents

Christmas was always a magical time but never more so than when the weather entered into the spirit, bringing snow at just the right time. Then it seemed that the world was hushed, wrapped in its protective white blanket. If it came before bedtime, I was allowed to peep at the flakes fluttering past the windows. I watched in awe as it fell steadily against the dark sky: clinging like beads to the bare bushes, the hedges and the roof of the bird table. I knelt on my bed, face pressed against the cold of the glass, mesmerised by the gentle motion until I could keep my eyes open no longer and had to be scooped gently into the covers. The warmth of my own blankets closed around me as I drifted into dreams of a sleigh gliding to a halt just beyond my window, the steam of reindeer breath hot in the crisp air.

If the snow crept down during the night, I might wake to a whispered voice suggesting 'Why don't y' 'ave a look out there?'

I knew what I would see as I scrambled to the nearest window but still the sight took away my breath. The bushes wore shrouds, as full and round as when they bore the foliage of summer. The paths could not be distinguished from the garden. The whole scene was a picture of white silence.

On Christmas morning, whatever the weather outside, the one bar of the electric fire already glowed, switched on in the bedroom before I woke. I leapt into the middle of my parents' bed and my pillowcase-sack was dragged onto the foot. One of the clearest memories I have from this time is of the blend of aromas that came from that sack. Before I opened anything I could anticipate the contents just by breathing in.

As I unwrapped bath cubes and talcum powder, there came irony. They were scented to evoke memories of special summer moments in a country garden but, for the whole of my grown-up life, I have stood in such gardens and the image in my mind is of a tin of honeysuckle perfumed talcum powder on a cold Christmas morning.

Then there was the glossy sheen of an unopened annual; the newness of a silk petticoat or cotton handkerchiefs; the soft fur of new slippers; the flowery print of a winceyette nightie; that special rubber or celluloid smell of a new doll; the cardboard smell of a game, perhaps beetle-drive or Ludo, or a boxed jigsaw puzzle.

My favourite jigsaw arrived on such a morning, a picture of a gypsy camp at night, illuminated by the glowing fire. It had a thousand pieces, way in advance of my age, and took me years to complete, but from that morning I was captivated by the scene on the box and I dreamed that one day I would join such a gathering; I would be the girl with ebony hair and golden hoop earrings shining, as I danced by the firelight.

Sometimes a present brings unprecedented joy. I thought my happiness was complete the year I unwrapped two large boxes, each with the word 'Rosebud' on the lid. The first one contained a beautiful doll with soft, curling hair. I couldn't guess what was in the second box but, when I tentatively opened it, there was an identical doll and suddenly I was the ecstatic mother of twin girls who I called Trudy and Tracy. I opened all my other presents with both dolls clutched in my arms.

Then my parents steered me up the passage to the front room. There, waiting for its new occupants, stood a shining Pedigree Triang pram with a metal body and two hoods. Sometimes you just know you are the luckiest child that ever celebrated Christmas.

Another year, as I reached the bottom of my sack, Mother announced 'Ooh, 'ang on. I forgot one. 'ev a look in the wardrobe'.

I scrambled off the bed, opened the heavy wardrobe door and met the steady gaze of the softest, fluffiest teddy bear. His fur was blue and white but I don't remember thinking that strange, I just loved him and he slept with me for years but there was a downside to that story. The following year I emptied my sack and then asked 'Can I look in the wardrobe now?'

I saw my parents exchange a glance but it was not the conspiring look of those with a trick to play. It was the hesitant look of realisation that they had not foreseen my expectations.

Greedy, selfish child that I was, I sat on that huge bed surrounded by more gifts than one child might ever expect and complained that there wasn't anything left in the wardrobe. I don't know what lesson I was supposed to learn from that; perhaps not to be presumptuous, but my parents must have felt guilty that I had been disappointed on Christmas morning because, from then on, year after year, my last present was always in the wardrobe.

After the pork pie breakfast, I was allowed to eat what I wanted for that one day of the year and I was usually too full of sweets and biscuits to enjoy much dinner, although I would recover enough by teatime to enjoy a fair-sized slice of that frosty scene on top of the cake. My only reservation about tea-time was approaching the table, knowing that there would be crackers beside each place setting. These must have been bought for the amusement of the grown-ups because I hated and feared them. Every year I was cajoled into holding one end as they were pulled. I grasped them with screwed up eyes, head turned away and a pounding heart. The bang terrified me and perhaps this added to their sadistic fun as I squirmed in my seat.

'Don't be s' darft' Mother urged, but I was always too nervous to even put my hand inside to retrieve the tiny piece of paper that told a joke, or the neatly folded paper hat that was placed on my head, falling over my eyes as I dived for cover at the next explosion.

Another very special memory for me is of the fire being alight in the front room. The chimney on that side of the carriages is more sheltered than the kitchen chimney, getting little draught, so the fire never drew well. It sulked darkly and emitted a menacing cloud of smoke every time someone opened the door to go into the room. For that reason it was lit infrequently. Mother usually got it going a couple of days before Christmas to air out the room, often the first time it had been lit for a year. She persevered despite its contrary behaviour until the room filled with a smell that I struggle to describe. It encompassed damp, as the layers of wallpaper, curtains and rugs started to dry out, the earthy elements of the soil in which sat the tree, and the overtones of wet coal and kindling. All these smells that I loved, came into the carriages and hung there. Then the heat from the fire took over and a new cosiness glowed in that room.

For these few days each year, I took my toys in there, sharing this experience with them and, on Christmas morning, Father joined me while the two women bustled in the kitchen. This was a short, precious interval when he had time off work. With no television or other distractions, we played together and shared stories and were probably as close as we ever got but, all too soon, the mirror above the mantel piece steamed up, the first sign that the potatoes were boiling on the stove in the kitchen and we would soon be called to eat.

I spent every moment I could in that room, even asking if I could have one more look in on my way to bed. I remember Mother opening the door slowly so as not to disturb the fire, and waiting behind me as I paused in the doorway in my nightie. The last glowing embers in the grate and the crimson light reflecting in the baubles on the tree are my picture of Christmas.

On Boxing Day night I had to be led from that doorway, feeling the stealth of a Christmas about to leave as I slept. Tomorrow it would be gone. The ashes would not be rekindled. The fire would not be relit. The lingering smell of wood smoke would start to fade.

Something held me in that doorway and I wonder if I sensed the presence of those who had stood there before me, just as real at a different time, their heightened emotions caught in the frame as they waited for the train to slow at a station somewhere so that they could alight and join their families for Christmas, or stepping up from a platform at the end of the holiday, turning on that step to wave goodbye.

12 Sweating Cobbs

Each year, as regularly and predictably as Christmas, came the decorating season, heralded by observations such as 'Ceilin's lookin' a bit dingy in 'ere...' and 'Look at all them fat splashes be'ind the stove...'.

After a winter of cooking, coal fires and Mother's intermittent smoking, it was usually the kitchen that was first on the agenda.

The search for a suitable wallpaper began with a bus trip to Manders' decorating shop on Long Causeway in Peterborough. Huge sample books were spread out on a counter that ran around the walls and Mother perched me on a stool with a book of my choice. She knew from experience that this tome, with pages so big that I struggled to turn them with my short arms, would keep me amused. This gave her the chance to deliberate and make a decision which did not involve my opinion.

Unaware of this subterfuge, I began the serious task of selecting something really impressive, with vibrant colours and dynamic patterns. I imagined the bunches of richly coloured fruit draped from our picture rails in the kitchen. I gasped at thatched cottages, set amid a plethora of multi-coloured flowers, their gardens spreading so far that they met the garden of the next cottage as the pattern repeated. I fell in love with elegant ballerinas in pink tutus who would have performed exquisite dances around my bed. Once I reached the boring, colourless, embossed papers at the back of the book, it was time to wriggle off my stool and see what Mother had discovered.

Sometimes, if she was feeling decisive, I was dragged away before I had made a choice. Then I protested loudly, indignant that if I had not been allowed enough time to view all the possibilities. I had not yet noticed the definite bias towards all the papers coming from Mother's book.

Once this did became apparent, I patiently deliberated over the papers which would grace the walls of my own house, once I was old enough to be free of the limitations enforced by the unimaginative grown-ups. For now I had to put up with the predictable mixture of pale colours and small patterns. My choice, which Mother described as gaudy, would have made our small rooms appear smaller, somehow, apparently.

I had to live again with the tiny posies of flowers, sprigs of lily-of-the-valley and miniature baskets with ivy entwined around the handles. Actually, these were very pretty and, many years later, as I stripped back the layers, I salvaged pieces of each, large enough to resurrect in frames. Now they live again on the walls of the rooms they once covered: each with a memory of a particular time of my childhood.

Amongst the twenty-six layers, left on for added insulation, I have discovered the heavy, hessian-backed flock papers of a previous generation. Some are still edged with strips bearing the roll and serial numbers. These narrow strips were meant to protect the paper if the roll end was knocked, then be removed by a special trimmer before the paper was hung. It seems that we had no such device and so they survived, pasted onto the wall and overlapped by the next strip, being revealed to tell their story so much later.

I also rediscovered the ones that I dreaded most - the mottles. We had mottles in all colours, sometimes following each other. Pink might be replaced by blue, covered with green and then yellow, representing four years of my life when I was surrounded with the same pattern.

Once 'our' choice had been made, the rolls were wrapped in brown paper and secured with string, then taken home for Granny's approval. It is perhaps testament to the shared taste of the two women that I never remember there being any hint of dissent.

Then came the preparation stage, always beginning on a Monday with the annual sweeping of the chimney. We did not employ the local chimney sweep, although I am sure he was quite capable and very experienced. The grown-ups believed he wasn't used to doing railway carriage chimneys and he might dislodge the pot if he pushed the brush too hard, causing the weight of the pot to fall through the roof.

Instead, Mother and Granny donned their oldest clothes: stained pinafores and cardigans where even the darning needed darning. Then they dragged the hessian sack of rods from the shed. These were the same rods that had an old piece of towel or sheet tied to the end and were thrust underground when the sewer pipe backed up.

On chimney-sweeping day, they were laid out along the path at the side of the carriage to establish the order, the first one having a rounded end and the last one having the brush attached. They were screwed together with brass fittings and I tried to help, loving the feel of the smooth wood, but I was shooed away on the grounds of hygiene. I don't think it was because of the residual soot that clung to them but, more likely, in fear of residue from their other task.

A canvas curtain was hung from the line under the mantelpiece to catch the soot. This had a hole through which the rods were poked, but the hole was not rod-size. It was a small, rectangular slit, neatly hemmed all the way round, and the size of our letterbox. I have a feeling that this is the curtain seen in early photos of the carriages, hanging on the outside of the front door, protecting the paintwork from the blistering heat of the sun, with this slit at the height of the letterbox, allowing letters to be posted through it. This was a time when junk was left out for the scrap-man; it didn't arrive through the letterbox. Post came in small, handwritten envelopes and this was reflected in the tiny opening.

Inside the carriage, Mother pushed the rods, always cussing because there was some kind of ledge in the chimney which hampered her heaving. It was one of the many times when she would mop a hand across her brow and proclaim that she was 'sweating cobbs'.

Outside, Granny watched for the brush, not to cheer that it had burst into the sky above the chimney, but to shout a warning that she could see the first bristles. Then it was hauled back in, with much relief that the pot had not been dislodged and we would survive for another year with an intact roof.

Despite the curtain, a certain amount of soot always escaped into the room so the rest of that day was spent cleaning, wiping, mopping. Everything was put back in place and tea cooked by the time Father got home from work. He took no part in this spring-cleaning. Mother and Granny were not women who expected the man of the house to do drains or be responsible for chimneys or gardening. They just rolled up their woolly cardigan sleeves and got on with whatever needed doing.

A second day of preparation saw the smaller furniture taken out of the room and the larger items moved to one end. Half the ceiling was whitewashed with a mixture of distemper that Granny had knocked up in a zinc bucket. She always applied this and Mother glossed the panelled doors and the window frames. They worked as a team but each responsible for their own task.

Dockey- time was about eleven. Then, after a pot of tea and a few rich tea biscuits, the furniture was moved to the other end of the room so that the second half of the ceiling could be done. Any spills were wiped up from the lino with a floor cloth, kept at the ready in another bucket. I don't remember much splashing although the liquid was quite runny and it was applied with a wide brush and sweeping strokes. Again, after they had stopped for fourses, the furniture was replaced. We could not function in this restricted space unless everything was back to normal for the evening so, as wallpapering day finally dawned, it all had to be pulled out again.

The most difficult room to paper was our bedroom, where a double and single bed had to be stripped and upended, a dressing table had to be cleared of its candlesticks and trinket set before it could be manoeuvred. Even the heavy wardrobe had to be lifted, not dragged, so as not to tear the lino. Every year Mother would swear to 'Git rid of the bleddy gret orkard thing'.

This wardrobe, which was too tall to stand against the side walls, where the ceilings curved downwards, was pressed tight against my dismantled bed and the door between our bedroom and the kitchen creaked open. This was the only time of year that the door was opened. Normally, the wardrobe stood in front of it and access was only from the passage. Now, it allowed lengths of paper to be sized on the table in the kitchen and carried through to be hung, with me ducking and squealing as it was passed over my head.

The team were at work again. Granny held the strip up to the wall and Mother cut it to the right length. Then, back in the kitchen, Granny applied the size, which she had mixed earlier in the pudding bowl. Mother held the paper up to the ceiling and Granny coaxed it onto the wall, butting the edges, sliding it up and down to get a neat match in the pattern and gently smoothing it out with a clean piece of old sheet. This pattern matching was an art. As each piece was cut, the position of the pattern left on the roll would alter. Sometimes they would work from up to four rolls at the same time, testing each for the closest match to minimise waste. This was why the mottles were favoured. They required hardly any matching, so were the least wasteful and quickest to hang.

Finally, Mother trimmed along the skirting board and round the Bakelite switches, while Granny took a breather before selecting the next length. Our walls were not straight, our ceilings not level. A narrow border complimented the paper and hid any gaps. These unrolled to nearly the length of the room and it took both women to wriggle them into position above head height. When they reached the last wall, Granny always announced, 'Well, I think tha's bruck the back o' it now'.

They worked with little conversation but an unspoken co-operation. The atmosphere was light as if, once the chimney was swept, the dirt and dark oppression of winter had been banished, replaced by the smell of drying paint and paper, bringing freshness and new beginnings. They were even tolerant of my coming and going, in and out of the door between the rooms, just because it was a novel new route. They only threatened to 'stick 'er up the wall be'ind the paper' with laughter in their voices.

By night-time, everything was finally settled back in place and the door shut again for another year. The wardrobe was forgiven for its bulky proportions now that it was refilled and Mother remembered how much storage it provided. I could fall asleep with the newness all around me, dreaming that perhaps next year it might be my turn to choose the paper and then the ballerinas would come to perform their dance around my bed.

13 Woolly Hats and Tea Cosies

As the bitter nights of winter closed in again each year, we spent long evenings huddled around the hearth, like true fen dwellers of the past. We considered ourselves much more advanced than those who had trod this land in an earlier time, wrapped in animal skins to ward off the biting winds, but still we pulled knitted shawls tightly around our shoulders. Granny pruggled the dying ashes with the poker, attempting to get the last of the heat out of the grate before bedtime. All traces of the fire had to be extinguished before the grown-ups could go to bed. We had still not forgotten Robert Sayles.

The north wind whistled across the fields, threatening to lift the zinc sheets from the roof and rain and hail beat on the glass. There were times when that room got so cold that the heat from the light bulb could be felt if you stood directly beneath it. I was at a real disadvantage as the shortest member of the family.

It was wise to wait until bedtime before going to the lavatory. The door to the passage was directly opposite the fireplace. Whenever it was opened, smoke belched into the room and the heat was lost.

This was especially true if it was me needing to go, because I wouldn't go on my own unless the door was left open. This stemmed from a time when I was quite tiny. I had toddled down the passage and reached the two big steps leading to the lavatory, only to see water pouring from the old tank that was mounted on the wall above the seat. The tank had burst in the frost and when the thaw came, the water gushed forth. It cascaded right down to where I might have been sitting. I recall being so shocked that I couldn't even run, but Mother claimed 'They must 'ave 'eard 'er 'ollering up town'.

I didn't stop even when she ran the length of the passage, scooping me into her arms, followed by Father and Granny who thought I had at least been murdered. The fact that I now went down the passage on my own as long as the door was left open was progress, but it didn't keep in the heat.

Visits from relations now became less frequent. Perhaps that could be attributed partly to the condition of the old fen roads, eroded by frost and even more rutted than usual, but I think the real reason was the dropping temperature on the thermometer. It rarely reached double figures.

A one-bar electric fire was switched on in the bedroom an hour before bedtime to take the chill off, and again just before I got up in the morning. My clothes were hung over a clothes horse in front of it. When they stopped steaming, I knew it was time to get dressed.

We all wore layers of clothes, meant to trap the heat, but I remember little heat to trap. I wore a woolly vest, a liberty bodice, flannel britches, a petticoat and thick tights before I even got to my top clothes.

Granny's layers consisted of a vest, a 'brazzier' worn over the vest, stays with rubber buttons to attach stockings, bloomers which reached the knees, a flannelette petticoat, a cotton frock, a wrap-around pinafore and at least one cardigan, knitted from recycled wool. She always wore a woolly hat, even indoors. These were knitted to the same pattern that she used for making tea-cosies. It was only at the stitching-up stage that a decision was made. A hat would be stitched from the brim to the crown. A cosy would have holes left in the seam on each side, one for the handle and one for the spout.

As scorch marks spread across the front of our calves and goose-pimples still covered the rest of our bodies, undergarments were patched. Missing buttons were replaced, often with odd ones. Socks were darned, each stretched over a 'mushroom', normally made of wood, although we once had a very modern plastic one with a battery and bulb, which shone through the wool, illuminating the hole that was to be mended. Strips of elastic were measured around my growing legs, then cut and stitched to make garters. Sheets were cut in halves lengthways and turned sides to middle, so that the most threadbare section would be nearest the edge of the bed.

Although these tasks involved a lot of sewing, the main industry of the women was knitting. A vast number of knitted items were produced each winter.

The sound of the clock was drowned out by the incessant click-clack of needles. The noise was never synchronised because Mother knitted faster than Granny, holding the needles differently and somehow pushing the wool forward with a flick of her finger in a way that I didn't master. I never progressed beyond the laborious, methodical strokes of Granny's style. I did, however, learn to knit early. I don't remember a time when I wasn't fascinated by the growing garments that hung from the needles, begging to join in until I was given balls of yarn from a bag of left-over oddments. I wound this round and round a pair of short, sturdy needles in an attempt to create something that I could wear. Gradually, I got the hang of basic knit and purl, opening my horizon to simple garter stitch, stocking stitch and rib. I could do row after row without too many dropped stitches, although I still needed a grown-up to cast on and cast off for me.

I was always impatient, wanting to see the results of my

labours tonight, not in a week or a month, though it was common to see the women spending this length of time, returning night after night to the same task. It was not necessarily the size of a garment that decreed how long it would be in the making. A pullover with no stripes, for my six-foot uncle, could be completed in less time than a first-size matinee coat with a lacy pattern and 'pie cot' edging.

I loved the colours: the pastel pinks, creams and blues of the baby clothes, the vibrant reds, greens and blues of the grown-up jumpers and cardigans. I enjoyed the feel of the different textures, especially the angora that was used to make tiny boleros. Baby clothes were made of two or three ply yarn and needles as fine as a size thirteen. Bigger clothes were a chunkier four ply.

As I mastered the art of knitting, I practised my counting. How many stitches did I have at the start of a row, how many were left at the end, how many had I lost on the way?

Each time I realised that a couple had escaped from my grasp half way across, I tutted 'Oh, cripes', and someone had to lay down their own work to rescue mine. Occasionally, if the response wasn't immediate, I tried to get Father to put aside his newspaper and help me out but his answer was always the same, 'I think yer best wait fer yer mother'.

Time was measured in terms of knitting.

'Are y' goin a' mek a cup a' tea?' might be answered, 'When I git up to the next button'ole' or 'I've just got six more rows to do on the rib'.

Bedtime was when something was safely cast off.

The items produced by the two women were different. Mother knitted all the baby clothes for cousins, friends, neighbours and many friends of cousins, friends and neighbours. She wore a clean pinny which she kept solely for this purpose, doused her hands in Smith's Cremolia, so they didn't get sweaty, and balanced a cardboard box on her lap, inside which bounced the ball of fluffy wool so that it could not fall onto the hearth. At one time she had a special ball for holding wool. This was green plastic. The wool was placed inside and threaded through a hole at the top but it never flowed freely and she soon returned to the box.

She produced copious amounts of tie-on bonnets in pink and button-up helmets in blue, bootees, mittens and matinee coats, from patterns by Emu and Patons. It was not unusual for a baby to be clad from head to toe in wool. A layette was the usual gift to a new-born. Leggings with feet and a double-breasted jacket with a pointed pixie-hood constituted a 'pram set'. These were worn by a baby tucked under a knitted blanket and amused by a pompom, made from left over wool, dangling on a length of wool, pinned inside the pram hood.

Once a child was toddling, they were zipped into a 'siren suit'. These originated in the war as a warm, all encompassing, garment which could be slipped on quickly over a child's day or night clothes as they headed for an air raid shelter, and were still popular in my childhood.

My worst experience of this woolly world, was the knitted vest that I was forced to wear even after I started school. I was conscious that the other girls wore soft, linen vests, not wool-cladding. I suppose I should have considered myself at least luckier than the fen children of a previous generation, who were reputedly sewn into their clothes as winter threatened their lives, and only undone when spring lifted the threat.

Mother's claim to fame was that a pair of her hand-knitted knee-socks, appeared on TV, worn by my second-cousin who was a guest on Miss Roslyn's Romper Room.

Granny was more likely to undertake the larger items; sleeveless pullovers for my uncles and twin-sets for my aunts. The same patterns, tried and tested on more than one generation, were endlessly repeated, often from memory. A jumper for a relation's child could be produced from a letter stating that he was a twenty-four chest, twelve inch arm and liked blue.

When someone visited, they often brought with them an old garment to be recycled. The work of an earlier year would be diligently unpicked, wound into skeins, then stretched over the back of a chair to pull out the kinks. A small ball of a contrasting colour could add a few stripes around the bottom and just above the cuffs. This had most likely been salvaged from another re-hash, so a 'new' jumper cost nothing. Even buttons and toggles were kept in a big tin and reused.

Granny's other speciality was toys. She knitted up whatever wool was left over into a garish array of woolly characters. There were dolls, teddy bears, dogs, clowns, monkeys, pandas, golliwogs, all in clashing colours. Their only common feature was their eyes. Once they were stitched up to the neck, and before the heads were stuffed, she used a big darning needle and black wool to add two bulbous eyes. This gave them all the same penetrating stare: quite unnerving when a number of them sat on her ottoman, steadily watching any small child who strayed into her bedroom.

When she had produced enough to fill a bag, she donated them to the children's ward at the Doddington County Hospital and I always imagined that a whole generation of children went home traumatised, not by their stay in hospital but by waking in the night to see those eyes staring at them from the foot of their bed.

With no television and no love of reading between them, Mother and Granny relied on their knitting to keep them amused as much as to produce a finished item. There were serious discussions as to whether they had enough wool to keep them going; particularly if it was a Saturday, at this time when shops did not open on Sundays. It was not unknown for one of them to decide that more supplies were needed just before the shops shut. Then I would be shoved into my coat to catch a bus up town. Town was always 'up', although the rise in the land was not enough to be discernible to the eye.

We headed hurriedly to Beryl Butcher's shop on High Causeway. This was the proverbial Aladdin's cave. The walls were lined with square pigeon-holed shelving. Each section held ounces of wool in a particular colour, ranging from the purest, white angora to the darkest shades of browns and black.

Labels read Sirdar, Robin and even Wendy. Posters advertised the newly fashionable nylon yarns. Mother did try these, although Granny was never tempted. She stuck resolutely to the traditional wool with its irritating fibres. My Granny-made hot water bottle cover gave me the choice between cold feet or itching feet.

Beryl and her husband took time to browse through patterns with their customers, discussing options and suggesting combinations. If there were a couple of customers waiting to be served, it was easy to spend an hour there. I loved the warmth and welcome in that shop. There were amazing glass drawers of buttons, cottons and everything needed by a generation for whom knitting was an important part of clothing the family.

They put by wool, too, so it was always sensible to order more than recommended by the pattern. Any excess was put back on the shelf if not needed. This also spread the cost; each ounce being paid for when collected.

Mother was a good customer and probably because of this, I was treated with smiles and polite service when I decided one day that I was going to knit Father a huge, polo-necked sweater that I had spotted in their book of patterns, and I ordered them to put by thirty ounces of wool: two red, two green, two blue, two black…

On these late afternoon forays, it grew dark before we left to walk the short distance back to the market place to catch the bus home.

The Butter Cross stood on the market place and we sheltered under it as we waited. This 17th century structure, worn by time and weather, was supported by sixteen stone pillars. Otherwise it was open to the elements. Whichever way the wind was blowing, it blew through the open sides, always finding its target: the space between the top of my knee socks and the hem of my coat, whipping my legs until they smarted as Mother cussed the bus and vowed that it 'Would a' bin quicker t' walk'.

Seats beneath the Butter Cross offered no respite as the wind curled and wound its way through every twist of the ironwork. Even on the coldest days, resilient old men in ancient overcoats hunched on these benches. There seemed to be little or no conversation between them, just the resigned silence of each other's company.

Without a word, one might catch my eye and exhale pipe smoke in rings to amuse a small child with chattering teeth; stomping her feet to keep at bay the spreading numbness, hoping that the bus would arrive before the need to go to the lavatory overtook the fear of maternal wrath if a visit to the dark and dreaded public conveniences led to a missed bus, and waiting all over again for the next one.

When the bus finally did arrive, it was only a five minute ride out of town, past the old mud walls that I loved to explore on a fine day's walk. I was always fascinated by the masonry bees, hovering in every crevice. Now the protective thatched hoods just dripped water dismally onto the path.

Back at the carriages, Granny looked out for the bus to slow as it passed. The kettle was on for a hot drink and everyone could relax for the evening. The crisis of running out of wool had been averted.

14 Equally Different

In the days before equality became an issue, let alone the perceived 'norm', roles were much more clearly defined, but I think our household was a little unusual.

Because Grandfather had been away for a lot of each year, and then died young, Granny and Mother had taken responsibility for all the necessary repairs and maintenance. This continued after Father came to live here. He was always the breadwinner: going out to work all day and coming home each Friday with a brown paper wage packet, to be handed over on arrival. Then his time was his own. He was free to relax with his newspaper or to spend time with me. He wasn't seen tinkering with a lawnmower or climbing a ladder to fix a guttering, like the other husbands along our road.

Mother, who had once worked in the Farrow's canning factory, after her time in the Auxiliary Territorial Service, never returned to work following my birth, but her and Granny were the practical ones. Together, they tackled all the jobs, inside and out.

Father did try to help but he was left-handed or, as Mother described it, 'kack-handed'. Her derogatory name for him was 'Useless Eustice', a cartoon character in the Daily Mirror. As he fumbled, probably nervous under her watchful eye, her scathing voice would be heard muttering, 'Git out th' road while I do it, yer like a fart in a culunder'. She was not a woman known for her patience or delicate turn of phrase.

He was entrusted to oil her bike chain and pump up the tyres but it was a family joke that mending a puncture was too complicated for him. Such technical jobs had to go to a neighbour. Despite this perceived handicap, he did have an array of woodworking tools, neatly suspended on a sheet of peg board in his shed, with which he produced an assortment of household items including cupboards, linen-boxes and flower tubs. In the lead-up to Christmas, he took orders from friends and family for forts and dolls' houses, pull-along toys and garages.

As winter nights drew in, he changed out of his suit after work and disappeared into the dark with a storm lantern, working for another hour or two in this shed that was his space. I lurked close to his side, angling to be allowed to accompany him for a while. I loved the shed. It was rich with the smells of turpentine, linseed oil and sawdust; cosy with a flickering light, which more than made up for the lack of heating. He wore a battledress, acquired from the Army and Navy Surplus store, with a woolly scarf tucked in the neck, and often returned to the carriages only in time for supper. His hands cracked and had to be soothed with cream, and later, with some new invention which came in a small bottle and was applied with a tiny brush, like nail polish. He called it 'plastic skin'.

Night by night, the toys took shape and I enjoyed being the elf who got to have the first turn in Santa's workshop. The garages were the ones I liked best. I was allowed to stick on the stickers, advertising Shell and Esso, and add a clock face which had been cut out from a catalogue of men's watches.

The showroom had a curved Perspex window and a ramp ran down one side from the parking spaces on the roof. Little cars were kept in the shed simply for the purpose of testing that they gathered enough speed to reach the forecourt and didn't get stuck halfway down. I took this responsibility as seriously as any test-pilot. How awful it would have been if some boy had cried on Christmas morning because I hadn't made sure his present functioned perfectly. Who says quality control is a new concept?

The forts were fun too, with crenellated walls, tiny steps leading up inside the turrets and a drawbridge which was drawn up with a length of string by turning a tiny handle. As these neared completion, it was vital to ensure that the handle turned freely and that the parapets were not too high. The three soldiers that also formed part of the testing gear, had to be seen peering out. I recall the way their uniforms shone in the light from the storm lantern, their features dark in the shade. I wonder if they were perhaps more realistic in these shadows than ever again in any playroom.

The dolls' houses never held the same fascination, perhaps because they were not finished to the same degree. They were dispatched with no dolls or furniture; the walls and floors left bare so each family could choose their own décor. When they left the shed, they were little more than painted boxes with holes for windows.

On Sundays and Thursday afternoons, when we were not out exploring, I followed Father to the shed, snugly wrapped in my siren suit, climbing onto a box so that I could watch what was happening on the work bench. I selected and passed the required nails and screws and learned their different purposes. Together, we glued pieces of wood at a time when the heady smell of glue could be savoured with no thought of health risks and we stirred turps into paint until it felt the right consistency. I learned to paint, not as an artist, but as an 'undercoater', where the odd run or drip would not be so noticeable, not getting disheartened even when Father sighed, 'Oh dear, another brush for the chimney sweep', as I pressed with too much enthusiasm and the bristles splayed.

All the tools were hand operated. Electricity never reached the shed. As I copied him, practising with hammers and screwdrivers, saws and planes, I followed his moves faithfully and still, today, I instinctively hold tools in my left hand although I am predominantly right-handed. My favourite job, and that took both hands, was wielding the axe when there was kindling to chop, as Granny scowled and shouted 'Watch what she's a' doin' wi' that 'atchet'.

I never saw Father lift any domestic appliance beyond a spoon to stir his tea. Cooking, baking, washing and ironing were solely the responsibility of the women so I was quite lucky, as a girl, to be allowed to skip between these two scenes. I was happy with a mixing bowl and spoon. I loved to bake buns, or at least stir in the currants or caraway seeds. If there was a bit of pastry left over, I flattened it into a 'policeman's foot', which was like an apple puff but without the apple or the puff. It was just two pieces of pastry with a lick of jam in between, sealed around the edge and baked until it was hard. I took great pride in these creations because they were mine. I was the chief bowl-licker at a time when everyone thought an egg contained a yolk, or sometimes two, but never salmonella. I basked in the unusual heat when the oven was hot and breathed in the rich aroma of pastries and puddings, but my heart really lay in the shed.

When we were not gainfully employed, meeting orders for Christmas, we went on exploring. Outings with Father were always for pleasure and leisure; probably more to keep me occupied than for any other purpose. Our Sunday rambles continued and, as I got older, we were less restricted by adverse weather. We wrapped up warm and headed out even when the little man and lady, who lived in Granny's weather-house and only came out alternatively, were not encouraging. My legs got stronger and we were able to venture farther afield, exploring the various roads out of town: the wandering banks of the Old River Nene, the curving walls of the Bower, the banks of Delph Dyke and the new cut, which now allowed the Nene to flow past the town in an arrow-straight course, speeding its passage to the sea.

In the fishing season, fishermen arrived here and set up their pitches at regular intervals along the banks. Our fen rivers were so well stocked and the catches so good, that men came from all parts of the country to compete in organised matches. They came by the coachload and the coaches, in a variety of unfamiliar liveries, lined the bank; appearing to lean precariously over the water, parked as close as possible to the edge, so as not to obstruct the narrow road.

This walk was particularly exciting in the first weeks of New Year. The fields of the Wash, where cattle had grazed all summer, were deliberately flooded as part of the defence system. Then families came to skate as they had done in history. With my hands tucked deep in my pockets against the frosty air, I listened, enthralled, as Father chatted to old fen men, who had come to watch. They were always happy to reminisce about their boyhoods when the area had been frozen for long periods, when the winters were more severe and remote farms could be cut off for weeks. They spoke of the old families whose sons had skated their way to fame from this very spot. The combination of their words, delivered with steamy breath, and the freedom of the frozen scene extending to the horizon, was exhilarating. This was when I briefly considered that a career as a long distance skater might be fun. I imagined the cheers as I glided gracefully along the rivers, first to reach Peterborough or Ely, as those heroes of the fens had done so long before.

My other most exciting memory of time spent with Father, is of the nights we went to the 'pictures'. He had regularly gone to watch a film on a Thursday evening, without Mother, who expressed no interest in films, saying they were all 'Too far-fetched and most on' it ent even truw'.

I think this had not always been her stance, as she talked quite fluently about Clarke Gable, Errol Flynn, and Humphrey Bogart.

Now, however, it was me who accompanied Father if he considered the film suitable. I saw a few grisly war films at this time but I was confused by the uniforms: never sure who were the goodies and baddies. I couldn't follow the plots, so gradually it evolved that I was taken when it was a comedy. This was the time I first saw Norman Wisdom and I loved him. I was captivated by his permanently puzzled expression. The frustration of knowing what was going to happen next, but also knowing that he was going to walk straight into another disaster, had me squealing from my seat.

On several occasions Father had to shush me, fearing that I might get thrown out, but it was an atmosphere where everyone got carried away with the slap-stick antics and I remember his laughter, more unrestrained in that darkness than at any other time in his life. It was an escape from reality where we bonded in shared humour.

On numerous occasions the reel of film broke and we were plunged into darkness. The crowd whooped and then booed until the lights were switched on whilst the man in the projector room did a quick fix and the film flickered onto the screen again; sometimes only running for a few minutes before the whole process was repeated.

Leaving the building at what felt like a very late hour; probably getting on for nine or even ten, we walked hand in hand through streets that were rain washed, lamps reflecting in the puddles, thinking that we were not yet back in the real world.

We called in the chip shop and I couldn't see over the counter but my nostrils filled with the steam of frying fat and I could breathe in the smells of fish and vinegar. Then we walked the mile home to where lights burned in the carriage windows and Mother bustled around, laying plates and cutlery, unwrapping the newspaper to reveal the steaming food.

When I had been too young to accompany Father, a portion of this supper had always been put aside for my breakfast next morning. Now I realised for the first time that fish and chips was a food normally eaten hot. I speared my chips with a fork and blew on them, waving them aloft as I described what had happened in the film, animating with my arms.

Mother shook her head and tutted, 'Too darft t' laff at' and I knew that the scenes of hilarity, still so vivid in my head, lost their humour in the re-telling. They could not survive this transition to the real world.

15 To the City

Shopping trips to Peterborough were Mother's domain and it was with her that I shared many Saturday adventures. Even as we waited for the bus, I was asking the first questions of the day.

'What's that writing say?' as we watched the Pickfords' low-loaders crawling out of their garage: Scammell printed boldly across their noses.

'Where they gewin'?'

Their split windscreens appeared as two eyes, looking forward to where-ever the day would take them. Then we would hear the sound of another engine: often an old Gardner or Bristol, chugging towards us even before the bus came into sight.

Once aboard, we passed the numerous brickyard entrances on both sides of the road: Saxon works with its own row of cottages on the left, Star Cottages on the right, a water-filled knot-hole on the left, the chapel and the school on the right, the little sweet shop on the left, the King's Dyke rows of terraced houses on both sides. My head must have constantly swivelled from side to side as I struggled not to miss anything.

We might stop where the railway line crossed the road, waiting impatiently as a man sauntered down the steps from the signal box and carefully pushed the gates into position. Then we watched as a slow goods train passed, often hauling more than twenty trucks. Once the crossing-keeper had pulled the gates back into position, he retraced his steps to the signal box, waving cheerily to the bus driver

Drawing away again, the road ran parallel to the rows of chimneys and the railway sidings. We bumped over the hump-back bridge across the old Nene and round the bend that still bore the name Horsey Toll, from when tolls were collected from travellers on horseback. On the right was the factory that built aeroplanes in the war.

Turnings to the left would have taken us to Ramsey, at the very bottom of the fen, or on to Yaxley and Holme, both ports in days before the water was drained. Now they were just sleepy villages where our bus didn't go.

Leaving behind the fields, we entered the built-up areas of Stanground and Fletton. Once they had been little villages but now they joined up to the city. Since the brickyards had brought hundreds of immigrant workers to live in this area, whole new streets had been specially built to house them. Stanground was now home to a large Polish community. Fletton hosted a similar community of Italians.

On the last part of the journey, I had to turn my gaze rapidly from one side to the other again if I was not to miss any of the landmarks. To the left was the Fair Meadow: always worth checking to see if an unscheduled fair might have arrived. Then there was the electricity sub-station with its fascinating tangle of wires and coils. I always thought it would be good to take this home and rebuild the intricate, industrial structure in our garden. It would have been far more interesting than cabbages, but this was not a time when such monuments of history were considered an important part of our heritage.

Equally impressive to my young eyes, was the iron bridge which carried East Coat Main Line trains to London. This crossed over both the river and the Midland

Line from Leicester, which swept in a curve under the Main line and the main road before entering the East Station. We followed the main road over the Great Eastern line, which runs through to the North station, parallel to the Main line in this configuration of tracks, bridges and roads which could have been a forerunner of Spaghetti Junction.

The river appeared again on the right, overlooked by the old Customs House. We passed within a pavement's width of the offices of Mitchells' Engineering. This boasted the largest mural in the country, made of Portland Stone, covering the entire height and length of the building, depicting art and industry from Archimedes to Newton. The figures towered above us even from our high vantage point in the bus and I reminded Mother that she had promised that one day we could walk back so I could study them in more detail.

Now we were at the entrance to the city, along with all those women who regularly caught the bus on a Saturday morning. It was quite rare to see a man on such a journey. The exception was the group of men who fascinated me with their dark skin and flashing brown eyes. I liked to sit close to them so that I could over-hear their conversation; listening but not understanding, because their accents were unfamiliar and their vocabulary a mixture of English and Italian. These were the men from Italy, now resident in Fletton, on their journeys to and from work. I don't remember the Polish men ever getting the bus. Perhaps they were less noticeably different and so did not capture my imagination in the same way.

Arriving at the bus station, we set out down Bridge Street, shopping as we went. Sometimes, as we entered a doorway, the smells and the lighting triggered the echo of a memory. We might only visit shops such as Broom's, the iron-mongers, in the Arcade, a couple of times a year, for a box of candles or a new wick for the paraffin heater, but it was one of my favourites. In this dimly lit treasure trove, some of the stock was covered in dust. High shelves towered above my head, accessible only by an elderly gentleman and his step-ladder.

We often walked around the market, listening to the men and women with cheeks reddened by the wind, calling out in hoarse voices, bidding passers-by to look closer at their wares. They vied for customers, offering the best deal in Peterborough, asserting that such an offer wouldn't be repeated. I slowed my pace, expecting Mother to step forward, purse in hand. She walked on, seemingly oblivious to the bargains that would never be seen again.

Behind this market was the cattle market where cows and pigs and sheep, all with frightened eyes, awaited their fate. This weekly sale had started back in the days when livestock had been herded along fen droves from the outlaying farms. I wasn't old enough to grasp the extent of their plight. I thought they were just nervous because they were moving somewhere new and I offered them a reassuring pat through the bars of the pen. This brought forth another scowl of disapproval as Mother scolded 'Don't touch them mucky ol' things. They're prob'ly got fleas an' all sorts. Let's get out o' this stink'.

She was happier back in the shops, especially Timothy White's: a comparatively new store, with a variety of goods displayed in a light, modern setting and entrances on two streets.

I preferred the smells and dim lighting of the older department stores such as Parrish's and Barrett's, where carved wooden staircases had to be climbed to reach the upper floors. They sold beautiful dresses of silk and satin, ideal for a Sunday school anniversary or a birthday party. The assistants spoke in lovely voices and nothing was too much trouble for them. They smiled kindly as they held aloft each delicate garment in turn and I never felt rushed to make a decision. I could examine and re-examine dresses, unsure whether I preferred pink or lemon, undecided whether I liked a belt or a sash. In fact, there were times when my decision making took so long that Mother's patience gave way and I finished up with two dresses, each carefully wrapped in tissue and then brown paper from a roll attached to the counter. Of course, this didn't work every time.

Just along the street were the Corn Exchange and the entrance to the cathedral. On days when she was in a particularly good mood, perhaps because she had managed to cross off everything on her shopping list early, or had found an unexpected treasure, she might allow me to lure her through the arched gateway and into the cathedral, although I had often heard her say to friends, 'We 'ad to gew round the c'thedral agen t' please 'er. She's a queer un'.

She never understood why a small child wanted to walk in silence around this vast building, staring upwards at the ceiling until my neck hurt, running my hands gently over the marble statues, begging her to read me every inscription. I don't know why I was drawn by this splendour. I didn't understand its significance. I just felt the glory of it all.

Once, when we had met one of her friends in town, the friend had suggested that I might enjoy the museum. I didn't quite understand the look that Mother gave her but she agreed, through gritted teeth. The three of us spent hours in there. There was so much to see: rooms full of display cabinets, passages hung with beautiful paintings, stuffed animals, jewellery, costumes, too much to take in on a first visit, but I did my best. I sensed, somehow, that it might be a while before we came back.

When she did indulge my pleas to walk around the

cathedral, it was usually just before mid-day, so she could get me out again with the promise of dinner. We always ate in the same restaurant, above a chip shop behind St John's church. These were the only times we ever ate out so it was another exciting experience. It was on these occasions that I thought I might become a waitress with a neat little cap to hold back my hair and a starched pinny.

I was allowed to browse the menu as if making a choice, before Mother ordered the meal from a real waitress who delivered the food to our table. The highlight of these visits was being allowed to put on my own salt and vinegar. Our order was always the same: two plates of fish and chips, with peas, a side plate of bread and butter, and two cups of tea. I don't think the prices varied from week to week but, when the bill was brought to the table, Mother studied it carefully and often said out loud, 'That were a dear ol' do'.

After dinner, we worked our way back up Bridge Street to Woolworths, where a floor-walker always went off to let Father know we had arrived. Then, leaving Mother to browse, he paraded me about the store, introducing me to his colleagues who stooped down to my level and asked me sensible questions.

Where had I acquired my new mittens?

Was red still my favourite colour?

They noticed my new shoes or commented on my new coat.

These girls smelled flowery, a mixture of scent and powder. I wondered if I might like to be a shop-girl with stockings, a smart blouse and curled hair. I loved their attention and left reluctantly, usually carrying a bag of sweets, to be clutched tightly all the way home and only eaten once we were indoors.

Mother always chose a fine morning for these excursions but occasionally the rain set in during the day and I huddled against her thick coat as we sheltered on the narrow, slatted seats which ran around the outside of the bus station 'caff', as we waited for the bus home. We were not allowed inside as she described cracked cups that other people had drunk from, and the associated health hazards. I could only peer from my coat-shelter, watching the miserable drizzle in the lights as buses came and went, praying that ours would come soon.

As it finally drew into Stand 5, the door of the caff opened and people who drank from the cups and didn't look any worse for it, surged across the road. I clung to Mother's hand, afraid of getting separated, scrambling up the steep steps into the bus, hearing the shrill voice of the conductress, calling 'Move along', even when there was nowhere left to go. I was often frightened that I would suffocate or be compressed. I tried to avoid the sharp edges of wicker baskets, poking at face height, and the pointed umbrellas that dripped on my feet. As the laden bus creaked out of the bus station, its cargo of buxom women sat in rows in their uniform of headscarves, kept dry by plastic rain-mates, and wiped steam from their spectacles.

Only if there was a home-match at the football ground, and Mother had badly mistimed the journey back, might there be men on board. Then the crush was even worse, as they hung from the luggage racks, swaying towards me at every bend. At least three or four more would be packed into the step well. One conductress proudly claimed that she had never left anyone behind and that was an accolade in times when getting everyone home, however uncomfortably, was paramount. Regulations on passenger numbers were not yet in force and sometimes the more agile walked along the edge of seats to reach the front when approaching their stop as the gangway was packed solid. Six people might have to jump off to let them through the narrow space near the door, leaping back on as the bus drew away again. On days like this I just concentrated on not feeling sick in the fug of smoke and steam and fumes, squashed onto Mother's lap, along with the zipped up shopping bag.

No matter how frightened I was, how uncomfortable, I would never have cried. Too many times I had squirmed as I listened to her tell the tale of how I had cried on an earlier journey.

'She roared 'er eyes out all th' way 'ome.'

She always started with that same line, before continuing, 'An' some ol' woman who sat be'ind us kep' tuttin' till I craned round an' gev 'er a look. That med 'er wuss an' she said, 'I know wat I'd do wi' 'er if she were mine', right out loud so ev'rybody could 'ear'.

'Well, she ent yers an' that's th' end on it,' Mother had supposedly replied but then, in her retelling, she came to the line that always made her friends laugh.

'An all the palaver were jus' 'cus I wouldn't let 'er gew upstuirs an' it were a single-decker.'

Despite the embarrassing anecdotes, I really did love these trips out. All thoughts of being a waitress or a shop-girl faded as I imagined the excitement of being a bus-conductress, just riding up and down on a bus all day. I would decide how many passengers to let on and no small girl would ever fear for her life on my bus.

Remembering how much I enjoyed these outings, it seems unlikely that I would have been obstinate enough to jeopardize one. However, there came a day when my will clashed with Mother's determination once too often. I refused, as always, to wear my ankle socks the right way out. She knew I wore them inside out so that the bits of thread didn't annoy my toes, but that day she turned it into a major battle. She actually said that if I didn't change them, she wouldn't take me.

I never seriously thought she would leave me behind so I sat on Granny's lap on my swing in the front garden, my hair and clothes neatly arranged, my black patent shoes over my inside out socks, as she walked out of the gate and vanished from sight behind the neighbours' hedge. Then I sat, defiantly staring at the hedge, waiting for her to run back and scoop me into her arms, admitting that I had called her bluff.

I waited until the bus went past, slowing at the bus-stop as if it was going to pick someone up. I heard it pull away again and then I cried because she really had got on that bus and left me sitting there in my silly, inside out socks.

16 Can you hear me calling?

Just up the road from us was Barker's small grocery shop. I had been there on numerous occasions with Mother, or sometimes Granny, to buy everything from bacon to paraffin. One day I decided it would be quite exciting to go there by myself. Even as I checked the handful of coppers kept in a little purse for playing shops, I knew instinctively that the idea would not meet with parental approval, so I snook out of the door and sidled up to the gate. No-one noticed.

As I headed along the path, I kept looking over my shoulder. The distance seemed somehow longer than before. I could still see the gate for most of the way but, just short of the shop, a slight bend in the road threatened to obscure my view. Now I had to make a choice. I could either turn back while the gate was still there, or I could risk it disappearing whilst out of sight. I remember how fearlessly I had left home to go and live in a blockhouse when I was smaller, but now I was a year older and more sensible: more aware of the danger of things disappearing if you couldn't see them. I hesitated momentarily, but the coins were warm in my hand and the thought of chocolate won. If I was to get the chocolate but minimise the risk, I needed to be quick.

With one last backward glance I ran for the shop, throwing myself through the door, bell clanging, as kindly Mr Barker looked up from the counter in surprise. I suppose he thought I was allowed to be there as I had money, so he served me without question. Within seconds, I was fleeing from the shop, clutching the chocolate. Reaching the bend I could see the gate had remained in place and I was safely homeward bound. No-one had even missed me.

I stepped up into the kitchen and announced 'I've bin to the shop'.

'Oh, 'ave yer?' Mother didn't even look up.

'Yer, really,' I persisted. 'Look, I got choc'let.'

Then she looked up.

'She's bin to the shop,' she called to Granny.

'Oh, 'as she?' Granny didn't even look up.

'Yer, really,' Mother persisted. 'She's got choc'let.'

Then Granny looked up.

I clutched the tiny chocolate bar, as she shook her head, exclaiming, 'In all my born days, did y' ever know such an out and outer, yer can't turn yer eyes fer a minit!'

There was no punishment for my intrepid venture and I got to eat the chocolate so I don't know what I was meant to learn. If there was a lesson, it was perhaps that this was to be only the first of many times when I had to produce evidence that I was telling the truth before anyone believed anything I was telling them. It was also a good indication of the difficulties I was to encounter as I struggled to communicate with these fen people who spoke so sparingly.

Living in such an insular environment meant that I was a naïve child in many ways, but I compensated by developing my imagination so as to escape from the mundane, away to my fantasy world, until the boundaries blurred. An early, though limited, exposure to the wireless honed my imagination in a way that television cannot. I listened to words but built my own pictures, improvising all the time to fill the gaps.

I listened to a BBC voice announce that the royal

carriage had just come into view and I saw it before my eyes, resplendent in gold, though not necessarily the right shape. I had never been to a boxing match or seen a televised event but as we listened closely to the commentary, I saw Cassius Clay land on his bottom in the fourth round of his match with Henry Cooper in 1963. I remember that he was white at that time, as I had no reason to imagine that he might be black.

Perhaps it was to compensate for this lack of visual information, that I developed my insatiable quest for answers. Mother's closest friend from her days in the Salvation Army, visited us regularly with her two daughters who were a little older than me and probably more fluent talkers, but she was always amused by my relentless need for explanations. She nicknamed me 'Little Miss Why'.

Granny, however, was not always amused. I filled every silence with my incessant questioning. I remember her warning me to be quiet as she turned the knob on the large old wireless on the sideboard and waited with her ear against the casing as it crackled into life, her neck craned to hear better, while she listened to the news.

She would nod her woolly-hatted head and sigh, 'Arr, Old Moore said as that'd 'appen', in reference to the predictions of the soothsayers in her almanac, but mostly she listened without a word. I never grasped this concept of listening. I just gabbled on as normal despite her mutterings of ' 'old yer tongue, will yer'.

One voice which did capture my attention read out crimes that were being investigated and asked listeners to contact Scotland Yard, on Whitehall 1212.

My favourite part of this evening ritual was the shipping forecast. I listened to this with the rapt attention that I had previously paid to the reassuring rhythm of nursery rhymes. It was comforting in its predictability and I waited for the familiar names. I dreamed of visiting places like Dogger Bank and Fair Isle, feeling the swell and breathing in the fog in faraway Finisterre. I was intrigued by the increasing wind speeds as gale force eight turned to severe gale nine, then storm force ten and violent storm eleven, building to the ultimate hurricane force twelve.

Another treat for me was to keep the wireless going long enough to hear the football results on a Saturday because, again, I imagined those far off places as the names were read out. Hamilton Academicals was my favourite because it sounded so exotic. I had no concept of distance but I had been told of other countries where the sun was hot enough to ripen oranges and bananas, and coconuts hung from the trees. That was where I placed Hamilton Academicals, epitomising all that was tropical.

It must have been irritating for Granny, having to share her space with a child who dreamed silently through these irrelevant details but chatted loudly over the weather forecast which told her whether she needed to pick peas or water brassicas. One day, in her frustration, she made a comment that changed my life for years.

She scowled at me and hissed, 'If yer keep on talkin' at this rate yer'll run out o' words and then yer won't 'ave any left when yer want to say somethin' as really matters'.

I froze in horror. I had not realised that vocabulary was limited. I had rabbited on with total disregard for the sheer quantity of words that I exuded from the moment I woke to the second I fell asleep every day. I tried to work out how many days I had been talking and how many hours there were in each of those days but my calculations were hampered because neither she nor Mother would elaborate on exactly how this worked. They wouldn't explain whether short words counted the same or less than long ones, and they wouldn't assure me that there were any warning signs when the limit was being neared.

This was a frightening period of my life and the more I

looked for reassurance the more I became frustrated that I was using up my words and getting no answers. I felt that they were being deliberately secretive, as if it would be some kind of justice if I was struck down mid-sentence. I even had nightmares that someone was standing over my bed. Mother came into the room and put washing away in the drawers without looking in my direction. I couldn't attract her attention because I was shouting and screaming and no words were coming out because they had all been used up.

I don't think it was a deliberate regime of torture. I think they were just pleased that they had quietened me to such a large degree, not realising how this could devastate an exuberant child. Father was out at work all day. In the evenings, he would sit with me on his knee and read me stories. It was my calmest time of day anyway, so I don't think he noticed or commented on my withdrawal.

Perhaps the effects were not as profound or long-lasting as I thought. Maybe it just felt like an eternal sentence to silence, but it wasn't until after I started school and observed that my teacher talked for large portions of the day without showing signs of verbal exhaustion, that I finally realised that the grown-ups had been mistaken in their understanding of vocabulary. Then I started asking questions again but I don't think I ever quite regained the former fluency of 'Little Miss Why' and I'm sure a few people remained grateful for this.

17 Words Alone

I was rarely lost for words, but there was an occasion. I recall sitting on the chair opposite Father one night and asking if I could look at the faded photograph of my paternal grandmother which he kept in his wallet. I had never met her and it was the only picture he had. I often held it and conjured up visions of what she would have been like. I knew she had been one of twin girls and had another set of twin girls for sisters. She was called Anselina, and her siblings were Beatrice, Esmeralda and Richenda. These were names I had not heard before and I found them beautiful.

As he held out the tiny, creased image and I reached to take it, it slipped from my fingers and fluttered, as if in slow motion, onto the fire between us. I remember shrieking 'Do summat', but time had moved on at its normal speed and a flame engulfed it even as I heard the desperate sound of my words. There was a moment when we both stared at the lost image in the ash before I flung myself onto Father, clinging to his neck, imagining how angry he must be with me. He wasn't angry. Perhaps it would have been easier if he had been. If he had accused me of carelessness I would, no doubt, have pleaded that it was an accident but there was no accusation to answer. All I saw was sadness in his eyes and even I had no answer for that.

My fascination with words and places continued to develop. The ones I cherished most were those that I could memorise and repeat. On day trips, I had Father reading out the names on every station platform and practising them with me at home until I could recite them off the cuff to impress visitors, sometimes to the rhythm of the train. The first was the route to Ely, perhaps because it was most familiar. Apparently the name of Chittisham had been changed to Chettisham in the 1900s but we never caught up and years later, when I saw it written in a book, I thought it was a spelling mistake. It still lived in my mind as Chittisham, the last stop on the Ely line as I rattled off: Whittlesea, March, Stonea, Manea, Black Bank, Chittisham, Ely.

Gradually my repertoire grew to include the lines to Cambridge, where we shopped for new winter rig-outs; to Leicester, home to one of my cousins; to Doncaster; where Father had cousins; and to the Lincolnshire resorts of Skegness, Mablethorpe and Cleethorpes. Listening to the announcements, I could imagine no job more rewarding than to sit in the stationmaster's office all day, reciting these lists as the trains came and went. I had found my vocation and after a day out I fell asleep in the carriages, hearing the voice in my thoughts: 'The train now arriving at platform two is the ten forty-five to Birmingham, calling at Leicester, Hinkley and Nuneaton.'

For a while this interest even distracted me from the atmosphere which I had already come to associate with stations. I felt fine on the platforms of those such as Whittlesea, which were open the breeze blowing through, the air fresh and constantly flowing. It was on the covered platforms that I suffocated, cloaked in a mist of tears and hugs and farewells from the past, which seemed to hang, suspended beneath the iron canopies, clinging like shadowy cobwebs to the supporting pillars. Before I had the vocabulary to question this feeling, I remember the same lingering sadness that I felt in the doorways of our carriages, but now I could chant my lists and keep the ghosts at bay.

A lot of the terms used by the grown-ups were puzzling to me at this time. Mother had a habit of saying that something was better or worse by a long chalk. In my limited experience, chalks came in a standard box and were of a uniform length.

Granny reminisced about the times when she had distributed the War-Cry, a Salvation Army newsletter, to the local pubs.

'Some o' them men wouldn't know when they'd 'ad enough t' drink. Then they'd 'ave a right set-to about sommat or nothin'. Yer never seen such capers.'

She would shake her head and add, 'It's allus better to give them places a wide berth'.

How wide was a wide berth?

Similarly, I never established how loud a stuck pig squealed, despite frequently hearing the term, 'He squealed loud as a stuck pig'.

Sometimes I adapted words which I thought I understood. Mother had a special noise that she reserved for cats that strayed into the garden. It was a sort of 'schchchch' noise as she took a deep breath and exhaled with her tongue against the roof of her mouth, always accompanied by flailing arms and pinafore slapping. I learned to copy these mannerisms as well as the sound. She seemed amused when I first did my impression of her but, for some reason, she was not amused when I started to do it on trips to town, every time I caught sight of a cat sitting on a wall or lazing in the sun in someone else's garden. I never understood how her sense of humour worked, especially as passers-by seemed to find it funny.

Another feat was that she could stand at the kitchen door, shove two fingers in her mouth and whistle me from the bottom of the garden. I never mastered that one;

neither did Father. Nor could he roll up his tongue from the sides like Mother and me. He could move his ears and I was impressed with that for a while but it was probably hereditary as I quickly learned to do the same. Then I wasn't impressed any more.

At a time when manners were of paramount importance and I got the wilting frown if I so much as hiccupped in public, Mother's most impressive noise was when she belched. One day, after producing a particularly loud example, which sounded like it originated somewhere lower than her kneecaps, she exclaimed, 'Ooh, 'scuse me, what a glutton'.

I had a new word. With my unquenchable thirst for new vocabulary, I seized upon it, thinking that I now knew the real name for these sounds. They were 'gluttons', as surely as coughs were coughs and sneezes were sneezes. It was a logical step to assume, therefore, that the corresponding verb was 'to glutton', but that earned me a withering stare on the couple of occasions when I noticed a lull in the conversation with visitors and tried to be helpful by urging her, 'Why don't yer show 'em how loud yer can glutton?'

This was obviously not going to be her new party-piece.

On other occasions, I misheard a word but faithfully incorporated it into my dictionary-lobe. One such word was 'salusa-cake'. I talked for months about one that I had seen. When questioned, I was sure I hadn't eaten any of it or even touched it but I was evidently enchanted by it. I wanted to go and see it again. This proved impossible as I hadn't the ability to explain where it was. Only on a subsequent visit to Wicksteed Park in Northamptonshire, the following summer, was I able to point excitedly and squeal 'There's the salusa- cake'.

Apparently everyone else called it a sluice gate.

At other times, I was just trying to make sense of a world too complicated for me to grasp. Although I was oblivious to their origins, unaware that their name was derived from Greek, I was always impressed by pylons. I saw their glinting silver girders as fine lines, drawn with a very sharp pencil against the sky. They framed and fragmented the scenery, reminiscent of the lead in a stained glass window.

When I asked 'What a' them for?' I was told 'They carry 'lectric' and when I asked how, I was reliably informed that they passed it along from one to the other. Now I thought I understood. It worked like pass-the-parcel. I saw their outstretched arms, gripping the wires as they waited: one reaching out to take the 'lectric, the other to pass it on. I waited, too, watching for a long time, but they stood in silence, silhouettes against the backdrop of clouds.

As I waited, I studied their geometric patterns, their legs splayed to balance despite the wind. This appeared to work well as they were not cowed by the prevailing wind; unlike the telegraph poles which often leaned precariously over the water from their roots on a bank. I liked the tapered tops of the pylons, pointing skywards like rockets poised to launch, but their feet were firmly in the ground. In summer, crops grew around their ankles, then up to their knees. I wondered if they, too, had been planted at some time and were now forging ahead, like runner beans above the rows of cabbages. Sometimes it looked as if they were clutching the wires close to their bodies, tucked under their armpits, but as I passed and looked back, arms were outstretched again. I could never turn quickly enough to see them move, and never realised that this illusion was only due to the angle from which I viewed them.

However closely I observed, I still couldn't see the 'lectric. I questioned this again and was told 'Oh, no, yer won't see it, 'cus nobody can see it'.

Now there was an element of magic, as well as intrigue and also a challenge: three of my favourite ingredients for any recipe, so I continued to play the waiting game, just as I had with the figures on the Christmas cake.

It wasn't until much later when I studied currents and voltage, that I realised the only magic had been in my imagination, but I still retain the affection for those sentinels of steel as they march out of the city, carrying the 'lectric' across the fields of the fens.

Another part of my language developing technique was to quote back what the grown-ups had said, with all the seriousness of their tone.

At the back of our garden and along one side was a cornfield where Granny and I spent hours watching the men reaping, binding, baling; the dust and scent of harvest blowing towards us as we stood, and finally seeing the low line of fires as the chaff was burnt. This was a time when farming was labour intensive and men were a more common sight than machines.

One day, however, a different breed of men appeared and commandeered the top corner of the field, nearest to the road. These were builders and we learned that two new houses were to be built here. I was drawn to this new activity, visiting the construction site at least once a day to monitor progress, accompanied by Granny.

The workmen were cheery chaps who humoured me and my constant questioning. Late one afternoon, whilst chatting to us, one of them dropped his hammer into the cavity of the wall.

'What'll 'appen now?' I wanted to know.

'Well, it'll just 'ave to stay there an' we'll just 'ave to 'ope nobody misses it.'

He looked very serious, adding quietly 'Don't you gew saying o'wt'.

I nodded equally seriously and we went on our way. The wall at that point was about three feet high. I expect he retrieved the errant tool as soon as our backs were turned but for months, whenever anyone visited us and the topic of the new houses came up, I put on my most supercilious voice to inform them 'There's an 'ammer inside the wall of that first one, but don't you gew saying o'wt'.

I'm sure that builder would have been amused, knowing that for a child like me, the possibility of saying 'no'wt' was an impossibility.

18 Untying the Apron Strings

I started school after the Easter holiday in 1961. At this time there were three intakes a year and I could have been going since the previous September, but Mother wouldn't hear of parting with me before my fifth birthday in April, so I missed two thirds of my first year. I'm sure the separation was more traumatic for her than it was for me; leaving a space where I had been her constant companion for the last five years.

I just saw it as a wonderful new adventure. I had always wanted to be a sociable child. Being born to older parents, meant that my cousins were all in their twenties when I was still quite small and I remember the loneliness of having no siblings.

There were few children along our road and none considered to be suitable companions. There was a boy in a house close by, but simply being a boy ruled him out. I recall Mother describing him as 'Do-lally' because he dressed up in different hats. I think she had a few funny ideas about the merits of role-play. The last time I saw him, he was wearing a very smart suit and heading for his job in the city so I think he turned out alright.

Starting school gave me my first opportunity to spend time with other children, time away from the carriages, away from the grown-up world in which I had been cocooned. I learned to share and co-operate and have fun of a new kind. There were many lessons to learn, and not all were on the curriculum.

I was bought a very smart, red, Triang tricycle with a metal carrier on the back. Each day I loaded it with provisions for the journey and Mother emptied it before we left the house. At the school gate, she waved me off and waited, along with all the other mothers, until we had gone indoors. If I looked back I could see her head over the wall as she sat on her bike.

School was close enough for me to be home-dinners and when I came out she would be in that same position, foot on the pedal, ready to push off. Arriving home for dinner on the following Monday, I learned the first of those unscheduled lessons.

As we wheeled our bikes down the gravel path and turned the corner next to the kitchen door, I had a clear view down the side of the carriages to the clothes-lines in the back garden. They were full: a billowing cloud of sheets and towels. This was extraordinary because Granny never did washday on her own.

'Who's done the washing?' I asked, never dreaming of the answer.

'Well, I did.' She seemed surprised that I was even asking.

Then the horror of the truth dawned on me. After I was safely through that school door, she had not waited just the other side of the wall. She had come all the way home, done the washing and only got back to pose in that position again when it was time to fetch me home.

'Did yer leave me there?' I needed reassurance that it wasn't true.

'Yer, course. Did yer think I wait outside all that while?'

This was getting worse. Now I realised that she was not just talking about today. She had been doing it every day and I faced the stark truth that life went on in my absence: my first clue to the fact that grown-ups had lives too. They were not there solely to amuse and accommodate the under-fives.

It wouldn't have been as bad if it had been shopping day or ironing day, but wash-day was my favourite. I had always been a part of this ritual: a crucial part, or so I had believed. From the time I learned to walk, I had toddled around carrying boxes of Tide and scrubbing brushes, loving the early morning bustle of activity in the wash-house.

Water was carried in buckets from the tank and poured into the top of the copper, a large circular bowl set in brickwork. The scent of wood-smoke drifted up as kindling was set alight in the grate at the bottom. A wooden lid kept in the heat but as the water got hotter, steam escaped between the slats. When the required temperature was reached, and this was a case of experienced guesswork, the water was taken out again. These old coppers had no tap so a copper-bowl with a wooden handle was used to ladle large amounts of water, a small quantity at a time, into the waiting dolly-tub.

As the soap-powder was added, I was occasionally allowed to sprinkle some from the box: a very responsible job because if it was tipped too quickly too much powder would fall out and this could not be retrieved, but if it wasn't done quickly enough, the steam dampened the cardboard box and the powder turned to clumps. Either result met with grown-up chuntering.

Then the clothes were added and the water agitated by a posher with holes in the bottom, sucking and spraying and pounding out the dirt. Again, I helped by standing on a wooden stool so that I could hold the long handle and push the posher down at least four times before my arms ached and I had to be lifted down. White bedding was washed first, followed by white towels and light coloured underwear, then paler clothing and finally anything in darker shades. Each load was carefully lifted out with a wooden copper-stick, the steam lessening as the water cooled. It was not changed too often as this involved the tedious tasks of refilling and reheating the copper.

After all the rinsing was done, a zinc bath was placed beneath the mangle and I could get the stool into position for my next job. This was to turn the mangle's heavy cast iron wheel, engaging the cogs as Mother fed in the linen and the rollers started to grip. Usually her patience lasted long enough for me to see the first handkerchief or tea-cloth emerge into her other hand, as I strained and grunted with the effort of balancing on the stool and stretching to push with both hands, my whole body-weight behind them. Then, having had my turn, I was happy to watch as she and Granny hauled massive cotton sheets and heavy towels out of the water and into the rollers, somehow producing neatly pressed linen which could go back on the beds without ever needing ironing.

The washing was carried along the cinder path to the line, in wicker clothes baskets big enough to sleep in. I trotted along with the bowl of wooden dolly-pegs, ready to pass each one to a grown-up who attached the garments to the line. Once the sheets were safely anchored, I could wrap my arms and legs around the clothes post, throwing back my head and clinging to this mast as I sailed across the ocean.

The sheets caught the washday wind like huge sails, straining the rope line to breaking point. Occasionally it did snap, allowing the whole performance to collapse in ruins. Sheets which had appeared to be set on a course for far off destinations, suddenly given their freedom, lost their impetus to escape and sagged to the ground. Still wet, their weight draped them forlornly over bushes and the next gust of wind failed to raise their enthusiasm. They just drabbled in the mud and wet grass until two pinafored figures rushed from the carriages and hauled them back into the wash-house, muttering words that I was not allowed to say.

Now I realised sadly, this same pantomime that had been played out over the years, pre-dating even my birth, continued every week. My lead roll had just been another fantasy.

Back at school, though, I thrived in an atmosphere of warmth and security, where the air always smelt of polished wood. We played with a sandpit, a water trough, a Bronco horse and an indoor see-saw with canvas seats. The desks were pushed together for afternoons of knitting and sewing and lined up against the outside walls when we stomped around on the wooden boards in Friday afternoon's country dancing lesson. Ceiling-high cupboards lined one wall of the Infants' class, opening to reveal treasures such as triangles, tambourines and castanets, which we always called 'clackers'.

We were learning with a freedom that has since been lost, encouraged to use our imagination and allowed to explore on nature walks at a time when a 'Blackberry' was picked from the hedgerow and an 'Apple' grew on a tree.

Wakelyn's lane, at the side of the school, skirted the knot-hole and took us towards Morton's Leam, named after Bishop Morton of Ely. We always called it 'Ball River', because cannon balls had been found there, filling our imaginations with battle-scenes.

We blew dandelion clocks and tried to guess the time as we went. Our route took us past the site of the old Boat and Anchor, a thatched pub which had burnt down over twenty years before my birth. Its fruit trees and flower garden still grew untended and bunches of wild flowers were brought back to fill the classroom with delicate scents, temporarily surpassing the polished wood smell.

Our feet were dirty where we had kicked up brick dust with our open-toed sandals and our fingers were stained purple from the blackberries we had consumed, fresh and unwashed. We were perhaps the last generation to be uninhibited by 'Health and Safety', unimpeded by regulations and constant testing. We learned because we were offered the opportunity. Homework for the under-elevens was unheard of and we left school each afternoon free of books or commitment, returning with keen anticipation the next morning.

19 More Lessons

High windows gave our room an ethereal light. In summer, bright shafts of sun pierced the air and an older boy from the class next door would be summoned to open the very top pane with a hook on a long, wooden pole. In winter, only the area nearest to the windows was illuminated by natural light, supplemented by electric lights suspended on chains from the lofty ceiling.

A boiler in the cloakroom heated pipes which ran along the walls. Glass bottles, containing a third of a pint of milk for each child, rested in rows along these pipes, waiting to be distributed by the milk monitor. As the frozen milk thawed, the rising column of ice pushed off the tops. Watching this slow process as I listened to the teacher, I remember the milk but not her words. At this time of year the aroma of summer flowers was a distant memory. Now the air was filled with the combined medications of winter: clove-oil, eucalyptus and mentholatum. We had chilblain cream on our feet and camphorated oil on the corners of our hankies.

On the coldest days it was not unusual to arrive to find the husband of our headmistress, who was also the only male teacher, already busy at work: not preparing the day's lessons but shovelling snow from the path so that we could reach the door. We came in through the cloakroom, sat on wooden benches to pull off our wellies, and hung our coats and hats on rows of pegs. This cloakroom was like a communal airing cupboard, warmed by the breath of the huge boiler, in a wire enclosure.

I never felt at ease in this confined space, with a beast so fierce that it had to be caged. It rumbled and shuddered and I always watched it with one eye as I quickly put on my indoor pumps and headed for the safety of the classroom. Sometimes the teacher poked very wet gloves into the holes in the mesh to dry but I didn't trust it not to eat them before playtime.

My other enduring memory of the boiler is that I was too scared to go near it while everyone else was in class. One morning, I was told to fetch a hankie from my coat pocket but fear held me in the doorway. I snuffled and sniffed and put up with the lecture when I arrived home with stiff-dried cuffs, where I had wiped my nose on my sleeve.

Another area of unease was the row of lavatories at the far end of the playground. We queued under the shadow of the brickyard chimneys, before entering the gloom of the poky cubicles with wooden seats and very hard paper. This was the first time I had ever had to shut myself in such a dark space. I was tormented by the fear that if I locked the heavy wooden door, I might not have the strength to unlock it again. As voices outside urged me to ''urry up, will yer'. I knew I could not perform under such adverse conditions; hence I developed excellent bladder control.

I loved playtime, with the hopscotch drawn in chalk and the brightly coloured hoops. We played lots of group games like 'The farmer's in his den' and 'What's the time, Mr Wolf?' and I relished all this company and interaction. My infant teacher was a lovely lady called Miss Steeper. She had no children of her own but mothered all of us. She had an open face and an honest expression. I would have trusted her with my life.

In her care, we were nourished, praised and encouraged. She instilled in us a love of words, numbers and music, as we learned sums and spellings that would take us through life. We benefited from individual attention and a curriculum, although that sounds too formal, which was tailored to our abilities.

I never felt that I was disadvantaged by my late start. My only regret about the unfortunate timing of my birth, was that each year we broke up for the Easter holiday before my birthday. In all the years of my schooling, I had only one birthday that fell in term time: just one occasion when I was able to have Miss Steeper read out my stack of birthday cards, and the class sung 'Happy birthday, dear Wendy', as was the custom for each birthday child.

Miss Steeper knew each child as an individual and had a good rapport with every family. Enveloped in this warmth, I developed my social skills and my imagination. There were times, however, when the easy familiarity between home and school could have disadvantages, especially for a child who was prone to confusion over where the boundaries lay between fact and fantasy.

One day she asked us what pets we had, and I had wanted a pet for so long. Mother, with her obsession for hygiene, thought otherwise. I had listened, with little regard, to her warnings that 'Yer'd be catchin' all sorts from dog shit', and 'How 'd yer like t' get in bed at night wi' a load a' cat fleas?'

I had seen a photograph of Mother and Granny with a dog lying on the front doorstep and, under cross-examination, she had admitted that a dog had once been part of the family, years before my birth. His name was Rip and she then told me the story of how he had jumped up at the kitchen door when he heard the dustman. This had been at a time, before the blight of black plastic bags, when a dustman came into the garden, collected the galvanised bin from the back of the carriages, hoisted it onto his shoulder and emptied it into the cart, before returning it to its home outside the wash-house. On this occasion the door had not been properly bolted and Rip escaped.

She described how he 'Frit the dustman 'alf t' death', and added 'Yer should ar' 'eard the clatter when 'e dropped the bin an' run'.

It appeared that this had caused her much amusement, but she would have been a lot younger at the time, perhaps a child, herself. It did not change her stance that I should have no similar tales to tell.

Eventually, I thought a compromise had been reached, with a pet who could live outdoors. Father built me a smart, detached residence for a rabbit. The front looked like a classic dolls' house with windows on two levels and a door with a knocker and tiny letterbox. The back was a large hinged door, opening to reveal two floors connected by a ramp so the lucky occupant could reach the upper floor. The roof lifted, with storage space for hay and food in the loft. It stood taller than me, resplendent in doll's house colours and was all ready for its first inhabitants.

Mother would not budge on her 'no animals' policy. I can only assume that Father had believed she would be won over by the regal house-hutch. His optimism was unfounded, his labours unrewarded. It stood at the back of the wash-house for years, deteriorating in the weather and was never occupied: a sad monument to the lack of communication between my parents.

Perhaps as some well-meant attempt at compensation, Father always let me bring home anything dead that we found on our walks. Despite Mother's loudly expressed fears that I would catch some dreaded disease, I was never made to leave a body, be it a bird, a rabbit or a field mouse, to the mercy of predators. All were borne home and buried with sombre respect at the bottom of the garden in the shade of the hedge. We thought of names for each one, which Father carved with his knife onto little wooden crosses. My cemetery marked the resting place of Wanderlust, Beauty, Furry and a number of Brownies and Snowflakes, all of which I had never known in life but had cried for in death.

It was against this back-drop, that I listened to the other children answering Miss Steeper's question about their pets.

'A cat' was a popular answer.

'A dog' claimed some of the luckier children.

So, as ever, when real life didn't live up to my dreams, I invented an alternative. Miss Steeper reached me and, without blinking, I looked into her kind eyes and said, 'A pig'.

She looked impressed, as I had known she would. She didn't know that we kept pigs, of course, as we didn't, but she was interested enough to approach Mother at home-time to have a chat.

I tried to pedal off, calling back to Mother to hurry, but she was happy to linger and I could only watch as the two women discussed my pet pig, or perhaps my loose relationship with reality.

I think I had an innate need to liven things up. If a drama wasn't happening, I would invent one. During this same period in Infants, biking home one dinner-time, I allowed Mother to get a little distance ahead, just to the point where a high hedge obscured her view of the knot-hole. Then I called, excitedly, 'Look. Did yer see that? There's a plane crashed right in the knot-hole.'

'Really?' She called back. 'I'll 'ev a look later.'

Her pedalling never faltered. I think she knew me well.

20 Bows and Books

For as long as I could remember, I had accompanied Mother to the hairdressers for her regular trims. I enjoyed the bright lights and mirrors. I breathed deeply, savouring the unfamiliar smells of products being used on other customers. Mother, of course, would never have let any of these chemicals touch her head.

I watched with envy as the scissors snipped her already short hair into a manageable bob. I wished so fervently that I could jump into that chair and be relieved of the heavy mane that hung past my waist and had never even been trimmed. I longed to be rid of the bow: always shiny and constantly interrupting boisterous games by slipping from its mooring. Most of all, I dreamed of never again hearing that dreaded summons, 'Come 'ere, 'air-wash-time'.

I had run. I had hid. I had begged for mercy, but I had never found any way of swaying Mother from her course. As a toddler I had been lain on my back on the kitchen table with a bowl on a chair at the end. This had been so uncomfortable. My neck was only supported by her left hand and took the full weight of my head every time she reached for the kettle or used both hands to squeeze out excess water. I pleaded to be allowed to have the bowl in the sink like the adults did.

I very quickly learned the perils of this position. I was hauled on to a chair and held there with my head hanging forward over the sink while bowls of water were poured over me. No-one heeded my squeals that I was 'drowneding' as water got into my ears and eyes. It only got worse as shampoo was added to the horror, bubbling around my face, no matter how close I tried to press my chin against my chest.

''old yer 'ead up, will yer,' Mother's exasperation could be heard in her voice as I instinctively drew back from the cascading water, causing it to soak the towel around my shoulders.

'Git further forrad.'

If the neighbours had ever heard of Child-line, I'm sure they would have rung them, unable to bear my distressed wailing, especially in summer when the carriage door was open and this tragic scene was performed with my chair right in the doorway. Mother could reach the kettle and the only tap we had indoors, ensuring that she did not lose her grip on me, thwarting any hope of escape.

In winter this ordeal was followed by shivering as I sat on the hearth rug in front of the fire until my hair-blanket was considered dry.

'Yer too far orf,' Mother scolded as she poked the fire into flames and I drew back from the heat on my face.

Too close, brought Granny's warnings of 'She'll be melting 'er gizzards'.

It was only when I started school and Mother heard of 'nits', although I never remember a case, that she became willing to consider my pleas for a trip to the hairdresser. I know it was a terrible wrench for her. When she died, almost fifty years later, my ponytail was still wrapped in tissue paper in her wardrobe.

I didn't notice her anguish on the day I leapt joyously into that chair. Today it was me having the black apron draped around my shoulders. I was to be transformed into a schoolgirl with a simple bob and a very straight fringe. I felt light and free and very grown up. Now I would be much more agile, able to run and climb better and, in the winter, I could wear close-fitting hats and not have a bulge where the bow distorted them, bringing a whole new meaning to the term 'poke-bonnet'. Now my coat wouldn't pull tight where my pony-tail was tucked in at the back, making me look like Quasimodo with cerebral complications.

With this new school lifestyle, my wardrobe grew. That's a slight exaggeration because I never had a wardrobe. The one in our bedroom housed all our clothes, but going to school in winter did bring about a change. We now had to leave the carriages on days which would previously have been deemed unfit to turn out. This meant having thicker clothes and more layers, all underpinned by the woolly vest.

It was a time when women were starting to wear trousers in this area. I recall overhearing a conversation between two mothers at the school gate. The first one, arriving on her bike, claimed 'They mek such a diff'rence. The wind don't git in a'tall'.

The second one replied 'My 'usband 'ud never let me wear 'em'.

I think times were changing because women and girls in trousers soon became a common sight. Mother and Granny were never converted but I had two pairs. They were called 'trews' and had straps attached at the ankle which went under the foot inside the shoe. These straps had seams which annoyed my feet so much that I would wail and flail every time I was forced to wear them.

One pair was green and the other brown. I also had two skirts, in two different plaids, and two Fair Isle patterned jumpers. I presume garments were bought in pairs so that they could be washed and worn alternately. This was not a time when still-clean clothes were scooped into a washing machine after one wear. A jumper and skirt might last all week if dinner was eaten carefully. Granny neatly folded each garment as she took it off at bedtime, placing them snugly under her eiderdown so that they were warm and pressed for the morning.

Mother always referred to our clothes as 'clobber', not to be confused with the term, 'He'll get clobbered', which meant caught by the police.

In summer I wore pretty, seersucker dresses, light gingham checks, and shorts with a matching tee-shirt for outdoor games. With bare arms and legs, we spent hours in the playing field under a relentless sun. Brown was considered healthy. Even babies were left uncovered in their prams, limbs exposed to 'catch a bit a' sun'. Tanned was synonymous with 'bonny', pale might be referred to as pasty or sickly.

A headache at teatime brought a vinegar-soaked flannel to hold on the forehead and muttered recriminations from a woolly-hatted Granny.

'I told 'er t' keep 'er 'ead covered up. She'll be 'eving sunstroke next', but we glowed in the fresh air, only occasionally needing to be doused with camomile lotion if our skin looked like it might peel. Mother would not have been amused by the chemical sun-screens available today.

'All tha' gunge bungin' up 'er pores, I sh' think not'.

On these hot, summer days, team spirit was built in games such as stallball, played with sashes over our clothes, proclaiming the colour of our team. Sports-days were competitive and races were won or lost according to individual ability. We were not psychologically damaged for life because our pot egg leapt from a spoon held in shaking hands and we lost the egg-and-spoon race. No-one sued the school because we tripped in the sack-race and landed on our noses. The terminology of the day was 'clumsy', not 'compensation'. Bruises healed and we developed a realistic view of our capabilities.

Those of us, like me, who couldn't run or jump, discovered other talents and concentrated on them, finding a niche in painting or writing or maths. It was not a time when everyone could be a winner.

We were, however, inspired by popular figures. As we began to realise in 1964 that Tokyo was a real place, not just a word on the globe, we followed the progress of our Olympic stars. We ran around the field like Ann Packer, jumped in a feeble imitation of Mary Rand and dreamed of following in the fleet footsteps of Mary Peters.

For the umpteenth time, a boy who had just passed the football successfully, could be heard shouting to the headmistress's husband - only male teacher - football coach - referee, 'What d' yer reckon Ron 'ud mek a' that one?'

Ron Ashman had grown up in this community, his grandparents keeping the only shop, before he went on to become a footballing legend and manager of the Norwich team.

Whilst I never excelled at sports, I did compensate by being a prolific reader. With this ability to read, and subsequently to write, came a new freedom to express myself, to put my thoughts to others and get feedback, both positive and constructively critical. I was constantly amazed by the words that appeared on the page. So many words took on a new shape in their written form.

'A nam samige' became 'a ham sandwich'. Some words, however, did not appear in my narrow range of reading material and it was many more years before I read the label on the familiar bottle that appeared every winter and realised that the comforting 'camphoraty doil' was actually called 'camphorated oil'.

The frustration of not being understood, because of my limited and sometimes obscure vocabulary, lessened rapidly at this time. Now that I had discovered the wealth of knowledge hiding between the covers of each and every book, I was unstoppable.

Before I left King's Dyke school at the age of eleven, I recall the headmistress regularly being summoned to help. I had handed another book back to the teacher, assured him that I had read it thoroughly and explained the plot in detail to prove the point. Now I was waiting expectantly for a replacement and there wasn't anything left on the bookcase that I had not read. On such occasions she would go off to search in dark, dusty corners, returning with an apology and some outdated tome. These books were no longer used in class as their phraseology was already dated. They had beautiful words that I had not heard before and fine illustrations.

I had never been allowed to join the public library as Mother was convinced that every book was contaminated by the previous reader who had 'mauled it with mucky 'ands', whilst bed-ridden with some fatal contagion, but now I was allowed to take books home, as this was part of our 'edgercation'. This further increased my rate of consumption.

School staff seemed not to share Mother's reservations about exchanging books. Each term a library van visited the school: greeted with excitement, as it cleared and restocked our small library corner.

One book captured my imagination to the extent that I read it over and over again, making sure that it was safely in my possession and missed the collection on at least two occasions when we were instructed to return books for the van's visit. This was Geoffrey Trease's 'Cue for Treason'. I was thrilled by the daring escapades of Kit, the girl who dressed as a boy and joined a travelling theatre group. This was exactly the spirit I loved.

However, the library van eventually caught me out and

it was gone from the shelves for ever. I pleaded with Mother to buy it for me but she said it was 'out a' stock'.

I sensed a reluctance on her part to spend good money on a book which she knew I had read countless times and was able to recount in a fluent synopsis, although she did assure me later, 'If I could a' got it I would a' done to stop yer ornging'.

Only in later years did I manage to acquire a copy and re-read it with an adult's perspective, immediately seeing why I was captivated by Kit. She had been another fantasy version of me.

21 Other Worlds

As I settled into school at King's Dyke, I slowly became aware that I was not quite part of that community. We lived less than a quarter of a mile away but our worlds were separated by more than distance.

The building was originally designed to accommodate seventy children but rarely saw more than forty at any one time. It had been built in 1904 to educate the children of the workforce of Arthur Werner Itter, who opened his first brickyard in the 1890s on a site between the main road into Peterborough and the Great Eastern Railway line.

More than seventy terraced cottages had also been built to house the workers and their families. These were rented out as 'tied cottages', playing an influential part in maintaining a core of regular, skilled men who might, otherwise, have become seasonal workers, happy only to work in the kilns and knot-holes in winter when work on the land was not so readily available.

Mr Itter was a man with vision. The scheme was successful and the cottages remained in the ownership of the brickyard for nearly a hundred years.

In blocks of eight, they stretched from the railway crossing gates to the school, providing solid, practical and comfortable accommodation but they never really lived up to their pretty names. Stone plaques in the brickwork identified them as Jasmine, Lily and Myrtle, Daisy, Primrose and Lilac, but there was a grim air of defiance about them as they faced each other across the road. The paintwork was always green as this was reputed to survive better than any other colour in the surrounding atmosphere, laden with sulphur from the chimneys just yards away.

In this dusty, smoky environment, children were raised and many stayed to raise their own families. Some of the houses were occupied from beginning to end by the same family. I only got to know these children at school, where they made up almost the entire register.

We had no uniform to identify us although, strangely, I did have a school badge: the sort that would be sewn onto a blazer pocket, but we never had blazers. The badge is still in its original envelope, silently proclaiming the name of the school against a backdrop of brickyard chimneys. Any sense of belonging to that community came from within, not from having the right badge or clothing.

Grandfather had once been one of Mr Itter's employees. My grandparents had lived at King's Dyke. Two of my uncles had lived there as boys and they told of playing in the road and hiding in the passages between the terraces. The eldest even recalled an incident when he was chased through these passages before being hit in the eye by a stalk of Brussel sprouts, wielded by another boy, but time had moved on.

Father worked in the city, not in the brickyard. He went to work wearing a white shirt, armlets and cufflinks with a dark suit. His shoes were polished: not the heavy, clay-caked boots that were the regular footwear of the brickyard workers. Perhaps I might have been considered more privileged as an only child of parents whose income was a little higher, but I never felt privileged. I envied those children who ran in and out of each other's houses, through doors that were never locked, calling for friends that they had known since birth. They appeared to exist as one huge, extended family and that familiarity carried them easily through school, equally supportive of their siblings, friends and neighbours.

These were the children and grandchildren of the members of the King's Dyke Silver Prize Band, formed at the turn of the century: another example of the community spirit that was so strong. They were the descendants of those who had fought for a place of worship, starting services in a tin tabernacle and progressing to a chapel built with bricks, donated by the same benevolent Mr Itter.

Some of the families here had seen two wars, twice watched their boys leave to fight, some never to return. Side by side, they had faced adversity and now came together to support those who had been touched by the tragedies that occurred from time to time, both in the kilns and the knot-holes, bonding as they waited for news, then sharing the rejoicing or mourning.

All along the road were other brickyards. Each had its own housing, workers and identities, but all the children were somehow bound by their common ancestry, from the time when men on ladders had hewn the clay with pickaxes and pushed it to the surface on carts.

At school, the children talked of what had happened the evening before and planned for the evening ahead. I could only listen and imagine how wonderful it would be to have a garden path that ran to the very edge of the knot-hole. The grassy slopes that led down to the exposed clay were their playground. Health and Safety inspectors would have such areas tightly fenced off these days but parents were happy to have their brood out of doors on warm summer nights and they probably didn't worry too much. The children explored in groups, the eldest looking out for the younger ones, aware of the areas to avoid. Wet clay sucked like quicksand and channels of deep water lay at the bottom but I don't ever remember a child being drowned or even injured in this landscape.

The grown-ups may have been more concerned that they might stray onto the railway lines and the sidings. These ran within feet of the houses, right up to the kilns so that bricks might be loaded directly for transportation by rail. Again, I have no recall of any child coming to harm there.

I did go to a birthday party once, in one of these houses. It was warm and cosy with coal fires and carpets. I was impressed by the stairs, complaining to my parents afterwards that I couldn't have a bedroom upstairs 'because I live in a stupid carriage'.

My only reservation about the house was the closeness of the railway track. With the vibration of each passing train, I caught my breath and waited. The family didn't even seem to notice. After tea and the traditional party games, we were allowed out to play. We skirted around the edge of that forbidden paradise before being called back because some of us had come in shiny, patent party shoes, not wellies.

Another group within the school were a handful of 'bus-children'. They came from King's Delph: a small cluster of homes, known locally as the 'Black Houses'. This name was left over from the original two houses built there to home the Lighter men, who worked the boats, called 'Lighters', on the old River Nene. They had carried wood, coal, bricks, corn and what-ever else needed carrying, hauling cargo inland to Peterborough and Northamptonshire.

This old river ran at the bottom of their gardens and an earlier generation had followed its twisting course, across fields to the school. They still told stories of floods and snow drifts and small figures in high boots, struggling through the winter. By our much advanced time, the children of King's Delph left in time to catch the three-twenty bus each afternoon. Class was interrupted every day to allow the teacher to escort them across the road to the bus-stop. I was envious of them because they left early and got two rides on a bus each day.

I spent a lot of my childhood not appreciating how much I had, but envying what others had. This wasn't a craving for material possessions: more a desire to live another existence. This envy peaked each year with the arrival of the 'fair children'. Their families parked up the wagons and living vans in a big yard behind the shop at King's Delph after the last fair of the season. They only ever spent the winter months with us, swelling our class-size by about seven. I don't know if the education authority or the school had any notification of their times of arrival and departure but we never knew.

We would just get to school one morning and they would be in the playground, bigger and stronger than the rest of us, their skins more tanned. They wore clothes that set them apart and had gold ear-rings.

'Yer back then,' the local children greeted them. 'Where yer bin then?'

Surrounded by an eager audience, they were animated and confident although they had not seen us for nearly a year. They spoke of places unknown to us and told stories of adventures in which they had played a part, speaking with an unfamiliar accent.

I was mesmerised by their presence. I wanted to make friends with them and dreamed of getting invited back for tea but it never happened. The closest I ever got was glimpsing the massive showman's vans in their burgundy and cream paintwork as we passed on the bus: high enough to see the chimneys smoking and the lace curtains that veiled another part of their lives. Then, as the days started to lengthen into spring, we would find one morning that their seats were unoccupied. I can still see the empty chairs and feel the sad realisation that the wagons would be gone too, that somewhere far away, they were starting their day in their other world.

22 Magic in the Air

The most exciting night of the year in my world, exceeding even Christmas, was in October when I was taken to Peterborough's last fair of the season. I jumped up and down, making it impossible for Mother to tie the bow of my hat under my chin. She wrapped the scarf around my neck, tucking the ends into my coat, an extra layer to protect my chest. The huge bulge strained at my buttons. I was the excited puppy, desperate to go out yet hampering progress by not keeping still while the lead was attached.

Mittens and stout shoes completed the ensemble and finally we headed for the bus-stop to wait for the bus that was inevitably late. The hedge behind us provided little shelter and I huddled between my parents as a keen wind blew from the north. My shivering was a combination of cold and excitement.

Eventually, the dim headlights appeared round Mile Tree Corner and we climbed into the warmth, finding a seat as the driver pulled away. It took about twenty minutes to reach the city. On any other day, this journey would have been an adventure in itself. On fair-night, it was just another part of the waiting.

I pressed my face against the cold glass of the window, seeing only my own reflection for much of the journey as we travelled mostly between dark fields. These windows were not the sealed units of modern coaches and the frames were always a little loose, the glass vibrating against my skin as every bump in the road brought us closer to our destination.

The nearest bus stop was just after the fair meadow, so my first glimpse was as we passed above it, over the water bridge. From this high vantage point I looked out of the window, level with the tallest attractions: the dome of the penny-on-the-mat and the seats that swung precariously in the sky, suspended from the steel structure of the big wheel. The noise of the bus engine blocked out any sound and the scene framed by the window was as silent as any painting I had seen, and more beautiful.

As we walked back across the bridge, an occasional squeal could be heard but mostly there was a blur of sounds, still muffled by distance. The strings of coloured light bulbs swayed in the wind and a haze of smoke drifted upwards.

Only as we went in through the gate, could individual voices could be discerned.

'Roll up. Roll up.' was a familiar cry from the men in charge of the bigger rides: the Swinging Boats, the Cake-Walk, Jollity Farm.

These men were always lean and tanned and I loved their confident voices, the nomadic accents.

'Try yer luck on the coconuts - darts - ducks,' shouted competing barkers from around the field.

Everywhere I turned were shining eyes and the flash of gold. Women with ear-rings, bangles and chains, smiled down at me from behind their stalls, inviting us to knock down a stack of tin cans or to throw wooden rings over a prize on the hoop-la stall. Their fingers were laden with heavy rings. They wore a leather pouch around their waist, into which they shoved handfuls of coins.

I walked slowly now. This was an experience that could not be rushed. My parents were probably conscious of the time of the last bus home, or rather the last bus on which Mother would travel. She always said, 'Only drunks git the last bus'.

They would try to chivvy me along, suggesting that I could go on a roundabout with a choice of an aeroplane, a fire engine, or even a two-wheeled bicycle, all securely bolted to the moving floor, or I could choose something from a stall which displayed fudge and nougat and bars of toffee that could only be broken with a toffee-hammer.

We always bought brandy snap to take home for Granny and, all in good time, I might have a toffee apple or a candy floss, but I was overwhelmed by all the activity, the brightly painted scenery and canopies, the cacophony of sounds. Surely this was the original surround sound system. I could only take in so much at once. Eating or riding were not my priorities.

As I stood before the big horses - I've always wondered why they are known as the Gallopers when they move with such controlled elegance - my parents seemed to assume that I was considering whether to have a ride. The thought did not occur to me. I saw the beautifully carved horses, with wild eyes, manes flying. I saw the gilded poles which supported them and the intricate artwork that decorated the top of the carousel as it turned, all hand-painted by steady hands. Sitting astride any one of those horses would not have afforded me this view and I would saunter off just as they stopped and everyone else surged forward.

Similarly, I was drawn to watch the swinging boats with their painted undersides, gradually revealed as they gained height with each pull of the ropes. I studied the cake-walk, trying to fathom out how it worked, gyrating so that it bumped people along, on one end and off the other, time after time, yet it still stood in the same place, just like the striped barber's pole. Another favourite was the bumper cars, before they became dodgems. I loved to see them glide over the shiny floor, spinning and weaving, creating sparks of electricity as they went.

My parents followed my lead, hopeful that I might decide to use up my allocated allowance for the night but I didn't reward their patience, unmoved by their prompts that the chair-o-planes looked fun or the little train chugging round a circular track might amuse me. Perhaps I was a little nervous about leaving the safe proximity of my parents to be carried away, strapped to some unfamiliar piece of machinery, but there was more than that. I felt something that I could neither understand nor resist.

I was compelled to experience more than these rides offered. With the grown-ups still wandering behind me, I remember trying to peep beyond the lighted circle of entertainment. There, in shadow, were the engines that drove the rides and powered the lights. They towered above me, my head not even level with the spokes of the wheels, but I never feared them. They were much bigger than the boiler at school but not so unruly that they needed caging. Getting close enough to breathe the smell of oil, I felt the rhythm of the pistons, regular, reliable.

Forcing myself to walk more quickly now, lest I was dragged back to the main arena, I reached the circle of lorries and living vans. The lights reflected on gleaming chrome and danced on the glass of high windows. I was fascinated by the odd bits that were left outside: a dog's bowl, an empty bucket, a length of rope, the chattels of another life. They all took on a strange significance. Dogs lurked here, straining at their chains. Not too comfortable with the expression on those canine faces, my parents hauled me back to the public area, but it was still the characters who held my attention.

I have very clear memories of a beautiful girl of about six, no bigger than me. Her curly hair escaped from plaits, her cheeks glowed and she wore no coat. She was obviously resident here. A group of boys chased through the crowd, hands in pockets, shouting to each other in accents that identified them as the sons of the men who called 'Roll up. Roll up'.

The most vivid picture of all is of babies in prams as big as mine, parked by the stalls as their mothers worked. Some snuggled under blankets, shielded from the cold night air. Others sat up, round eyes staring at the scene as if mesmerised by the lights and movement. One drank what looked like cold tea from a bottle clenched in tiny white hands, or perhaps it was warm tea.

As the night grew later, although it couldn't have been much more than eight o'clock, Mother would become restless, insisting that I decide if I was going to have a ride 'afore yer miss yer chance'. We always had to leave before the tarpaulin sheets were pulled over the rides, before the prams were wheeled to their respective homes, before those straggling children with hooped ear-rings were rounded up for the night.

I trailed back to the bus-stop, filled with the thrill of what I had seen. Back at the carriages I was still too excited to sleep but dreamed of being a fair-child. I imagined what it would be like to fall asleep inside one of those magnificent showman's wagons, sharing a cosy bed with a number of siblings, knowing that my friends and cousins were with their families close by, and that the big dogs outside would keep us all safe through the night.

23 Revelations

I was once taken to the circus and for a while this captured my imagination, replacing the fair fantasy. Enchanted by the girls who performed on the trapeze, I spent the next few days wearing my bathing costume over woolly tights. I posed on chairs, arms outstretched in readiness to launch myself into the air above the crowd. The smell of the canvas was in my nostrils as I flew close to the roof of the big-top. The footlights sparkled on my sequined costume and picked out the jewels in my tiara.

The living vans that encircled this world were very similar to those of the fairground people and the lorries that pulled them bore the same bold artistry, but I think the romance was overshadowed by fear. Late at night, I worried that if I really joined the circus, I would be sleeping in close proximity to the lions. I hadn't felt comfortable sharing the confines of the big-top with them. I didn't think I would sleep too well if I could hear them prowling up and down their cages while it was still dark. Perhaps I wasn't destined to be a trapeze artiste with a waist-length ponytail and glitter around my eyes.

Other images carried me away for a while. Weeks were spent practising on my roller skates, holding the fence with one hand, when I decided that I was going to be a professional skater with long legs and a very short skirt. A wonderful ponytail now brushed the ice as my handsome partner swept me upwards, holding me aloft as the crowd cheered ecstatically. This particular phase followed a coach trip to Wembley where we watched the pantomime, Ali Baba on Ice.

Another distraction was when Robinson Crusoe was performed as a pantomime at the Embassy Theatre. I just wanted to sail away to a deserted island and share a camp with the charismatic Jess Conrad but, as a child who didn't belong to Brownies or Guides, I never even got to experience the thrill of sleeping under canvas.

I think my parents waited for my fascination with the fair to fade and pass, but all these distractions were only temporary. Year after year, my love affair with the fair resurfaced. I always drew pictures and invented stories where I was one of the central characters in that world.

Eventually it must have dawned on them that my instincts were stronger than their logic, or perhaps they denied it but always knew.

I had sensed from an early age, from snippets of conversation overheard, that I didn't know the whole story of my roots. Towns as far away as Nottingham and Burslem featured somewhere in the memories of both Mother and Granny. I was also puzzled by some half-heard, half-forgotten comment that Mother had not always gone to school during the summer, but my dreams and their recollections floated in my mind without ever being connected.

In the bottom drawer of Granny's tallboy resided a doll who was never allowed out to play. He was a hairless baby boy who Mother had named Paul. She spoke fondly of having had him since she was five years old. He had a pot head and hands, eyes that swivelled open and shut, and a stuffed body. He was always wrapped in a soft flannelette sheet and secured in a strong cardboard box. Only on very rare occasions, such as when the drawers were emptied to make the furniture lighter to move for wallpapering, would she listen to my pleas to unwrap him. Then I held him briefly and gently stroked his expressionless face, under her closest supervision. I still have him now and he is not an attractive doll. He has the pallor of a very poorly baby.

When I questioned his origins, I was told simply that he came from Nottingham Goose Fair. This, of course, prompted a dozen more questions and the answers were a little strange. Mother, at five, had seen him on a stall and wanted him desperately, but he was never meant to be won. He was the unobtainable prize that drew in the public. Perhaps she was as determined and relentless as I was at that age, because her father had bought him for five pounds. The year would have been 1926 and I had no concept of the value of five pounds at that time. What was strange was her wording of the story. Her father had bought him from his mate on the stall.

Why had Grandfather got a mate with a stall and why was everybody in Nottingham?

I could no longer be diverted from hearing the whole story and I think now that maybe she had allowed me to lead the conversation to this point.

Why had he got a mate with a stall?

Because Grandfather was a showman, too.

Why was my five year old mother in Nottingham, so far from home?

Because, for part of the year, she had lived this life of which I dreamed.

Why the Goose Fair?

Because it was the last fair of the year and all the families, even those who did not travel regularly, turned up for this last extravaganza before the men disbanded and went home for the winter.

Slowly, over a long period, other comments that I had heard and not understood, but never questioned, began to make sense.

'I didn't like 'im coming 'ome 'cus then I had to sleep in my own bed,' was an answer I had heard more than once when I had asked Mother about the grandfather I never knew, as he had died before my birth.

This was the most profound revelation of my childhood. Initially I was thrilled. Everything made sense to me now. Those children with the flashing eyes and earrings, those babies that captivated me from their prams, they were my kindred spirits.

I danced around in excitement. All I had to do now was organise the grown-ups, motivate them so that they saw what we had been missing. Even without Grandfather, we could find our way back to what was our real world. I wanted to pack immediately. I had no reservations, but I sensed resistance. The reason Grandfather had bought the carriages was that Granny did not wish to travel with him. He returned there for winter. It was his base, but it was Granny's home and Mother's home and they were not planning to go anywhere soon.

At first I pleaded and cajoled. Then I became increasingly angry. This was unbelievably unjust. I had now grasped the enormity of the situation. I was living my life here, hemmed in by fences and a garden gate which had a latch on the far side so that I could not reach it and escape. I was bound by school and regulations and routines and this wasn't where I should be. I should be travelling to far-off places, my long hair shaken free, blowing and tangling in the wind as I ran until my cheeks were rosy and I looked at my reflection and saw the real fair child that I was.

I was frustrated and resentful and stamped around no end, but all to no avail. Granny had not been persuaded by her husband and she certainly wasn't going to be convinced by a small, petulant child. Perhaps it was a part of her life that she wished to forget. She never refreshed her memories by accompanying us to the fair.

These visits continued but now took on new meaning. My parents lessened their attempts to persuade me to go through the motions of a normal child who pleaded for money to go on just one more ride, time after time. They no longer tried to pacify me with a balloon on a stick or a bag of Bulls' Eyes. They allowed me time to stand and gaze; time to breathe in the heady smells of oil and steam and spun sugar; time to imagine that when the crowds went home I would return to a little bunk somewhere in that circle of showman's wagons.

The fleeting magic of the fair extended to two fields. Between them, were the blackened arches which supported the railway tracks, carrying trains overhead. Some fair families parked in this dark space. Straw and sawdust were strewn on the ground because water collected there. I always thought I would not park there because those arches were very old and might give way under the weight of a train. They are still standing and still bear that weight today but I was never a child to take risks. I always listened for approaching trains before I would venture to make the short crossing from one field to the other.

Hearing the them rumbling slowly because they had not gathered much speed after stopping at the nearby Crescent Station, I stood and waited until they passed. It was here that I first noticed the people in the carriages, their faces illuminated by the lamps above their heads. They were observing the activity below them. It occurred to me then, not that I was just a dot in the crowd, but that if I could see them so clearly, they must also see me, my figure lit by the backdrop of the fairground bulbs.

I wondered if I looked as if I belonged there. Did those people imagine a family who would make sure I was safe in one of those huge lorries before they hooked up my home and towed it through the night, the artistry announcing that the fair was on tour?

I tried to sidle away from my parents. I claimed to be hot on the coldest of nights and insisted on taking my coat off. I needed to look like a child who lived in this world. I wanted those strangers on the train to believe in my fantasy.

If they believed, I would live in their minds as a fair child. They would carry that image to their destination and it would be as real to them as the girl with the curling hair was to me. Reality was only real if someone believed it.

This reality, however, was fragile. I was always prised from it in time to catch the bus back to the carriages, walking backwards to savour every last moment of that life that could have been mine: that life that had been stolen from me.

Sometimes I wondered if I had imagined it all. We travelled to the city on the same bus another day. I looked out of the same window, but the fair meadow was empty. Had it all been just a dream?

Had I so desperately wanted it to be real that I had merged the edges of fantasy and reality?

It was only after Mother's death, nearly fifty years later, that I found Granny's death certificate and read the words, 'Widow of George Holmes Travelling Showman'.

24 To the Other Side

Moving up to Juniors can mean a traumatic change of school for some young children but in our small community, we were lucky. We stayed at our same school until the age of eleven. It was not unusual to find three or more children from the same family on the register, working their way up the years. This also meant that a frock or coat often made more than one journey through the classes.

Of course, I had no siblings in whose steps I would follow, nor any that would follow me. My clothes were exclusively mine, always 'bran' new', but I never felt that was much compensation. When I saw a tiny child fall and an elder sister appear at her side as if she had been watching over her from a distance, or a bigger boy shouldered his way into a situation where a little brother might have been threatened, I felt very alone in my frills and bows.

After the demise of the original 'tin-tabernacle' Methodist chapel due to subsidence, the school had been used for services on Sundays. The two rooms were separated only by a wooden, panelled partition which could be easily removed to accommodate worshippers. A new chapel had been built in 1929 and the partition between Infant and Junior classes now remained closed except for Christmas parties. Then the whole school celebrated around a huge rectangular arrangement of desks, with chairs facing inwards and outwards.

Each of us carefully transported our contribution to the fare. Cakes and sausage rolls, biscuits and mince-pies, all homemade and often a little battered on arrival, were washed down with large gulps of fizzing pop. The teachers hovered, handing around plates, gently intervening in disputes when the last sandwich on a plate was seized by two hands not belonging to the same child. They also seemed to have a knack for spotting a child who had suddenly stopped eating and turned a funny colour, briskly escorting them out to the cloakroom.

The role of the partition now was to provide a buffer between those who played and those who worked. Although our journey to becoming a junior was just a few steps, there was a definite shift in our experience and in the expectations of the teachers. We sat in more formal rows, moved around the room less, spent more time listening and less time chatting. The nature walks and the cosy afternoons of knitting and sewing became a happy memory.

In Miss Steeper's class I had knitted a Goldilocks doll with a blue frock and long, golden plaits of woollen hair. Three others had made the trio of bears. We had taken home dressing table mats and felt rabbits. Most of these items had now been put aside but we still carried our plimsolls in little calico bags that we had made ourselves as we practised various embroidery stitches.

Now we had the headmistress's husband as our teacher. We swapped the motherly protection of Miss Steeper for the quietly spoken Mr Greetham, as the emphasis shifted to books and paper, pens and paints. I recall clearly the individual tins containing blocks of paint. Each had a distinctive smell. I could tell the colour of the paint by the smell and recall that yellow ochre had a particularly pungent odour.

Colours were very important to me at this time and it

caused another battle of wills when Mother bought me a pair of brown sandals. I exploded at this blatant attempt to turn me into a boy. Whoever heard of a girl wearing brown sandals?

I'm not sure where this association came from but it was probably very closely related to my reluctance to celebrate my seventh birthday, begging to be allowed to remain six until I reached eight because seven was definitely a boy's number.

In our new role as juniors, we listened in silence to programmes for schools on the wireless. Science, history and music came to us over the air-waves. I was never able to sing a note in tune, being the daughter of a father who carried a flag, not an instrument, but I loved the hymns and carols with their powerful words and reliable rhythm. We sang John Bunyan's 'He who would valiant be', and we all avowed to be pilgrims. We sang 'In the bleak mid-winter' and I felt the chill of Christina Rossetti's snow on snow.

We were also allowed to join a savings bank at this time. Mr Greetham explained that we could each bring in a sum of money every week, say sixpence, to be invested for our future. This sounded exciting. When he added that we would get even more back than we put in, this concept of interest became of great interest. I took the letter home, gabbling about the content before Mother could even open it. She looked as if she was having to weigh up its merits as she read it, frowning and sucking in her cheeks. Her misgivings were based on a previous experience when she had visited the bank and been asked to discuss her finances with a 'walk-about'. This was a derogatory name for someone not important enough to have his own office. In a fit of indignation she had shut her account, vowing, 'They won't be 'aving no more o' m' money', and declaring, 'I sh'll keep it under m' bolster where I know as it's safe and I can see what I got'.

This seemed unreasonable to me at a time when the only 'Crooked Bank' I had come across was just a turning off the road to Wisbech, but it took a lot of persuasion before I headed off to school with my first 'tanner' in my bank-money purse.

By now Mother had agreed to allow me to eat at school some days. I loved putting my hand up to be a school-dinner when the morning register was called. Father ate his mid-day meal at work and I only ever remember Granny coming to the table for Christmas dinner. Normally she balanced a plate, or sometimes a pudding basin, on her lap in her armchair beside the hearth. It was much more fun to eat with my friends in a small group at a large table, rather than at the kitchen table in the carriages where Mother and I sat at opposite ends.

I think she was pleased, too. This new experience of eating in company, speeded up my progress towards the appropriate use of cutlery. A lot of meal-time friction had arisen from my refusal to use anything but a particular fruit spoon. Its crinkly edge served quite adequately as both a knife and fork. She knew I was perfectly capable of handling a full size knife and fork because I conformed when we had visitors. Her frustration was evident in her voice as she threatened 'Yer won't be gitting no pudding if yer don't eat this proper fust'.

As juniors, in the classroom at the front of the building, we were first to know it was dinner-time. We heard the arrival of the van that delivered hot food to local schools. Cooking was done at the big school in town and then transported in large stainless steel containers. I enjoyed all the dishes that are generally mocked: the cabbage, pale and limp; the custard, pale and runny; and rice pudding, especially the skin on the top. The dishes were nutritional, locally sourced and varied with the seasons. We were not offered a choice, except to eat it or not, but there was always enough for a second helping. My favourite dish was goulash. The smell drifted into my nostrils as soon as the containers were opened, always on a Friday. I have never since tasted goulash as good and I struggled to stay in my seat as the smell pervaded the classrooms and we all waited for the call to the table.

The other vehicle which arrived regularly at the school gate during the summer months was the mini bus which took small groups to the local swimming pool. This only happened in summer because the pool was outdoors. Even on sunny days it was freezing, but we still went eagerly and never quite understood why we were ordered out of the water at the first plop of rain. Perhaps it was the teachers who didn't want to get wet. The pool was quite primitive. Plastic chairs stood on a slippery, paved area. We placed our clothes in supermarket-style baskets and ran from the changing area in our ribbed and ruched costumes. Our heads were squeezed into stretchy rubber hats that never stretched quite enough to be comfortable. They covered our ears, deadening all the noise to a drone.

Mother wasn't too keen on this part of my education but it was classed as a lesson so she never stopped me going. She just chuntered to Granny 'In th' wa'er wi' all them boys and all on us knows what boys do in wa'er.'

I know she worried because her and Granny would exchange frowns and comment on how 'nearly an 'undred folk died in that last cholera do, an' that were 'cus o' th' wa'er'.

That had been before Granny was born, but fen folk have very long memories, especially for the bad experiences.

25 Look Out

During this same period, I finally learned to ride a two-wheeled bike. I say finally, because it was a slow and painful process. I had been so accustomed to gliding to a halt on my trusty trike, pausing to study whatever had caught my eye, or just to savour a moment. The new, stupid bike, which I had loved when I saw it in Mr Marson's shop, proved to be incapable of accommodating this. Every time I stopped pedalling, I finished up in a heap on the floor, wheels still spinning, my legs bruised by flying pedals.

For the first time, I now understood Mother's complaint about the flex on the new-fangled iron. This machine had cable brakes which hung from the handlebars and grabbed the toe of my sandal on more than one occasion, tipping me onto the gravel before I was even seated. I hated cable brakes and pleaded to have them taken away. I hated the whole bike and avoided getting on it. I wasn't in control any more. My life would never be the same again. I think part of the delay in the learning process was due to my refusal to accept that this would ever get better. The other part was my complete ineptitude. I couldn't balance, I couldn't steer, and Mother seemed to think that I should do both at the same time, as well as pedalling.

For weeks her voice rang in my ears as she trailed along with me.

'Steer, steer, left a bit, keep yer 'ead up, look where yer going, don't stop pedallin', steer, gew right, look out...'

One day she was right at my side, holding the tie-belt

of my dress, when I hit a stone wall. I went over the top into the hedge beyond and left her still clutching the belt that had ripped from the dress. She just wouldn't give up.

Another attempt found her banging on a school-friend's door for help because I had landed on the path outside the brickyards. Blood was pouring down my face and every cut and graze was filled with grit and red brick-dust. The kind lady bathed my wounds with a flannel and a pudding bowl of warm water, tweaking a sliver of brick from my left eyebrow, but I was still left with a scar that has never since grown hair, haunting me every time I look in the mirror and see my eyebrows that don't quite match.

Mother didn't even relent when I nearly beheaded myself. On a visit to one of her friends, she let me play outside on bikes with the friend's children. They were riding across the garden, ducking under the clothes-line. I did this successfully a few times before I lost concentration, or maybe my lack of spatial awareness clouded my judgement. The rope line caught me right under the chin and threw me to the ground.

She rushed from the kitchen and had the good grace to make sure that my head and body were still attached to each other before she began to berate me for my stupidity. That incident left me with a red weal right across my neck for weeks, looking like I'd had my throat cut; particularly as I quickly learned to sit with my head tilted back so that even strangers would comment and offer their sympathies.

Still the bike-battle went on and eventually I must have overcome my reluctance. I was tempted into a game with two other children who had built a ramp in their yard, using a plank of wood and several old bricks. Each of them rode their bike up the ramp at speed, over the top and down the other side as the plank pivoted on the bricks. Not wanting to be outdone, I rode slowly to the top before the old fear took over and I tried to get off.

This meant having to explain not just the cut hands, the scraped legs and the torn clothes, but also the buckled wheel. Just as I was gaining enough confidence to take my smart new bike out on my own, Mother was deciding that perhaps this was not to be encouraged.

I was, however, expected to pedal sensibly at her side on the way to school and back. I did try to concentrate but it wasn't the easiest of routes. Windy days were the worst when we suffered what Granny called 'brickyard blows'. These were not on the same scale as the traditional 'fen blows', which could see the surface of a whole field rise into the air, but they occurred more regularly, stirring up the dust from the kilns and the straw used to protect the facing bricks. This debris swept across the road as I tried to steer my bike with eyes scrunched to slits, the grit stinging my face and bare legs, the spiky straw settling on my hair and coat.

Another hazard was the cracked and displaced kerbstones that jutted into the road, crushed by the heavy vehicles continuously turning in and out of each yard. Ruts in the road here could be as deep as furrows and broken drain covers waited to unseat the unwary rider. I clung to the handlebars with white knuckles. Just to make me feel entirely comfortable, there was Mother's voice shouting over the wind as the lorries rushed past in a whirl of straw and exhaust fumes, 'Keep in the side, they'll knock yer off soon as look at yer'.

Gusts of wind from every gap in the hedge wobbled me, but I never thought of complaining. This was the way to school and I knew no other environment. Like the smell of sulphur in the air and the smuts on the washing, it was all part of living near to this industry which was at the heart of the local economy. A large proportion of the population were employed directly. Other businesses such as lorry firms, building contractors and even shops employing people like Father, relied on money generated by the brickyards, so no-one ever grumbled about these little inconveniences.

I was happy at school and known as a cheerful child who arrived with a smile each morning. I'm sure I was pleased to be there but I can't help thinking that the smile was at least partly one of relief that I had survived the journey.

Most people who did not work in the brickyards, were employed for part of the year in the other industry which put our town on the map.

As early as the middle ages celery had been known for its medicinal value, used in the treatment of arthritis and rheumatism, so it was not surprising to find it growing in areas such as ours where these ailments were so prevalent. Since the fifteenth century, it had it been recognised and cultivated here in the fens as a vegetable.

In February, seeds were planted in trays in greenhouses, nurtured by a boiler and a system of hot water pipes. From these sheltered beginnings, the plants were hardened off in cold frames which could be opened by day and closed at night. Then, in March, came the army of celery prickers with their dibbers, pricking out the inch high plants to carry on growing in manured and raked beds. These were spread with soot to deter worms. The workers were mainly women who donned bib-and-braces and secured their hair in headscarves, in true land-army style, for the short season. They knelt in trays and jumped themselves backwards along the beds. These trays had a raised front on which the women placed a cushion to support their ample bosoms. This caused us much stifled giggling because they were always known as tit-lobs and we would refer to them just to be able to say such a word aloud.

In spite of our mocking, this was a serious business, often giving these women their only opportunity to contribute to the family purse or to earn themselves a little 'pin-money'. It was piece-work and they toiled in all weathers, often behind improvised wind-breaks. They were paid for each thousand plants and could prick out twenty thousand plants on a good day, in beds where the rows were twenty five across and forty rows long. In a season, eighty million plants could be reared here and by June they were forward enough to be taken up and put into bundles ready for their journey to Ely and Soham. The rich soil in which they were replanted was so dark that the whole area was known as the Black Fens.

Whittlesey became the capital of this production and several local families had large numbers of greenhouses, collectively called 'nurseries'. This is a term I will not forget again, as once I did and it led to a very cold, wet experience.

I had become friendly with the children of one such family and spent time in their play-room, where there was a lovely slide, as large as those in the park. On a subsequent visit, hopeful that I might be able to go on it again, I asked casually if we might look at the nursery. Only as we donned wellingtons and headed out the back door did I realise my mistake. A nursery in the fens is not the same as the cosy retreats found in story-books. It was too late then, and I learned everything there was to know about the celery industry in one very long afternoon. It was an informative tour but all I really wanted was another go on that super slide.

26 Nights by the Sea

'Yes,' Mother affirmed. We were going away on holiday for the whole week.

'No,' We were not coming home each night.

'Yes,' We were going to sleep at Hunstanton, in Uncle's caravan.

'No,' He wasn't going to be there. He was going to entrust the key to her so that we could actually live there as if it was ours.

There were so many questions to ask. This was just such an incredible idea that I struggled to believe in it. I knew that we had all stayed for a week at Skegness in Mother's aunt's caravan when I was three, but I had been too young then to realise what a holiday actually meant. That first time, Granny and her sister had come as part of the package. This time she was going to stay behind and look after the carriages and a good neighbour was going to come in each day to check that she was alright. This felt like a once in a lifetime experience and, actually, it was exactly that. It was the only time Mother, Father and I had a family holiday, sleeping away from the carriages.

My excitement was frightening because I feared that my chest might burst, rendering me unfit to travel, so I made a conscious effort to stay calm. I stood up straight and breathed slowly but it was difficult to maintain this posture for a week and I found my heart pounding whenever my thoughts slipped back to the days counting down. I tried to concentrate on the daily routines that normally kept me occupied but a new light shone over me.

I was the child who was going on holiday. The other children at school came back in the autumn with stories of what they had done during the summer. This year I would be able to join in these conversations. I would be the child who had gone to the seaside and stayed there all night, eating my food and sleeping there.

I stretched out on the back lawn, as I always did on lazy summer afternoons, watching the passing clouds. Normally, this relaxed me so effectively that I was often woken from this position when Mother came to call me for tea, but not now. Watching the sky, I saw a gently lapping sea. The blue was striped with white, ridges of sand pulled by the tide. I peered into a deep-blue hole surrounded by the crinkly, puffing clouds and it was a rock-pool with crabs and star-fish.

I saw curving bays, long spits of sand, jutting rock faces, everything that was seaside related. The whole experience of a holiday where you watched darkness fall over the sea and got up again early enough to see the sun rise before breakfast, played to me in vapour on a screen wider than any cinema.

Occasionally an aeroplane passed across the scene and I smiled smugly. I knew these carried holidaymakers to exotic destinations but I also knew they couldn't be going anywhere more exotic than Hunstanton - well, unless it was Hamilton Academicals, of course.

I had overheard Mother telling a friend that this holiday was going to be 'buckshee' and, not being familiar with this term, I assumed that it meant something really glamorous.

Beyond Father's first shed, where he carved and sawed, he had built another, planning to dry newly painted pieces away from the dust. It had two windows and under one of them was a bench, at just the right height for a bunk bed. I had immediately seized the opportunity and moved in my tea-party table and chair, plastic tea-set and as much bedding as I could drag behind me from the carriages without being noticed. I was never allowed to sleep outside at night but my parents had seen the logic in allowing me a space where I was not under their feet all day. Father painted the panels inside in my favourite lilac and yellow. Mother donated two pairs of ancient curtains. I had retrieved Toby, my old push-along dog on wheels, and for several summers I had sat in the doorway of this shed-caravan with Toby's reigns laying loosely in my lap as we trotted along leafy lanes, always on the lookout for a good place to set up camp. Now all lanes led to the coast.

I wore my bathing costume and a towel draped around my shoulders for days, resisting Mother's attempts to pack them, although I was busy packing essential toys in my 'tatcha-case'. I remember the happy anticipation as Mother bustled around, organising both a family holiday and supplies for Granny. Father just went through his normal routine of catching the bus to work each day and returning in time for his tea.

This was actually the best part of the holiday: imagining how good it would feel when we got there, visualising a series of the day trips that I loved, all running in succession. In reality, it was always a dream that couldn't be lived. There were no sweeping bays at Hunstanton, no sand-spits, no crabs and starfish in rock-pools, no rocks.

I had wonderful memories of those day-trips: the lunch-time queue at the door of the chip- shop, steam carrying the smell out to those who waited, making everyone so hungry that the largest portions were ordered. We had arrived at Uncle's caravan bearing fish and chips, so fresh that it tasted of the sea.

On holiday, though, the schedule was different. Mother

argued that fish and chips every day would not be healthy. She had brought food with her and when this ran out we had to go food-shopping, instead of browsing in the gift shops. It quickly felt too much like being at home. She cooked too, taking up time when I could have been in the sea. The beach was tantalisingly close but I was not allowed to wander off by myself so I hung around indoors, listening to the fair-ground music calling to me from the end of the caravan site. I tried to persuade Father to take me out but he was not always co-operative, sometimes delaying me until he had read the paper and been over to the lavatory block for a shave. All this felt too normal. What was the point of going on a holiday if it felt like being at home?

Worst of all, the lemonade had run out. It was here that Auntie had poured me my first fizzy drink of white lemonade, in a glass with a frosted green pattern. She had held up a hand to hush Mother's protests that I would surely choke, allowing me to savour this new experience. I had held the sweet liquid in my mouth, the bubbles dancing on my tongue, gargling until my throat tickled too much to bear. Auntie wasn't here now and Mother showed no inclination to replenish the stock.

On day-trips I had always felt sad that we had to leave before dark, dreaming that one day we might stay overnight but now it had become a reality and I wasn't quite so confident. On that first night I began to feel uneasy. There was no bus home, the last train had left without us. Uncle wasn't there with his car. We were stranded. Unfortunately for my parents, it was then that I chose to remember that among all the happy memories of being a day-tripper, there lurked some memories that were still quite terrifying.

I lived again that bright, sunny day when we had relaxed on the beach, listening to the sea lapping slowly onto the sand. There had been no warning of the violence that was about to erupt into our afternoon. In the very moment that we became aware of raised voices, we saw a rush of figures converge at the water's edge.

Rocks rained around us and even as we jumped to our feet, the danger was upon us. I was too big now for Mother to scoop me into her arms so she just grabbed my hand and we fled towards the promenade. As I glanced over my shoulder to make sure Father was with us, I glimpsed his outstretched arms behind us, the shopping bag held aloft, his only means of trying to shield us from the hailing pebbles. The beach was a battleground and young men charged forward with menacing cries, fresh blood on their faces.

After an age, we reached the bottom of the long concrete steps that led steeply up to the promenade but we were meeting another surge of youths descending to the beach like a water-fall of black leather. Right in front of us, one of them leapt from the fourth step and even as his feet touched the sand, he flowed into a crouching position, grabbing a boulder in both hands and rising before us in one fluid movement. Straightening to his full height, he towered over me, over Mother and Father, and I looked up into his scowl. If I was destined to 'die a' fright', that would have been my moment. We were not his target, of course. We were merely in his path and he stepped quickly around us.

With our heads bent low, we scuttled towards the safety of Uncle's caravan. Auntie and my cousin sat outside in deckchairs, totally unaware of the scenes that were playing out just a few hundred yards away. I was in front now, urgently pulling both parents. They had slowed down once we were clear of the beach, confident that we would not be followed, but I still had visions of warriors in black leather leaping the sea wall and springing up at my feet.

Mother described what was happening but everyone was calm. I was distraught and didn't stop sobbing until we were all inside the caravan with the door not only closed, but tightly locked. Then I listened to Auntie's account of how the radio was reporting similar incidents around the coast in that summer of 1964, when the Mods and Rockers revved into town and turned our resorts into the sands of Aliwal.

I had held these images in my mind for a long time, causing me to shiver whenever I recalled the details. It was probably near to the end of that summer before I was able to fill the basket on the front of my bike with the largest stones from the gravel path and ride my bike down the garden, my bathing cap as tight on my skull as any crash helmet as I steered my Harley Davidson towards the shore of conflict.

Now these images rose again to torment me and my parents believed that a simple reassurance would calm me down.

'That were then, they 'ent 'ere now.'

Before bedtime we walked the few yards to the sea wall. It was starting to get dark and the sea looked different. Earlier in the day it had shimmered in the sun and played a gentle game of catch with my feet as I had squealed and teased it by running away. I had taunted it, dangling my toes like a toy on a string for a kitten, keeping them just out of reach. It didn't look playful now. The kitten had turned into a heaving beast, hurling itself against the concrete, trying to wear it down, so that it could sweep forward and cascade down the slope to the caravans. I wondered if it had been such a good idea to laugh at its attempts to wash sand onto my feet. Was it looking vengeful now? It was certainly sounding more determined, rushing and churning up the stones that lay right at the top of the beach.

I held onto my parents' hands and pulled them back from the edge. I wasn't altogether convinced by their assurance that this was normal here, that it happened every night and it knew it must not encroach any further, turning round at a pre-arranged time. It looked an awful lot of water to turn and how did it tell the time?

I didn't want to be this near to it now that it was getting darker but I was also dubious about going back to the caravan, where we couldn't keep an eye on it. I dragged my feet to slow our progress across the narrow strip of grass.

Back indoors, the gas lamps had to be lit. These were new to a child who had grown up with electricity. The mantles were white but turned to pink as the match ignited the fragile honey-comb. They burned brighter, then softer; the glow wasn't constant. They were unpredictable and the hissing frightened me. I didn't know if I would feel better if they went out, plunging me into sudden darkness, or if I was more afraid of them popping into a ball of fire if they were left on.

Mother made the decision. Lights went off at night. We all huddled in the one big bed and I knew it would be impossible to sleep. The caravan creaked, unfamiliar shadows lurked in the corners. The cooling mantles expanded or contracted. I couldn't see which, because I couldn't see anything in this suffocating darkness, and all the time the sea was crashing against the wall. Images of that carriage, seen from the railway line, lying beaten and broken against the hedge, were etched inside my eyelids. The sea hadn't listened to instructions to turn round that night, had it?

Thoughts of train journeys were not conducive to sleep either. It had been on the long journey home from here that another of my nightmares had been born. One evening, we had just settled ourselves into our seats and were watching through the window as other passengers boarded, when we saw two sisters who lived just up our road, get on the train on the opposite platform.

'Look a' them silly sods, they're got on the wrong train,' Mother pointed.

'We gotta tell 'um.' I was always the good citizen.

'We can't,' Mother explained, 'If we git orf now, this one'll gew wi'out us and then we'll all be stuck'd.'

I'm sure I saw her smirk as she added 'They'll find out when they git there.'

Their train pulled out first and I watched with mixed feelings: uneasy that we had let them go away into the unknown, but relieved that we hadn't got off and missed our train because it would be dark soon.

Our train pulled out and I forgot them as I watched the houses and sprawling caravan sites give way to open countryside. We were on our way home. It was only by chance that I turned to my parents as they exchanged a look, but I caught it. They weren't smirking now.

'What's up?' I wanted to know.

'Nothin', yer alright.' Mother tried to look reassuring but I had glimpsed that frown.

'Tell me,' I squawked, panicking now. Had this train got no brakes? Was there a fire in the engine? What had I missed?

'Yer gotta tell me,' I pleaded, already close to tears.

'Don't blub,' Mother spoke quietly. 'It's just, I think we're on the wrong train.'

Now I really panicked. Those girls were safely on their way home and we were hurtling towards the unknown. I wanted to pull the cord and tell the driver we were here but, instead, Father went to find the ticket-man. I huddled up to Mother, not looking at the window because the scenery had become menacing. The trees and fields looked the same as ever but now I knew they were the wrong trees and fields, and with every passing moment the steaming train dragged us further away from home.

Eventually the ticket-man came back with Father and explained that he could hold up the overnight train to Edinburgh. I think he said Edinburgh although it was difficult to hear through my snuffling. This wasn't scheduled to call at Peterborough but he could arrange a special stop for us. I'm sure he was trying to help and Mother was trying to keep me quiet so that she could hear but I was becoming hysterical. The overnight train, which sounded terrifying anyway, might forget we were there and we could finish up in Edinburgh. I had never heard the name before but I knew it must be a long way away – it wasn't even mentioned on the shipping forecast.

Surely now was the moment to ring Whitehall 1212.

I clutched Mother tightly, screaming at her to ask the man to stop the train now. We could walk. I would gladly have jumped down onto the dark track and watched this monster roar off into the night, no longer holding us captive. We could have trudged back to the station and started the endless walk home down the right track. I had no knowledge of how the rail network operated, no concept of branch lines and connecting trains. We were just going the wrong way and every moment that the jump was delayed meant a longer way back. Mother was fighting free of my grasp, listening to the rational options. He was shaking his head, telling her that this train ended up in Ely.

I heard the name and gasped with relief. I had been to Ely. We had relations there. Mother quickly made the decision that we would stay on this train until it reached Ely. Then we would alight with what was left of our dignity and make our own way. She probably thought that this would be a better option than having me wailing all the way home and possibly 'dying a' fright', so we never caught the overnight train and none of us ever went to Edinburgh.

Instead we got off at Ely, with its familiar iron canopies supported by sturdy, reliable pillars and we walked the two miles to my cousin's house, arriving unannounced in this age before mobile phones. They were astonished at such an unscheduled visit but Mother just greeted them on the doorstep and asked 'Can we cadge a lift 'um?'

In the back of their van, I dozed contentedly for thirty miles across the dark fens.

Now, in the suffocating darkness of the caravan, I shivered as I relived all this fear and only fell into an uneasy sleep after Mother assured me that she would stay awake until two o'clock, waking me to take over the watch before she went to sleep.

Father had long since gone quiet, his eyes closed but probably not sleeping, more likely doubting the wisdom of bringing this family for a holiday fifty miles from the carriages. At home I would have been asleep hours ago, safe in my familiar bedroom. Maybe he just offered up a prayer of thanks that next week he would be back to the sanity of work.

Each morning of that week, I woke to the sound of seagulls strutting on the roof, welcome because they proclaimed that I had not 'drownded' in the night. I had survived to enjoy another day's holiday. I trampolined on the beach and roller-skated on the fairground rink. Sometimes I led Father to the gloomy back wall of the penny arcade where some dubious machines lurked. He was so easily persuaded to push a penny into the slots that I believe he enjoyed them as much as I did. Together we watched a prisoner hang and other dark deeds, until Mother caught us and led me away to be bored by a mechanical clown who rolled around looking very silly and hooted with false laughter.

She played bingo and accrued enough half-wins, which meant a shared prize if two people called on the same number, to be able to get me the doll which I had spotted on the first day. She was stuffed with straw and had dangling legs, huge eyes and shining blonde, plaited hair. I haven't got her now so I expect the mice ate her but for the rest of that holiday she was my constant companion, sitting astride the big horses as we rode on the fair, helping me collect stones and shells in my bucket, watching over me from the foot of my bed at night.

Towards the end of that holiday, my cousins came to visit and brought the joy of new opportunity. On our day trips, I had always watched in awe as swimmers not much bigger than me, waded out to sea, then raised their arms and plunged forward into the surf. I wanted to strike out for Skegness, which I knew was on the other side of the Wash. Father couldn't swim and Mother had no inclination to do so, limiting my exploration to water no more than knee-deep.

Now the limits changed. My cousin was a strong swimmer and her husband was a champion diver. They were deemed competent to ensure my safety. I remember the force of the water as it reached my thighs, making it difficult to walk, and the unaccustomed cold as it rose to my waist. The shingle shifted underfoot with every wave and I teetered nervously, clutching the grown-ups. At chest-height, it became too frightening and I had to be towed, squealing, back to the ankle-deep ripples. I didn't trust the sea any more. I had seen its other face. I decided that a visit to Skegness might be fun, but perhaps not just now.

27 Widening Horizons

When we reached our final year as juniors, we moved into a tiny room at the back of the school for more in-depth tuition from the head-mistress. There were only seven of us in my age group. I loved this additional attention and worked harder than ever, soaking up as much new information as time allowed. There was already an air of changes coming. We were being primed for the next stage in our life stories: the move to 'Big School'.

We still played our normal succession of childhood games: chasing hoola-hoops and throwing beanbags, chanting Hokey Cokey and skipping in and out of a line of girls jumping over a rope as it was twirled. This rope reached right across the playground and sometimes there might be six or more girls skipping at once. The ultimate embarrassment was to get a foot caught and hear the groans as the rope tangled and dropped to the ground so everyone had to start again.

Amongst all these childish pleasures, new interests were slowly emerging. At the beginning of the spring term someone had brought in a 'pop' magazine and we all pored over pictures of some boys who called themselves 'Monkees'. Apparently, it was acceptable to be bad at spelling if you were famous. According to the children who now had televisions, these boys were famous because they played very loud music and danced about, singing at the same time.

I managed to get invited home to tea with a girl who lived in the Star Cottages. She thought it was quite normal to go home, turn on the television and make a sandwich to eat whilst we watched this early performance. I was enthralled by this different lifestyle.

I chose my words carefully as I described the scene to Mother, knowing instinctively that a description of food in the front room would not create a good impression. Jigging around the furniture to the music, singing with our mouths still full of bread, would not enhance my chances of being allowed out for a second visit.

These songs took over from the old chanting in the playground just for those last few weeks. We were all 'Believers'. As the oldest among our peers and the most socially aware, we believed without question that we were superior. We were the leaders: leading the way to the grown up world that lay beyond King's Dyke.

On my 11th birthday, the last I would celebrate at that school, my parents hired the Sunday school room in the chapel and invited the whole school. It was the biggest party I had ever seen. We played games such as musical chairs with the Sunday school teacher on the piano. The chapel ladies made urns of tea in the little kitchen next to the vestry for the parents. Squash for the children flowed freely, accompanied by sandwiches and a mountain of cakes, all spread on trestle tables covered in starched, white tablecloths.

I had a beautiful satin frock and felt like a princess. I was showered with so many presents that I struggled to know where to put them. The wide, stone window ledges seemed to be the best place to display them. Trying to make sure that I had collected them all up from the tables before tea was served, I yelled in my loudest voice 'A' there any more presents?'

Mother grabbed me by the neck of my beautiful frock,

hissing into my ear 'Yer don't say that, y' greedy little sod, don't y' think that lot's enuff?'

I was just beginning to feel the clash between school and home. At school we were encouraged to question what we heard, to discuss and debate, and to have our opinion taken seriously. At home I was still expected to conform without question to the wishes of parents and Granny, trusting in their judgement, relying on their superior knowledge, born of experience and wisdom. I knew that now was not the time for debate. I just needed to free myself from Mother's strangling grasp.

I had only been trying to get organised. I wasn't asking for more. In fact, I would have been satisfied with just the one present I had received from my parents that year. They had bought me a pair of white leather skating boots and I probably had more fun on them than with anything else I have ever owned. I might have been the village idiot on my bike but I wasn't born in the fens without the necessary ability to skate.

At this age I was still a little rebellious but my resistance was tempered now by so many confrontations with the family, which I had inevitably lost. This is illustrated well in my last school photograph at King's Dyke. I had started to tuck my hair behind my ears, believing that this made me appear more sophisticated. Mother just chided me, 'It'll mek yer ears stick out so yer need a n'operation, then yer'll know about it.'

On the day of the photographer's visit, I went into school with the warning ringing in my hair-covered ears that I was not allowed to tamper with the neatly-brushed arrangement today but, of course, Mother wasn't there when we lined up to take our turn before the camera. I tucked back the controversial hair and pulled it forward again several times as I moved up the queue, wrestling with both my conscience and my wilfulness. Finally, just as

I was called forward, the answer leapt from my subconscious – a compromise. I had two ears, Mother and I could both be happy, but she was never that easy to please.

As the day when the photos were due to arrive drew nearer, I was filled with apprehension. Even as she opened the envelope, I knew from her expression that my fears had been justified. Her anger almost reached a state of tears. She didn't do compromise as well as I did. That felt so unfair that I cried too. She was unmoved. For months she showed the photo to everyone who came to visit, snatching it from its envelope, holding it aloft as an example of my disobedience.

'Look a' that. One side forrad and t' other not. Did y' ever see such an 'alf-baked do?'

She glowered at it before thrusting it back into its dark hiding place, never allowing it to grace the mantel-piece, where earlier photos of me as a compliant child were displayed with pride.

Our time at King's Dyke was running out. We had enjoyed the last autumn term, the last Christmas party and had returned for the last time after the Easter holiday. Now there was the excitement of the coming eleven-plus exam. I don't remember feeling nervous, perhaps not fully understanding what a life-defining moment this would be. I just watched the proceedings with the detachment of an onlooker.

There were only two of us taking the exam that year and we were escorted into the small room at the back. A long table had been placed in the middle. We sat at opposite ends and waited in silence as the papers were given out. When we turned over those papers, we had the key to our future before us but I still didn't grasp the enormity of the day. I just read the instructions and realised that I was allowed to write a story.

The theme was the recapture of an escaped lion. My escapee caught a bus and terrified the passengers but was eventually persuaded to go back to his home by a very calm and heroic bus-conductress. This was the first time I had been faced with exam conditions and it was great fun. We returned to normal class afterwards and life didn't feel as if it had changed.

Then it was May and the letters of allocation arrived. As I ran onto the playing field, Miss Steeper called to me 'I bet you're dancing on air today,' and I realised that I was.

For the last six years I had played and grown in this field, reached by an iron gate, leading from one side of the walled playground. We were only allowed here when an adult escorted us across the lane outside. This was a busy route for lorries entering and leaving the brickyard, and a constant stream of dumper trucks which stirred up clouds of dust from the crushed brick surface, clouding our vision and our judgement.

At the edge of the field was a narrow strip of land cultivated by the older boys as a school garden. A blockhouse, similar to the one in which I had planned to live so many summers before, stood regally against one hedge. This housed the headmaster's gardening tools and the machine with which he marked out white lines on the grass. On countless hot days we had sat on the cold concrete of its plinth, the solid walls shielding us from the sun. Through the years we had run until we were red faced with raging thirsts. Then we had sprawled on the grass, watching the shadows cast by the clouds drifting above. Resting on our elbows, talking earnestly as we constructed daisy chains to take home, we had exchanged ideas and formulated new theories on life. Occasionally someone had caused us all to look by calling out "Ey, I got a four leafer 'ere,' in reference to the elusive four-leaf clover, but they were invariably fakes.

Now, as Miss Steeper's words brought home to me the importance of the change ahead, I realised that from this same field, I was going to launch myself into a bigger world. I was the only child to have passed the exam that year. In fact, I was the last child in the school ever to go on to Grammar School. I would be going to March. I had never been there. It was twelve miles away, across the fields of the fens and I would be travelling alone for the first time in my life, on a bus with all the children from other schools in the town, but alone because I knew no-one outside this community.

The rest of that last term passed slowly as I dreamed of the adventures that lay ahead until, finally, one hot day in July, school broke up and I bade farewell to those children who had shared my Infant and Junior days, and went home to the carriages.

All the other children were moving to the local secondary modern school and I was on my own again. The new friends with whom I was going to spend the next few years, lived only in my imagination. They wore gymslips and starched white blouses, had curling hair and carried hockey sticks. They were a blurred group with no individual names or faces but I recognised them as the figures that Enid Blyton had described in Malory Towers.

During the holiday, I accompanied Mother to Templeman's, the one shop in town which stocked the necessary items of uniform, right down to the bottle-green knickers and socks. We came home with more new clothes than I had ever owned.

On numerous occasions in the following weeks, I modelled them for visiting family, or sometimes just for my own amusement.

'Git out th' road, will yer,' Granny snapped as she tried to manoeuvre around me. The only full-length mirror was in her bedroom so it was her bed that was strewn with string and brown wrapping paper as I strutted in my new gymslip. It was rough to the touch but I felt very grown up. Matching blazer, knee-socks, and the regulation brown, lace-up shoes that smelt of delicious new leather, were regularly pulled out of their packaging. On days when she was occupied elsewhere, I even got as far as the belted gabardine mackintosh and the odd-shaped beret which had to be flattened on one side of my head. A green and yellow scarf completed the ensemble and I was ready to leave with my satchel, ready to walk confidently into my future, weeks before the start of the new term.

For the first time in my life I had my own pencil case and a geometry set in a tin, although I had no idea of the purpose of a protractor or a set-square. I had a yellow and green striped tie and, as I practised tying it neatly in front of that mirror, I knew I wouldn't look out of place on the hockey-fields and tennis courts of Enid Blyton's other fictitious school, St. Clare's.

My only regret was that I had no midnight feasts to look forward to, no prospect of late night frolics in the dorm, nor food hampers arriving mid-term. Every night I would have to return to the carriages, to being an only child in this adult world.

28 The Art of Communication

 I had always loved to sprawl on the grass, hands cupped beneath my head, watching the kaleidoscope of clouds passing over. I never knew their names. Cumulus, stratus and nimbostratus were not words in my vocabulary. They were just boisterous, bouncing ones which bumped and cajoled, lively ones which skipped merrily on their way and cowardly ones that tried to slip past, skulking behind others.

Sometimes they were wild beasts with shaggy, feathered manes, sometimes halos, perfectly round and fallen from the hands of a careless angel. Elegant fairies in wispy lace might follow a bellowing elephant with an impossibly long trunk. I wove them all into the tapestry of my imagination, each with a brief role to bring alive before they passed off-stage and out of sight, lost forever. I always took for granted this canopy of clouds, and the stars which took their place on clear nights. The sky was darker and deeper before light pollution. I never considered how privileged I was to have this vast skyscape above my garden. Unlike today's children who watch a harsh, flickering screen, rewind button in hand, I knew that these moments were irretrievable. When I was absorbed in this manner, my mother often had to call me several times before I responded with a reluctant, 'I'm comin', 'ang on.' I couldn't leave just as a scene was unfolding. I had tried to explain to her but my logic was lost in the communication.

As with so many aspects of my play, she never seemed to grasp the concept. We fought similar battles over my perceived lack of obedience on a daily basis. A particular irritant to her was that whatever I was doing, I could not stop until I reached sixteen. I don't know why I had fixated on sixteen but that was the number. If I was hitting a tennis ball against the lavatory wall and dropped the ball, or maybe leaping over a flower bed and tripped on the edge, then I had to start from one again. There were days when she called me in because it began to rain and I was soaked before I reached the elusive number.

On other days I made her late, then suffered the indignity of rushing to the bus-stop, hauled along by my coat collar. I knew I would incur her wrath but this was not my intention. She just didn't understand that sixteen was non-negotiable and the fear of a wallop was outweighed by a greater fear of retribution if I flaunted the self-made rules.

I was perhaps unduly influenced by a family who were frightened by so many superstitions. I saw no sense in being unable to play with my umbrella indoors or lay my shoes on the table if they were clean, but I had seen both Mother and Granny launch themselves across the room to avert such catastrophes. I had been clipped round my ear so many times; the blows delivered with a force born of fear rather than anger, but still fierce enough to make my ears smart. It was usually forgetfulness that led to my troubles, rather than any wish to deliberately break the ancient rules.

Much of the history of these superstitions had already been lost, along with the origins of the old wives' tales and traditions that were still observed, passed down the generations by word of mouth.

Dialogue was sparse in the fens. Exchanges were still limited by the isolation of lonely farms and poor roads. The written word was not always easily available. Books were not encouraged in the carriages. We had the family bibles, prayer and hymn books, and Granny's 'Doctor's Books'. I only recall two other grown-up volumes. One was John Bunyan's 'Pilgrim's Progress'. The other was Donald Peers' autobiography, 'Pathway'.

Father always bought a newspaper to read after tea and once a week he bought 'Reveille'. He recognised my enthusiasm to share these at a time when I could only enjoy the pictures so he started to buy me comics, along with his newspaper, on his way home from work.

On a rare occasion when we were in the city as darkness fell, I accompanied him to make these purchases from a paper-seller in the bus station. I believe his name was Mr Green. He was an elderly man in a heavy coat and thick gloves. He moved slowly and his breath steamed in the night air.

A single lantern hung from the roof of his stall. The newspapers and comics were laid out on a table at the front where the light was brightest. As the draught swayed the lantern, shadows shifted across the front pages. These were probably sold and replaced regularly but, further back in the gloom, was older stock with the timeless smell of old paper. Years later, I recognised this as familiar in second-hand book shops, where even the humblest volume carried the hallmark of age in its scent.

I imagined how difficult it must have been for Father to make a selection from this cave of treasures, marvelling that he managed to do so and catch the bus home, his trophy rolled up under his arm.

I loved the time we shared each week as we looked at these comics, even if the suitability of their content was perhaps questionable. The first comic I had was 'Buster', with its characters who spoke in bubbles. This was perhaps an odd choice for a young girl but it was Father's choice. There is probably some significance in the fact that Buster was the cartoon offspring of Andy Capp and his wife, Flo, who made Father chuckle every day, from their short strip in his Daily Mirror.

One of my favourite bed-time stories was 'The Adventures of Charlie Peace', based on the infamous Charles Peace, arch-rogue of London's East End, hanged in 1879.

Later, my reading material was extended to include the 'Beezer' and I would go to bed with images of Dennis the Menace, wishing that I could be a member of his audacious gang.

Mother raised an eyebrow and sighed as I mimicked some of these dubious characters. She undoubtedly questioned this early diet of testosterone laden bravado, but her misgivings were probably outweighed by the fact that I sat still on Father's lap and didn't demand her attention for relatively long periods. Perhaps her concerns had some justification as I never developed a taste for more traditional girls' books. I still have, and treasure, my 'Legend of Custer' annual from 1968.

In the absence of television, and with Granny firmly in charge of the wireless buttons, one of the best birthday presents I ever received was a musical box. It had a ballerina just like those on the forbidden wallpaper, who twirled when the lacquered lid was open. I possessed no jewellery to keep in the tiny, velvet lined compartments and I had no interest in checking my face or hair in its tiny bevelled mirrors. My joy came from being in charge of making it play. I headed out into the April sun and spent the whole day listening to a tune I didn't recognise, the name of which I still do not know. Even at tea-time, with the party table laid and the relations in their seats, I had to be hauled, protesting, indoors.

The tea was interspersed with bursts of the tune and pauses when I had to rewind it. By bedtime Mother, seriously irritated by the repetition, confiscated it so we might all get some sleep. Next day, I seized it back and headed outside again, out of ear-shot, where I could play it over and over and over again. I waited for it to finish, then rewound it with all the authority of a DJ, making and implementing the decision with no deference to grown-up taste. I was completely the master of my one-piece music collection. On the eighth day after my birthday, it died.

I was distraught and Mother quickly took it back to the shop, explaining calmly, 'She's only 'ad it a week. It must a' bin faulty.'

The smiling assistant duly handed over another identical model and all was happy in the garden again, although I think we all knew that it had died from sheer exhaustion. I rationed the time I played the new one as carefully as I had rationed my words when I had feared that I could exhaust them, too.

In later childhood, Christmas brought me a record player and six records, which dropped one by one onto the deck and the carriages resounded to their first experience of a new beat. Now I really was a DJ. I had six choices as to which record to play first and I tried to remember the order in which I played them so I could change it each time. This was another freedom and I was ecstatic: dancing around the front room with thundering feet and no sense of rhythm, pounding the boards until the needle jumped a groove. The smell of new plastic mingling with hot dust was a heady combination and I controlled the volume knob. Louder equalled better and full-blast was best of all.

This was my first real encounter with songs that were not hymns. The music was faster and accompanied by new voices. I can't remember all six of the original records but Engelbert Humperdink invited me to share his last waltz and The Scaffold told me their tale of 'Lily the Pink'. Other early additions were Val Doonican as he walked tall and my favourite, Yellow Submarine.

My cousin donated a few of his old records so I was able to catch up with some treasures from an earlier era. Perry Como advised me to 'Catch a falling Star' and Lonny Donegan enquired if my chewing gum lost its flavour on the bedpost overnight. Such an idea was outrageous. I had never been allowed to chew gum, let alone save some for the next day. This was a time when I glimpsed an unknown, and undreamt of, world out there waiting for my arrival. I set my course to be a pop star. All I had to do was avoid tripping over my feet, or the furniture, and turn a deaf ear to Granny's scathing 'Just 'ark at that racket,' and 'I'm sure she's got St Viper's dance,' by which I presume she meant St Vitas' Dance, as associated with rheumatic fever.

Another brush with technology, not too well received, was when one of my uncles bought a cine camera and returned from holiday with a reel of film. Mother loved her two brothers, who both visited regularly, but she hated disruption to her routine. When he suggested that we might like to watch the film, she was quite put out, chuntering 'I s'pose all the chairs 'll 'ave to be moved an' we'll all a' to sit in the dark.'

When he started to unpack the cumbersome equipment, it just got worse. He had a white screen which had to be hung up, meaning that pictures of relations had to be taken down from their usual position on brass hooks hanging from the picture rail. The last straw was clearing the table and pulling it out from the wall so that the offending cine-camera could be mounted in line with the screen. Mother tolerated the viewing but a repeat performance was not suggested.

Sometime afterwards, I was given a Chad Valley slide projector. I don't remember who bought it for me but I'm sure it was not my parents, as Mother stoutly refused to repeat the furniture-moving procedure and I had to crouch in a shadowy corner, watching the fuzzy cartoon strips of Roy Rogers and Popeye play out against a back-drop of flowered wallpaper.

Photographs played an important role in our lives. Along with a tea service, already antique and never used, the sideboard in the front room housed a collection of albums. I loved to browse through these on rainy Sunday afternoons, enjoying a rare closeness as Mother turned the fragile pages, protected with sheets of fine tissue. Every picture had been labelled with care and affection. Each told a story of an era which, like the sepia photographs, had faded through the years. Mother read aloud the captions, taking me with her on a journey back to times that she recalled and even beyond the reach of her own memory. My parents' wedding took up a whole album. A single photograph captured the day of my grandparents' marriage. Relations who had died before I was born, came to life on those pages, giving faces to the names I had heard. Uncles, who I had only ever known as middle-aged, appeared in the long, white smocks that baby boys had worn at the time of their births. Their prams appeared to be quite regal, but were, no doubt, typical of the time. More recent albums showed an uncle in his army uniform during the war and Mother posing proudly in her ATS uniform with jaunty cap. Two brothers evacuated from war-torn London and given refuge by Granny, played in the garden that was now my playground.

The queen's coronation in 1953, was marked by Granny posing with one of her sisters in front of the carriages which had been decorated with flags and buntings.

The arrival of each of my cousins and my own birth, as the youngest of that generation, were documented here and every year the collection grew as my childhood was recorded. The carriages featured over and over again as a backdrop to three generations of our family, filling me with the comforting sense of continuity and security.

My first foray into the world of photography was less successful. When Mother finally tired of my badgering her to 'Let me 'ave a gew,' every time she took her box-Brownie camera from its case, she bought me my own camera and my first reel of film was taken to the chemists' shop to be developed. I waited eagerly for its return, but Mother collected it with much muttering about how many pictures I had wasted. With a sinking heart, I thought I had not operated the camera properly and the pictures had not come out.

Finally, she handed me the envelope and I saw with relief that this was not the case. They were safely there: all the clouds that I had captured, all the puddles that I had snapped. Here were moments that were unique. No-one would ever see that cloud formation again or find the water's surface pierced in exactly the same way by the jagged pieces of bricks that littered our landscape. Trees that were too tall for me to see clearly, were brought down to my level in those reflections. Each had its own beauty but they were not passed around visiting family, as was normal with new photos, nor were they assigned to the albums. They didn't survive as early evidence of my artistic flair, probably finding their way discreetly to the fireplace.

As she glowered over my shoulder, I realised that they were not what she had been expecting. They were not pictures which she would have taken. This was not the collection of relations usually immortalised, stiffly posing by the carriages.

My next batch was more carefully monitored and conformed to the expectations of those who brushed their hair and put on a clean pinny when a camera was brandished, or offered themselves up at a portrait studio with an unblemished frock and an unsmiling countenance.

It seemed that I was destined to limit my repertoire to a portrait gallery of familiar faces, like those staring down at us from their position on the wall: secure again on the brass picture hooks, now that the threat of the cine camera screen had been removed.

29 Good Health and Good Fortune

I was not a particularly sickly child, perhaps because of the fear of remedies being offered from a collection of dark glass bottles. Words like Paraffin Oil and Boracic Acid on labels were enough to ensure a prompt recovery. There were tins too, usually small and round with names such as Red Indian Ointment. Just a sniff of the pungent cream made the affected area suddenly feel quite better.

In cases of spots, blisters or rashes, Granny dug out the 'Doctor's Books' from the bottom of her wardrobe. The illustrations in these heavy tomes were perused to confirm a diagnosis of measles, German measles or chicken-pox, and I did have all of these. Once Mother and Granny were satisfied that they had identified the symptoms, they allowed the doctor to be summoned only for the purpose of recording any notifiable illness.

At one time, the fens had the dubious reputation of being home to the highest child mortality rate in the country. Fortunately, some of the earlier cures had now fallen into disuse. I wasn't expected to sleep with mole's foot dangling from a piece of string around my neck, nor forced to swallow a fried or baked mouse. Dried toad had also been taken off the menu. In less serious cases of feeling unwell, the old remedies still prevailed: a vinegar-soaked rag for headaches, salt-water gargle for a sore throat, clove oil for tooth-ache.

Vaccinations had only recently been introduced and

were treated with great suspicion, then dismissed as far too risky for a precious only child. I never succumbed to anything more serious than a chesty cough, a sore throat or the dreaded 'runs', so I was held up as evidence that the 'old ways' were best as Granny passed judgement.

'Them new-fangled injections'll cause some trouble. Mark my words. Just 'cus them 'oity toity doctors say they're safe, don't mean they know it all. Some folks'll try owt s' long as it's free.'

Although the doctor's wisdom might have been doubted, he was treated with the same reverence as the headmaster and the preacher. Washing up could never be left until the next morning, nor an unfinished game spread on the floor ready for the next day.

'Wha' if one o' us were took bad in the night and the doctor 'ad to come?'

There was a standard response, too, to the thought of going out shopping or visiting before the kitchen was tidy.

'Wha' if yer got knocked uver and somebody 'ad to bring yer 'um?'

I was never a visitor to the Welfare Clinic. Mother considered the place to be full of snivelling babies, each rife with germs, and the threat of those 'jab needles'. I have no memory of ever being taken to see a doctor. Surgeries were contaminated by sick people.

'Yer likely to catch summat worse than what yer went with.'

House-visits were more usual but even these were rare. The doctor was only summoned if I took to my bed and couldn't be revived by Lucozade. This was bought in dire cases and served in a glass egg-cup.

On these occasions, and they did feel like occasions, the trouble taken to prepare for the brief appearance of the doctor was often more debilitating than the illness. I recall feeling really sick and dizzy as I was pulled out of a perfectly good nightie, washed with a warm flannel from a bowl on the dressing table, then clad in a clean nightie. I was lifted and held aloft while my sheets and pillowcase were changed. If I felt ill when the doctor was called, I certainly felt worse by the time he arrived.

I say 'He' because the traditional doctor was male, middle-aged to elderly, and always dressed immaculately. I was amazed on the one occasion when I was tended by a female doctor. She insisted that I should not be allowed to eat only bananas, despite Mother's explanation that I was refusing all other food and would surely starve. I forgave her for this harsh judgement because she was young and pretty and smelled of summer flowers. I was so in awe of her that I pledged to be a 'lady doctor', immediately recovering enough to start treating all my dolls, who had now developed the symptoms which had confined me to my bed.

Medicine prescribed by the doctor was actually quite pleasant, pink with a sticky, almond taste. I was allowed to take this without question, perhaps surprisingly. Mother had once been prescribed iron tablets 'to improve her appetite', and she had boiled the first one in a saucepan of water to check that it did not contain a worm which would make her hungry.

Having to stay in bed was akin to a punishment. When I was feeling unwell, it was the time I least wanted to be alone. I was happy if Mother sat on the edge of my bed and chatted to me, but she kept leaving me to do less important jobs: to make up the fire or pay the milkman. At the first sign of improvement, I pleaded to be allowed up. Once I was deemed well enough to leave my bedroom, I was content to snuggle up on the old leather, horse-hair couch in the kitchen, covered with a chenille tablecloth, drifting off to sleep with the hum of voices in the background. This was the time to relax and exploit the moment, asking for just one more story to be read aloud as my arms were far too weak to hold up the book, or being fed dippy soldiers because I couldn't be expected to juggle an egg in an egg-cup as well as a plate of neatly cut bread and butter.

My worst memories are of bouts of sickness in the night. I recall the cloying darkness of the bedroom, relieved only by the dim glow of Mother's torch. We were not able to turn on the light for fear of it being seen from outside. Each time I squealed 'I'm gunna be sick agen,' Mother struggled to hold the torch, balance the green plastic bowl and hold back my lengthy hair. Between these bouts, retching and wretched, I crawled into the big parental bed and shivered in the crook of Mother's arm. The length of such nights was unbearable. The only glimmer of hope that morning would eventually come, was Mother's whispered 'Listen fer the first lorry'.

Then I strained to hear the rumbling noise of an approaching engine, heralding the start of the day's traffic from the brickyard. Gradually, the number of these passing vehicles became more regular, each bringing the dawn a little closer.

As the grown-ups suffered from corns, needing Union Jack Corn Paste, or a boil which required the application of magnesium sulphate cream, as well as the weekly ritual of swallowing tablespoons of cod-liver-oil, I sailed on in fairly robust condition. I would have welcomed an occasional bout of croup, so that I could have slept with a linseed poultice, savouring the smell that I enjoyed by sniffing the putty in Father's shed.

Some of my most painful experiences resulted from time spent in that shed. In fear of being banned, I hid scraped knuckles, resulting from over enthusiastic use of a rasp. I concealed bruised fingers and thumbs when I had been caught out by the hammer. I tried to divert attention from splinters too, until they turned septic and I finally had to admit, reluctantly, 'I got a green finger agen'.

Mother then held me by the wrist, waving the offending finger at Father, all but accusing him of neglect.

'Look at what she's gone and done agen now, it's startin' to gather. Yer'd better sort it out afore it gets any wuss and gews up 'er arm.'

He then heated a needle in the steam from the boiling kettle and held my hand gently while he lanced my finger and let out the 'green'.

I tried to be brave so he didn't get any more of those wilting looks, but I'm sure he lived in fear of hearing me whine, 'I got a green finger agen'.

Granny looked on in amusement, often repeating to relations, 'wi'all 'em green fingers, she'll mek a good gard'ner'.

As if this suffering was not enough, I regularly bit my nails down past the end of my fingers, resulting in a painful 'ang nail.

Good health was not taken for granted at this time. The cemetery housed many tiny graves of children who had succumbed to illness and everyone remembered someone who had been crippled or faced early death due to the elements. While cities had grown up with their own threats to health, we were still entrenched in the old fen ways, knowing that ailments such as rheumatism or bronchitis were an ever present danger. To go outside with wet hair or to put on a garment that had not been aired overnight would have had Granny throwing up her arms in despair, and no-one in their right mind would have washed their hair when it was 'that week'.

We lived in an area where fields often lay waterlogged, crops were regularly beaten to the ground by torrential rain, and one of the roads out of town was called the Wash. We took our health very seriously. Although fen ague now lived on only in the memory of the older generation, damp and mist were seen as harbingers of ill health. Frost was the blessed cure for winter germs, collected in a bowl for immersing feet with chilblains, as well as being considered necessary for Brussels to reach perfection.

'Feed a cold and starve a fever,' was the rule that made it important to know the difference. We adjusted our activities and our diets according to the season and developed a natural resistance from our environment.

Some of the unlikeliest of old wives' tales have now found credence in modern science and some have been lost to history but, at a time when research was limited and evidence was not available to us, we trusted more to insight and instinct. We saw nature as the cause of many disorders but also recognised its ability to heal. We were homeopaths before it became fashionable. Nettle stew and herbal teas didn't come from the health food shop, they came from the garden.

Neither Mother nor Granny would have considered applying deodorant. Long before the danger of aluminium in these products was recognised, Mother insisted, 'Yer don't wanna g' bungin' yer pores up so as they can't breathe'.

This logic did not appear to extend to the Fuller's Earth powder, with which they both dusted themselves after their morning strip-wash. My protests that I wanted to smell nice, were countered with the assurance that 'Only dirty folks as don't wash, 'ave to wear scent and such t' cover the stink'.

Again, this reasoning didn't seem to follow through to the perfume bottle, shaped like the Eifel Tower and bearing the words, 'Evening in Paris', which sat on Granny's dressing table. It did sit there for many years without becoming empty, so perhaps it was just an unwanted gift or an ornament.

One area where there was an unusual dissent between the two women was in their perception of hygiene. Granny believed in the theory that 'Y' 'ave t' eat a peck a muck afore yer die'. She was often seen eating unwashed vegetables and fruit straight from the plant, only ever washing her hands under the cold tap before meals. Mother washed everything excessively.

The dentist's surgery was another place considered to be best avoided. Mother believed that all dentists were corrupt, pruggling healthy teeth with their instruments, causing pain and damage so that treatment would become necessary and business would grow.

Father dealt with this by seeing his dentist in his dinner hour and not mentioning an appointment to Mother. Occasionally, after having a tooth pulled out, his gum bled onto the pillow. I recall the raised voices then as Mother berated him, not only for omitting to mention the visit but worse, for bleeding on a perfectly good pillowcase.

I was another victim of Mother's fears and was not allowed near a dentist until I was nine. Then our neighbour and close friend, Winton, announced that she was visiting her dentist in Peterborough. I pleaded to be allowed to go with her, grasping at the chance of a day out, a bus ride and the thrill of being grown up enough to accompany her, without parental supervision. Eventually, Mother agreed that I could go along for a check-up. I can only imagine Winton's trepidation as she returned me to the carriages with the news that all the sweets and chocolates, consumed with perceived impunity, had rotted my teeth to such an extent that I was booked in for a full week's treatment. Even this did not persuade Mother to subject herself to the chair. Perhaps it made her more reluctant.

Throughout the whole scenario, Granny just continued to smile at us with gums which had been bare of teeth, real or false, for years except for one front tooth which she retained until her death at ninety seven, chewing tough beef and biting apples to the end.

Death, like health, was a much less formal affair at this time. Most people died at home and a local woman would be entrusted to 'lay out' the deceased. Granny, who had worked for an undertaker when she was barely out of school, was called on to perform these last duties and she had a deep reverence for the dead. I recall repeating a term I had overheard once, referring to some poor departed soul as 'a gonna', and the lecture that ensued.

Even those who died in hospital were normally brought home to spend their last few days in the front parlour, surrounded by flowers and candles and grieving relations who could sit by the coffin in privacy and quiet. On the day of a funeral, the curtains of all the houses along the route remained closed to show respect for the procession. These often passed the carriages at walking pace with a top-hatted gentleman leading on foot, followed by whole families in their funeral garb. I waited impatiently on these mornings. There was no compromising with Granny's stance that I would not open the door or even look out of the window until the cortege had passed. I hung around the kitchen, hankering to be let out, but heeding her warning.

'If yer set foot out a' tha' door, yer and me'll 'ave a right set to.'

She was not one to be disobeyed. Her words were scarce but each loaded with meaning. Sometimes she didn't even feel the need to explain herself. A simple action could take the place of a volume.

I recall one such incident when there had been a falling out of some kind between Granny and a close neighbour. The woman had hurled a shoe at the carriage door. Granny did not dignify this with a retalliation. She simply put the shoe on the tank outside the door and set a plant in it.

Births, too, were different then. It was not usual to be admitted to hospital unless there were some complications. Normally, the baby was delivered by a local woman who was considered experienced in confinements. Granny had also taken on this role and described many occasions when she had been called from her bed to attend to a woman who was 'laying in'. Seemingly, she alternated with ease between the 'laying in' and the 'laying out'.

She held a darning needle over the bump whenever someone in the family was expecting; informing them, with uncanny accuracy, as to the sex of the baby, according to which way the needle swung. This was a skill she had learned when keeping chickens. Sexing the eggs was an important job, necessary for enabling the female eggs to be hatched to give laying hens, and the ones containing male offspring to be eaten. She also had a knack for predicting an imminent birth, claiming 'She's about to kittle'.

One of her most treasured possessions was a caul which was wrapped in tissue and kept in a leather pouch under her bolster. This was a membrane which had covered the face of one of the babies she had delivered. They are reputed to bring good fortune, particularly to sailors, who carry them to sea as an insurance against drowning. She often told the tale of how Grandfather had taken it with him when he set off on a voyage to Canada with grand plans to earn his fortune on a canal building project. He had been offered a hundred pounds for it by the ship's captain.

At the turn of the century a man such as Grandfather, taking a step away from convention, seeking a better life in the uncharted territory of a new country, planning to send for his family if the venture was successful, might have been considered quite a brave man, but he was not brave enough to come home with a hundred pounds in his pocket and no caul. At that time such a sum would have been a small fortune to the average family, but he must have weighed up the worth of the money against facing Granny's wrath and the caul was returned safely to its home under the bolster.

30 Fears and Fascinations

Grandfather was not the only one whose bravery wilted in the presence of Granny. I have a fear of the dark which probably originated from her habit of creeping around with a candle on a saucer, although there had been electricity in the carriages since a time before I was born. Mother was in hospital for two weeks when I was eight, and Granny moved me into her bedroom. She was no doubt trying to keep me safe but she escorted me down the dark passage with the unreliable, flickering light of her candle, put me in her double bed which had a feather mattress and then blew out the candle.

Those mattresses were renowned for their warmth and comfort but my tiny form sank in so far that I thought I would drown. There was nothing to hold on to. I lay rigid, petrified that moving would cause me to sink even further. If I had known of quicksand I would have compared it to this. My instincts told me to keep still until it was light and I could find my way out. As I listened to her getting up to use the commode that always stood beside the bed, I prayed for a moment of light but she felt her way, not even re-lighting the candle.

On Mother's return, I tried to explain how frightened I had been but she was surprised that I felt fear when safely inside. Her fear was of outsiders and she defended Granny's behaviour as being quite rational.

'If somebody's goin' by and sees a light on, they might come an' knock on the door.'

This was the first time I had any understanding of her struggling with a torch when I had been ill in the night. I never learned where her fear of outsiders came from.

Perhaps that, too, had been inherited from Granny, who always had blackout blinds, as well as curtains, covering the windows. My fears were the opposite; wondering what might lurk in the shadows in every corner, mistrusting anything that obscured my view.

This has manifested in my life as a reluctance to shut doors or curtains, or to be anywhere indoors without a light. I am the one who leaves on two lights overnight, the second as a back-up in case the bulb goes in the first, and I will never sleep on a bed that sinks in. I have boards under my mattress.

I will happily walk through the countryside, unperturbed by the noises of nature or the flickering light as branches cross the moon. I am calm as I drive along the unlit fen roads, where the night is purest. I love those dark fens with their openness and wide skies. They have nothing to hide and I have nothing to fear, but put me in a dark, confined space and I am eight again.

Some of the old fears seem irrational now but they were undoubtedly based on the beliefs of the time. I recall a visit to my Godmother's house. She had a new fish tank to show me. She left me at the door to the front room, whispering, 'Wait there', as she went ahead in the dark to flick on a switch.

I just managed to get a glimpse of the illuminated tank as Mother scooped me up and ran back to the kitchen. The light was inside the tank. The electricity was in there with the water. Her horror at that dangerous combination haunted that room for the rest of my childhood and I was never allowed back in to see the fish.

At the time when Granny was growing up, medical evidence still cited fear as a cause of many malfunctions. Women were barred from 'freak shows' as it was thought that pregnant women should not be allowed to see those with deformities, lest maternal imprinting resulted in the deformity being passed on to the foetus, as was believed to be the case in the story of the 'elephant man'.

In the fens we were not so mollycoddled, and a report from 1938 tells of a two-headed woman appearing in a waxworks show put on by the women's guild in our town, but old fears, like old habits, have grown from limited knowledge and misinformation and are not easily dispelled. Granny often quoted 'proof' of this theory as we had a relation who was born with a deformed arm after a neighbour dropped a dustbin lid.

'The clatter frit 'is mother 'alf to death when she were 'aving 'im.'

It was also a common belief that one could die of fear so being 'frit to death' was not an empty threat. There are some occasions in my early life when fear blotted out every other sense. I have clear memories of being a bridesmaid when I was three, being reluctant to carry a large basket of flowers, and squinting because the sun was hurting my eyes as we posed for the photographer, but I have no recollection of the wedding at which I was a bridesmaid for the second time. I know it was in Ely but I remember no church or registry office, no hymns or reception. All this was lost to an incident that happened on the way home.

Mother and I had travelled back from Ely by train. It was evening and already getting dark. As we got off the train in Peterborough, it was raining.

'Come on, if we're quick, we'll catch the next bus.' She took my hand and we started to run.

I can't imagine us running very fast but the paths were

already wet and I was still wearing my slippery-soled bridesmaid shoes. I don't know if I tripped or slipped but I felt myself falling. It was not unusual for me to fall. I always had grazed knees or bruised shins and Mother always picked me up, hugged me better and administered ointments and plasters.

That night I felt her falling too. I don't know if I pulled her with me or even if she had lost her footing and took me with her. I heard her hit the path and I was still holding her hand.

Neither of us suffered anything like serious injuries, just a few cuts and scrapes, but I was mortified. This wasn't how it worked. Mother was always there to look after me in a crisis. Now I was on my feet first and I didn't know how to deal with it. She was struggling to get up and there was blood running from a cut on her knee. I was panicking because this role reversal was not in the natural order of things. Father might have known what to do, maybe, but it had always been Mother who had taken charge, whatever the situation. He wasn't there anyway as it was a Saturday and he had worked.

A man coming behind us had seen what happened and stopped to offer help, but Mother wasn't about to accept help from a stranger.

'We're alright, ta,'

She was smiling and wincing at the same time and he went on his way, leaving me feeling more alone and frightened than I had ever felt before – because I had seen a vulnerability in Mother that I could not have imagined.

Sometimes fear of consequences was used to moderate my behaviour. At one stage I was even frightened of custard cream biscuits. It was after I had been ill and not eating for a few days. Mother, fearful as ever that I might starve, tempted me with a custard cream biscuit. It tasted good and I decided to continue eating them – but nothing else. After a day or two on this novel diet, Mother announced, in exasperation 'If yer don't start eatin' proper, yer innards'll git wangled up and then yer'll know about it. Yer'll eat one a' them biscuits and then yer'll run t' the lav and out it'll come, the same biscuit, 'cus y' ent digestin' it proper.'

The next biscuit didn't taste so good and I now noticed how sharp were the corners of a custard cream biscuit; so there ended that battle, like so many others, with me conceding out of fear of the threatened consequences.

On other occasions temptation was so great that it overcame these fears. I had been warned not to use Father's shaving cream and brush because it would surely result in me growing a beard. One day, left unsupervised in the kitchen, I seized the opportunity to work up an impressive lather and spread it from ear to ear. No-one caught me and I wiped it all clean before anyone knew but it caused me such angst, checking my face each morning in the mirror with dread that the threatened bristles would have appeared overnight, that I was never tempted to do it again.

It didn't, however, stop me from similar experiments. Despite warnings that my hair would fall out, I found the tantalising smell of Brylcreem too tempting to resist and slaumed it all over my hair, only realising too late that it would be that unique smell that gave me away.

Father was the only one in the carriages who owned a toothbrush and a tube of toothpaste. One day, after he had left for work, I noticed that he had left his toothbrush on the draining board. Wanting to savour the taste of the toothpaste that always made his mouth smell of delicious mint, I dragged over a chair and reached a tube from the cabinet over the sink. This time I was pleased to be caught as Mother rushed in and rescued me from the awful taste. She gave me cups of water to rinse my mouth, with the firm instruction not to swallow. Then she exclaimed to Granny, 'Whatever next, she's only tryin' t' clean 'er teeth wi' the chilblain ointment now.'

Perhaps the most worrying time for the grown-ups was when I decided that I wanted to be a blood donor. Father had arrived home with a badge for donating a certain number of pints and I wanted a badge, too. They frightened me with tales of needles, adding a warning of how easily I might bleed to death, but I'm sure they still had a few sleepless nights, imagining that I might pierce an artery in an attempt to acquire a few pints of the precious badge-procuring red stuff.

There was always a pessimistic comment to be made whenever someone was going to try something new. The mention of Uncle taking a holiday abroad brought forth recollections of the tragedy at the 1952 Farnborough air show and the loss of the 'Busby Babes' in 1958. The December smog of 1952 which resulted in the loss of over four hundred lives was also recalled each year at the first sign of fog and I had to keep my mouth in my scarf just in case.

Unnecessary travel of any kind was considered unwise. There had been two major crashes on the mainline crossroads at Murrow and the 1963 Great Train Robbery was the last straw for rail travellers. In that same year, motoring was proved to be dangerous when John F Kennedy was shot and killed in his car. I don't recall knowing anyone buying a boat, but I'm sure the first response would have included the word 'Titanic' and gone on to a plea to consider the fate of Donald Campbell and Bluebird. I don't remember any reference ever being made to the Paupers for Science scheme, where bodies were bought from workhouses to be used in research and transported in railway carriages. This may have been because the grown-ups were not aware of it themselves.

Had they have known of it, I'm sure it would have come up in conversation along with all the other unpleasant anecdotes that were dropped in at opportune moments.

Then there were the never-ending list of superstitions to trip up the unwary and bring bad luck crashing down on us: breaking a mirror, crossing the knives or walking under a ladder. It was important to know the significance of flowers, too. A handful of daisies was welcome but a similar bunch of dandelions was shunned as a sign of a wet bed. Lilac was grown outdoors but not allowed indoors and some tasks could not be performed on a Sunday. The most embarrassing of these superstitions was that it was unlucky to change a garment if it was accidentally put on inside out. This meant that a rushed attempt at dressing in the half-light could result in being teased all day for wearing a jumper with the label protruding just below my chin.

Because fen people had traditionally lived in small groups and were largely isolated, these customs had been passed down the generations, unchallenged. Their influence on everyday life depended on the theory that 'tried-and-tested' was always better. Tradition was a trusted guide and change was the unknown enemy.

My grandparents had been raised by parents who had lived in an environment threatened, yet nurtured, by water. Foreigners had brought schemes to literally suck their way of life from beneath their feet. Local heroes were those who had sabotaged the efforts of strangers seeking to change the landscape, until even the most heroic were finally conquered by the army of progress.

Although the fen folk were forced to adapt to this new way of life, their reluctance and resentment lived on, passed down in the tales of mistrust and betrayal, that were shared on long winter nights. Their descendants were just as adverse to change as they were suspicious of the unfamiliar. From this fear was born prejudice. In such small communities, prejudice or old-fashioned values, depending on one's viewpoint, survived throughout my childhood and well into the era of political correctness. These people would call a spade by no other name.

Culture was local, familiar and specific to our area. Even neighbouring communities had their own versions, which we found strange and sometimes amusing.

'Them from Lincolnshire,' might refer to a family that had relocated within the fens.

'Them from Yorkshire,' or any hilly county would certainly have been treated with caution.

This was a time when the term 'multi-cultural' had yet to be invented, along with 'multi-pack' and 'multi-task'.

Since the 1960s, many words which were in everyday use have passed into history or their meanings are now defined quite differently. Some have come to be associated with a prejudice which was not intended at the time. Homosexuality was a word unknown to children and whispered by grown-ups. Such relationships were illegal and electric shocks were still being used in aversion therapy. We had not moved on very far from the 1950s when the 'condition' was considered by some to be contagious. When we spoke of 'outing', we were describing a trip organised by the chapel. 'Trannies' were small, portable radios, carried by trendy teenagers. As a child born on the Sabbath day, I was often regaled with the rhyme, 'Happy and bonny, blythe and gay'. In the company of a whole generation of Enid Blyton children, I romped gaily around the garden without any thought that, within a few years, the term would become so controversial.

Sirdar, the makers of knitting wool, printed a Sunshine Series of patterns and across the front of number 99, leapt a smartly dressed gollywog. These were knitted by mothers and worn by a generation of children with no more thought than would have been given to a jumper with a Peter Rabbit motif.

Another word we commonly used, with no racial malice, but merely to identify folk about whom we knew no details, other than the colour of their skin, was 'Darkies'.

I recall one summer afternoon, on a trip to the town park in Peterborough, Father musing quietly, as was his way, 'I've been watching those Darkies. They're not talking to each other'.

Mother and I turned to follow the direction of his eyes, to where two family groups were in close proximity to each other but each engaged in its own activity. One father was pushing a toddler on the baby swings as the mother looked on. The other couple observed as a number of older children climbed up the steps and slid down the slide.

I had not noticed any of them before but, now my attention had been drawn to them, I quickly realised that they were not only different to us but different to each other. The group at the swings had very black faces, almost shiny in the bright sunlight. Their clothes were patterned in vibrant colours and the toddler had frizzy hair which was parted into several short plaits, so tight that it looked painful. The other family were better described as brown skinned and their clothes were different: less colourful but trimmed with beads.

It didn't seem strange to me that they didn't communicate with each other, any more than they didn't approach us. I wondered if they even spoke the same language. I remembered the animated voices of the dark-eyed men on the buses, and Mother's explanation that they had learned to speak in Italy and used different words from us but understood each other. Perhaps Father was just musing aloud but I felt that he was not critical, just curious. I wondered later whether he genuinely believed that these families from foreign lands would have known each other and embraced the each other's children in the park, as we would have done if we had met our cousins from Ely or Doncaster.

While Father may have been curious about these unfamiliar people, I believe Mother had a degree of affection for the children that often outstripped her feelings for me. I brought home from school little books with tear-out pictures of children, which could be bought for a small donation to Dr Bernardo's, and Mother always chose a black child, usually a boy, who looked at her with wide, innocent eyes.

All these children: black and white, boys and girls, had an air of serenity which I lacked. I had too much curiosity for my own good and the speed of an opportunist. I was wilful and obstinate. Granny described me as the 'little davil', and no amount of smacking curbed my defiance. On days when I pushed Mother past the end of her tether, and there were many such days, she lamented, 'I knew I should 'ave adopted a little picinnini,' and I could hear a wistful fondness in her voice.

In some ways, I think perhaps she had a quite progressive attitude for her time. Her closest friend, Winton, was a lady originating from Derbyshire, way up in 'them 'ills', who had only lived in the fens since the 1940s.

31 Under the Weather

Long before conditions such as Seasonal Adjustment Disorder became fashionable and studies showed that fluctuating atmospheric pressure can have an effect on concentration and memory, common sense told us that we all feel better when the weather is good. Here, in the fens, we perhaps noticed the changes more than those in urban areas because we were always exposed to the elements and many people's livelihoods were dependent on the whims of the weather for successful harvests.

Growing up in the late 1950s and 1960s I never experienced the fens at their most vulnerable, when inundations of water regularly drowned crops and cattle alike. I only heard the stories of farms turned into islands and torrents that carried away homes in the night, but I listened to those who had lived through such desperate times. Then I added my own dose of imagination and came up with awful images that haunted my sleep and drove me to seek reassurance whenever the weather invaded my thoughts.

I was always afraid of the rain. On wet days I would play happily in the kitchen as long as the internal doors were shut. The extra layer of carriage ceiling deadened the sound but if the door to the passage was opened, I ran from the noise of the water. Rain pelted onto its zinc roof, like rapid gunfire. Mother would drop down the top half of the outside door and rest her elbows on the ledge, leaning out to breathe the freshness of wet grass and flowers. Sometimes she pulled a chair to the door and coaxed me into kneeling up at her side.

'Oooh, that's lovely,' she smiled, 'just what them gardens need.'

I watched as the water plopped onto the concrete and formed tiny rivulets that ran onto the gravel. Puddles became pools and there was no sign of it slowing. I grew more anxious and tried to pull her inside, away from this perceived threat.

'What if it floods?'

I don't know how many times, over how many years, I asked that same question but I always got the same answer.

'Don't be s' darft, we won't flood 'ere. It'll all run into the knot-'oles and have to fill them fust.'

When this did not satisfy me, Granny reminded me how lucky we were to live in a wooden carriage.

'If it got to the top of tha' step it 'ud be straight in their door.' She pointed at the neighbours' house. 'But we're wood. We'd just float away like Norr's ark.'

The fact that the carriages were anchored on three sides by brick chimneys attached to the woodwork was never mentioned, nor was the weight of the ironwork. I didn't question her superior understanding. I just felt uneasy at the idea of this uncontrolled floating.

At night I lay awake as rain pounded on the zinc sheets. I had heard talk of water finding a weak spot in the river banks and surging forth across the fields so I waited, expecting it to burst through the roof at any moment to fill the passage and pour into the carriage through the vents as we slept.

Like a true Romany, Mother listened to it from the warmth of her bed, reassuring me that it was good to hear it, when we were all tucked in for the night. I was torn between burying my head under the covers to deaden the furious beating, or keeping my ears out in case it got worse and I didn't hear the grown-ups calling me as they ran in panic.

The only time I might have welcomed rain was in the summer of 1959, on that caravan holiday at Skegness. My parents had bought me new wellingtons just in case and there was, of course, no rain for the whole week, but I had new wellingtons and it is clear from the photographs that I was not going to be distracted from wearing them by something as trivial as hot sun. I posed on the beach, at the park, in the caravan site, always in my frilly dress, my sun-hat and my new wellingtons.

On wet Sunday mornings, I waited impatiently, knowing that we would not set out on our walk if there was the slightest mistle in the air. When the broody clouds cleared and a pale sun broke through and Mother deemed it fit, I launched myself out to the shed where Father would be tinkering about, waiting for me to collect him.

I was never a child who ran through puddles with such haste that a wake washed over the surroundings, nor did I stamp my feet so hard that the surface was broken into sparkling droplets. I felt no need to make particles of grit rise from the depth in a murky cloud, dispersing slowly, obscuring the clarity of the water. I was more likely to drop to my knees on the track where ruts and pot-holes, caused by the weight of dumper trucks, had become a landscape of lakes. Then I could peer silently into another world. As long as there was no breeze to ripple the surface, the image held steady and I could examine the detail of each rock-face, the crevices and seams in every crushed brick. These were my coral reefs and the faces of the Eiger. It is perhaps ironic, given my uneasy relationship with water, that I had developed such a love of puddles.

If we had ice at the weekend, Sunday morning found me hanging hopefully out of the kitchen door. Would Mother's fear of me slipping and breaking a limb be outweighed by her wish to hand me over to Father, taking the opportunity to get me from under her feet?

I waited for Mother's verdict, with a few of my little people secreted in my coat pocket. If her need for a short respite won, I clutched Father's hand and concentrated on my feet. I knew she would be watching from the kitchen window, ready to call us back if her conscience was touched by my unsteady gait.

Safely out of sight, we headed for the lane and soon reached the puddle 'lakes'. Then I took the little people out of the snug protection of my pocket and they shivered at the edge of the frozen expanse before being propelled across the icy surface with one deft flick of my thumb and forefinger: an ungainly re-enactment of the scene on the Christmas cake.

I never noticed at the time how patiently Father waited, just stamping his feet to ward off the cold, occasionally blowing into his cupped hands with the double benefit of hot breath on his fingers and a moment's heat against the skin of his face. I knew instinctively that I could not have enjoyed such quiet moments in the company of Mother, who would have shattered the silence with her impatient grunting, 'Come on, stop yer muckin' about, let's get gewing afore both on us get frez.'

Nor with Granny. 'Yer'll git rheumatics in yer knees.'

Only with Father could I lose myself in these fantasies, safe from being interrupted, until a growing numbness in my knees and fingers brought me back to reality.

In the days before temperature was measured in Celsius, we calculated it not only in Fahrenheit, but also in our own fen measures. It wasn't unusual to be told, 'It's cold as 'old 'arry out there,' or 'It's six overcoats warmer th' s'morning'.

The sky could get 'as black as Newgett's Knocker', and rain threatened 'over Will's mother's,' although I never worked out who Will was, or his mother.

On the occasional Sunday morning, when Father had a 'lay-in', I crept into the warm double bed and snuggled close to him as Mother bustled about in the kitchen, preparing breakfast. He always tucked my feet between his, urging, 'Come 'ere, yer like a frezzled wilk'.

I just savoured the warmth and never did find out what a frezzled wilk is.

Although we didn't live quite as close to the elements as previous generations, our lives were still governed in many ways by the weather. With no tumble-dryers or radiators on which to air clothes, it was really a matter of seizing the moment to do washing. Towels and sheets that had billowed against the morning sky had to be hauled indoors by late afternoon before they turned to boards of ice, swaying to and fro like plywood. At night a washing line was stretched between two hooks close to ceiling height in the kitchen. Even small garments hung so low that the grown-ups had to duck under them. Mother referred to this as her 'Chinese laundry' and often claimed that she wouldn't 'be washin' no more 'til summer'.

Despite this same struggle every winter, she was most indignant when someone suggested she use one of the newly opened laundrettes.

'Not likely,' She snorted, 'Yer won't catch me dead in a bag-wash where all the mucky folk put their washing in one machine.'

So, her endless battle went on and we all froze as an ancient wooden clothes horse, the two sides hinged together with binding, steamed in front of the fire, blocking any heat. Windows streamed and doors had to be kept closed so that the condensation could not spread down the passage and into the bedrooms. I can only imagine how much worse it had been at the time when I had supplied her with endless terry-towelling nappies.

These images remind me of one moment of humour, years later, by when Mother had a telephone installed. She was called by an old friend who chatted incessantly.

'Arr, yes, that'd be right,' she said.

Then she carefully laid the mouth-piece on the sideboard, came to the fireplace, turned all the washing round to air on the other side, returned to the sideboard, picked up the telephone again and continued the conversation, 'Arr, right, I know'.

As she had predicted, her friend was still talking and had not noticed her absence.

Granny often cited the old saying that 'the wind in the east is no good for man nor beast,' and I had heard people talk of a fen-blow, saying how it can last for just a few minutes but wreak destruction that is discussed for a whole season. I kept an eye out for changes in the wind, imagining that I might not find my way home should I be whirled into the air in the grasp of such a phenomena and I was never silly enough to be outside in anything more than a light breeze. This was a fear reinforced by Mother's reassuring gasp as the wind took away her breath.

'Yer alright. Yer won't blow away s' long as yer keep 'old of me 'and.'

As if she thought there was a danger that I might release my desperate grip.

Another fear that I had perhaps inherited from my forefathers, was of being lost in the fogs and mists which had once made the fens so perilous. One tea-time, after I had started high school and was allowed a little more freedom to roam, my friend and I left the town, biking out on the road towards Ramsey. This was a route we had taken many times before on hot days when the unforgiving sun scorched the treeless earth and we rode our bikes like camels across the desert. It was probably a little later than usual for us to be heading out but we were not going far so we felt quite confident as we passed the last of the houses. The fields opened out before us, sloping away from the town, dropping towards the bottom of the basin in which we lived.

We had only gone half a mile or so when the sun seemed suddenly to have left the sky. A chill struck our bare arms and our necks prickled. Swathes of mist form quickly in this area, especially at the end of a hot day when vapour rises from the water. We decided not to go any further, pulling into the verge to dismount and turn around.

In the instant that we turned, we panicked. This mist wasn't falling or coming in. It was rising out of the dykes on both sides of the road, like smoke from a bonfire that burned all the way back to the town, swirling to waist-height across our path home. The shapes of the buildings were vague. Already the mist had smoothed their sharp edges, blurring the distance so we could not judge it. We didn't exchange a word, nor glance backwards. Fear overtook the logic that would have seen us jumping on our bikes and pedalling furiously. Instead, we just ran, clutching the handlebars, half pushing, half dragging the bikes but not stopping to mount.

The familiar landmarks, the smoking brickyard chimneys and the imposing silhouette of the water tower, were lost to us. The railway crossing lay just ahead, adding to the urgency, lest the gates should shut before we crossed the line. We got back safely, of course, regaining our composure as we made out the outline of those first houses, irregular as crooked teeth, but with the welcoming smile of familiarity, still as solid as when we had passed them earlier.

For a long time we talked of ghosts who rose from the dykes in shrouds, obscuring our view of the town, threatening to trap us out there in the fen, at the mercy of the Will a'Wisps and Jack a'Lanterns that lurked in dykes, known to waylay those who were not indoors by night-fall.

Fogs always seemed worse here, too. I recall not being sure that we still had a gate as it could not be seen from the kitchen window and, later, hoping that the pale glow of the headlights on the school bus would pick me out as I waited at the bus stop. Granny was often heard lamenting, 'It's a right pea-souper 's morning'.

I don't know if that was just a term she borrowed from reports of the weather in London, or whether we did experience something similar here. As the clay burned, the brickyard chimneys belched sulphur, the ingredient necessary to turn a fog into a choking smog. Nearly a hundred chimneys once circled the town, so I think smog was a likely consequence.

Even more frightening than the mists and fogs, which at least could be shut outside, were thunderstorms, from which there was no escape. The first sign of an impending storm was the changing light: the blue fading from the sky, the grey taking on a yellowish hue. A wind began to stir the trees, leaves rustling as if swept by a growing tide. I began to feel uneasy. Mother busied herself in the kitchen, the door chained wide open as the air became heavier.

Confirmation that the 'eavens were about t' open', came in the shape of Granny's figure in the doorway. It was unusual for her to appear when she had not been summoned for a tea-break or dockey time, but she could sense a storm coming long before the first raindrops fell.

'That'll put paid to any more 'oing 's artnoon,' she would sigh stoically, peering at the ragged clouds. By now, all her tools were stowed in the shed. No fork or hoe or rake was left uncovered, and certainly not the shears with those long metal blades. Storms and metal went together like children and mouse traps.

Indoors, knives were secured in dark, baize-lined

drawers and there were no mirrors hanging on walls opposite windows where they could catch the lightning. I had heard, so many times, the stories of thunderbolts which could come down the chimney and blow the carriages apart if they couldn't find a way out. I never got between the hearth and the open door.

A thunderstorm over the fens is a sight to be seen. Mother was always in awe of such powerful drama and she took perverse pleasure in standing in the doorway, delivering details which I would rather not have heard.

''Ave yer seen 'ow black it is over Mucky Benwick?'

I don't know why Benwick was always referred to as 'mucky', but it was.

'Cor, look at that one, forking roight over the knot-hole.' Her voice bored into my head but I didn't want to see.

'I only counted to five that time, it's gittin' nearer,' she enthused as the thunder exploded overhead but, somehow, I never caught the enthusiasm from my foetal position under a blanket in the armchair.

Although I perceived the weather as threatening, always assaulting me with a new challenge, it wasn't all gloom and more gloom. I wondered why people spoke of the pot of gold at the end of the rainbow, intimating that a rainbow had only one end. Here, in the flatness of the fens, we often saw quite clearly where both ends reached down into distant fields as the rainbow arced across the sky in a splendid, transient, flourish of colour.

Even bike rides were an adventure when there was no mist. We could pack our baskets with food and have a picnic lunch, not just by a river, but by two rivers which lazily crossed each other without any fuss.

We could bike for miles along tracks where only tractors ventured. We followed the shadow of wires, strung like hammocks from one telegraph pole to the next.

As each pole was reached, the shadow took us out past the crest of the road. Then, as it dipped again to the lowest point, it brought us weaving back to the verge. As the melting tar stuck to our tyres, I was at the circus again, balancing my unicycle on the high-wire, imagining that I might teeter and fall into the chasm beneath the shadow.

The summer days were longest here in this flat landscape. The sun rose early from the horizon, far away across the fields to the east, bathing us in a pale light of promise, then dawdled across the sky, rising to a glorious midday summit before the burnished gold of afternoon. It resisted night like a child never ready for bed. A round, florid face flushed red with anger, was confined behind bars that could have been a cot, but were really the brickyard chimneys to the west.

32 Cultures and Confession

On Tuesday September 5th 1967, I finally set out on my journey to the new world. For the first time in my life, I left Mother at the bus stop and got on the bus alone. During the next five years Eastern Counties Service 343 carried me into town to catch the school bus, on which I made almost a thousand round trips across the fens to March. As two coachloads of boys headed for the Grammar School, I boarded one of the two coaches full of girls bound for the High School.

This had evolved from a tin tabernacle with less than forty pupils in 1905 and had moved to its new, purpose built site near to the town centre in 1909. Compared to the only school I had known until now, it loomed large and daunting with a red brick facade and two stories of windows that watched my approach.

This was my first glimpse of what lay ahead. Before education became child-centred, parents, not children, were invited to view the school and meet the headmistress prior to enrolment. I had waited at home with Granny, with a sense of trepidation and wonder, on the night that a neighbour with a car had driven my parents to this event. This was the only occasion that I recall them going out together after dark. In circumstances not dissimilar to an arranged marriage, they would combine first impressions, intuition and their dream of giving me the best start in life, to reach a decision that would set my course to the future.

That night was surreal. I felt the gravity of this decision

in the air. I imagined them taking in all the details of a conversation I could not hear and whispering their thoughts in the darkness of the car on the way back across the fens. They were gone for an unbelievably long time and, most unusually, I didn't talk much. I didn't know what questions to ask and Granny would have had no experience on which to base answers, so we just sat very quietly.

They must have been impressed because their decision was made before they reached home. I never asked what convinced them. I wonder now if it was the air of the building: if they felt the same sense of awe that I feel in museums and art galleries where the history and achievement can only be breathed. Perhaps it was the presence of Miss Shepherd, the headmistress: a tiny figure with shining, white hair and a face wise, yet kind. I think they would have loved her soft voice, which she never needed to raise, and the authority which she carried in her demeanour.

She had an office next to the dining area and we were not allowed to walk past in case we disturbed her. Sometimes this meant a lengthy detour, outdoors and back in again, even on wet days, but we would never have considered our task so urgent that it might justify taking a short cut and disturbing the important work of a headmistress.

So, I was no longer the only child, the centre of my family's life. I was a small, insignificant figure in the green uniform which united and identified us as the privileged pupils of this establishment. We wore our green, yellow and white ties with pride, symbolic of the school's emblem, the snowdrop, heralding the spring of our inspiration. I can't remember the exact words of the school motto but I do recall chanting 'With one accord, we pursue the common purpose,' and 'Each for all and all for each'. We looked to the prefects, with their prominent badges, for guidance and revered the head girl as a queen.

I became one small part of a moving community. We rose as a wave of green every morning for the next two years as the headmistress appeared in assembly. We stood and sat at the unspoken command of teachers and responded as one body to the sound of a bell, following the lead of those already established. Filing from classroom to classroom, always on the left of corridors and staircases, we walked in the footsteps of a previous generation of girls who had borne the responsibility of proving that a good education for girls was a worthwhile investment at a time when the emphasis was on educating boys and there were only three such schools for girls in the Isle of Ely.

With our privilege, came the knowledge that we had a duty to uphold the reputation and honour of those first pioneers. We quickly became integrated into the culture, unknowingly moulded to set an example to each new intake as we stretched ourselves towards the goals of achievement and success. Every moment followed a pattern, tried and proven over many years. I felt safe with this level of structure but, whilst I conformed to the discipline and respected those in authority, I think I may have remained a little detached.

I had spent my whole childhood, so far, carefully observing what went on around me. In the carriages, I had watched the grown-ups. In the garden, I had studied the creatures. At school I had compared the different lives of the other children. Now I had a whole new environment to watch. Trying to do maths or study a map was a distraction. I had enjoyed the unstructured approach of my earlier learning, thirsty for knowledge and the stimulation of new challenges, but I was not so impressed with this new rigour, sitting for long periods facing a blackboard.

We now had a different teacher for each subject and their expectations were never quite within my grasp. I avoided eye contact, dreading the moment when the voice paused, the gaze scanned the room and a question was posed. Once a victim had been picked I could breathe again but, occasionally, I was that victim. Then I blushed and stammered and it was obvious to all that whilst my green-clad body was trapped at that desk, my mind had gone travelling. Consequently, my first report states that I was 'A puzzling child, not always achieving her potential'.

As Mother read that report aloud, Granny shook her head and sighed, 'She'll allus be a fly b' night'.

I thought that sounded quite exciting but her tone of voice did not suggest that it would meet with approval as a career choice.

Exercise and sport took on a new meaning, too. PT lessons saw us leaving the changing-room on pale, wobbling legs, exposed beneath bottle-green shorts, before struggling to throw ourselves over a leather topped, wooden vaulting horse or balance precariously on a very narrow bench whilst attempting a forward roll. I never saw any potential disaster that would befall me at some point in my future if I did not master these skills so I spent a lot of time hovering close to the wall, hoping that the gym mistress would not notice that I was always at the back of the queue. I was the ever-polite pupil who waved others past with a discreet hand gesture and a whispered, 'No, really, you gew fust'.

Although I hated these lessons, they were not as bad as outdoor sports. To partake in these, we filed, two by two, out of the school gate, along County Road, across the road, down a track and onto a field beside the railway line. In our shorts and aertex tee-shirts, we braved the scorching summer sun to practise athletics and learn to throw a discus and a javelin. Again, I never grasped the concept that our futures would have been bleak without acquiring those abilities.

We were never quite posh enough to play Croquet or Lacrosse like the Enid Blyton girls, but in the mud and wind of winter term, we plodded in hockey boots, swinging our sticks at our sides, to the shrill instruction, 'Keep those sticks low. We don't want to have to go back because someone gets injured.'

Surely she must have realised how much we wanted to go back to the warmth indoors, even if it did mean that someone had to get injured. By February, I'm sure most of us would have volunteered to be the injured party.

On the field, I tried to run slowly enough to avoid any contact between my stick and the ball. I had no wish to be confronted by a group of eager girls, waving their sticks with enthusiasm, right next to my ankles. I never learned when to 'pass', nor understood where each position was supposed to lurk.

On days when the field was waterlogged, we were subjected to 'Hockey Theory', where we had to construct plans of a field, both teams at the ready, and chart the progress of the ball. The one thing missing from these plans was the only feature of interest: the railway line, where trains passed regularly on their way into and out of March. This had once been the largest marshalling yard in Europe, and was still a busy junction. At least, on those long, dull afternoons outside, it was good to know that the rest of the world was still going about its business and I could take a moment to listen to the clacking of the track and imagine journeys just started.

Within the classroom, I think I was perhaps hampered by the clash of cultures between home and school. At the carriages, everything had a practical purpose. All my experiences had been hands-on and led to a tangible result. I had no idea of the importance of theories and no appreciation of the value of knowledge stored for later.

I never had the luxury of a desk or even a designated space where I could concentrate. My 'study' was the end of the kitchen table nearest to the stove and the kettle. Mother grudgingly pushed the clutter further back against the wall, pulling the tablecloth over it to allow me a limited time with my school books. I regularly struggled to finish an essay as she glanced anxiously at the clock, muttering 'Ent yer nearly done that yit? It's nearly nine and the kettle's not on. I need t' git t' th' stove'.

When the kettle was boiled, I had to move from my chair so she could reach the tea caddy, always full of loose tea leaves, as she claimed to know for sure, 'them ol' bags, tha's where they put all the sweepings-up'.

Cholesterol had not yet been discovered and food 'good enuff t' stick yer ribs t'gether', was considered nutritious. As she dished up an improvised supper of bread and dripping or butter-puff biscuits with an added layer of butter, I lost the thread of my thoughts and had to stow a half written essay into my satchel to be finished next morning on the bus.

Despite these disadvantages, I enjoyed writing stories and, within the first year, I was granted extra time for English homework so that my natural exuberance was not curtailed by deadlines. I never managed to master the Modern Languages that were offered to us. French, German and Spanish remained forever foreign, but I loved the challenge of discovering a new English, spoken beyond the fens, a language that was still largely unfamiliar to me. I quickly grasped the concept that words such as 'bath' and 'path', although written as I had always spoken them, took a new shape when read aloud, now rhyming with 'hearth'. A distinct vowel sound had to be learned before 'cue' and 'pew' ceased to be 'coo' and 'poo'. Eventually I even recognised the subtle difference between 'do' and 'dew'.

Some of our teachers took on the thankless task of trying to refine, not just our fen accents, but our choice of phrase as well. I recall one conversation overheard at the end of a PT lesson.

'Cor, I ent 'arf sweatin', Miss.'

'No, dear, ladies do not sweat, they perspire.'

'Well, Miss, I'm perspirin' like a pig.'

We must have been a hard crop to cultivate.

Again, changes were not always welcomed into the carriages and I was often berated for 'puttin' on yer airs and graces wi' yer posh new talk'.

I learned to compromise. Food at home was 'et' and at school it was eaten. Illnesses were either 'tret' or treated. It was just a matter of who was listening and I'm sure I wasn't the only pupil at that school who became almost bilingual.

Another of my favourite subjects was Latin. I was enchanted by the rhythmic reliability of the verbs as we learned by rote, reminiscent of those earlier chants of station names. I was fascinated to discover the roots that made sense of our own language. I had no appreciation of poetry at that time and the complex language of Shakespeare was not yet on the curriculum, although I still have a letter from Miss Shepherd to parents, dated April 3rd 1968. It states, 'There is a strict school rule against borrowing...as indiscriminate lending and borrowing has a demoralising effect', so perhaps the influences of characters such as Polonius were being subtly introduced without us being aware of their origin.

We were also grounded in social awareness and the importance of world affairs and politics. We were not taken to County Hall to hear election results, as had been the tradition for earlier pupils, but we were in no doubt as to the importance of political decisions. We had debating societies which gave us a floor where our voices could be heard. We all held strong opinions, culminating in a mock-election, where girls represented each party and put forward a good case as to why we should vote for their policies.

From the recesses of earlier childhood, the words of an uncle with a business, surfaced.

'If the government don't look after the men who give work to the workers, there won't be any work for any of us.'

His words echoed now with a simple logic and I voted Conservative with all the confidence of the newly converted. I relished this opportunity to gather facts and figures that supported my new-born allegiance, proving that I could listen even though my attention span was limited and quite selective.

I tried to carry this exciting propaganda home to the carriages, but it did not travel well. Mother had been a staunch Liberal all her life and her allegiance was not to be swayed by my enthusiasm. Politics were not really discussed at home, but I do remember one occasion when matters became, literally, quite heated.

We were suffering the effects of power cuts. I quite enjoyed the romance of getting off the school bus to see the glow of a candle in the kitchen window because the miners were on strike, but Mother was not a romantic. One evening, her patience snapped. She had tried to heat soup on the paraffin stove and the bottom of the saucepan, normally scoured to a shine, had become blackened.

'Look at this, will yer? Black and Buggered,' she screeched, waving the pan dangerously close to my nose. 'See, that's what yer get from yer bloody Conservatives.'

I had no answer. That blackness symbolised all that she saw wrong with the government and strengthened her long held beliefs.

In those first years of High School, my biggest achievement was to make good and loyal friends, often based on little more than luck as we were seated alphabetically by surname. We got little chance to engage in conversation with those whose initial meant that they were seated out of ear-shot for a whole year.

As day-girls, we may not have had the opportunity to enjoy chocolate cake in our pyjamas when a trunk arrived from home, but we did enjoy a few day-time japes.

On one occasion a friend lay down in a lavatory cubicle, her feet sticking out under the door. I waited for a 'victim' to come in, then pretended that I had just arrived on the scene.

'Quick. Get 'elp,' I urged. 'Somebody must a' fainted.'

The girl rushed out. The plan was that she would return with a teacher who would be cross to find no-one there. However, luck conspired against us. The gym mistress was passing in the corridor and flung herself into the cloakroom before we could escape, finding my friend retrieving her feet from under the door and me standing by the sinks, unable to think of anything to say.

On another occasion it was the same teacher who caught me with the same friend, paddling through the snow at the far end of the playground with no shoes or socks. Perhaps our previous encounter coloured her judgement because she refused to believe our story that snow worked better than chilblain ointment and we were just bathing our heels. We were sent to explain our behaviour to the headmistress.

There were not many occasions in my school years, that I recall being caught and called upon to explain why I thought I knew better than those who taught and commanded respect, but my closest friend and conspirator does tell the story of us being thrown out of Ely Cathedral on a school trip because we were hiding in a coffin.

Perhaps there are some things that I have forgotten for good reason.

We had now left behind the innocent playground games of junior school. Huddling together at break time, we created a new kind of entertainment. We had more scandals in our school than even St Trinians, though I must quickly add that they played out only in the heads of pubescent schoolgirls with vivid imaginations. There was the male teacher who was fired because he touched the headmistress in an 'inappropriate' way, with much whispered emphasis placed on this word that was new to our vocabulary. It sounded so full of intrigue, especially when delivered with the head bent forward and eyebrows raised.

Then there were the two unmarried female teachers who shared a lodging, giving us the opportunity to try out another newly discovered word, 'lesbian', spoken with the same relish that we had mentioned 'tit-lobs' a few years earlier. A pretty young teacher with not much experience got the job only because she was the illegitimate daughter of one of the governors and the number of fights we overheard as we passed the staffroom was matched only by the number of illicit affairs that bloomed beyond that door.

None of these rumours ever reached the authorities, of course, or even the parents. They arose from boredom not malice. It's surprising how quickly a morning of Geography and Maths could pass if one had the distraction of knowing that a member of class has returned after a sickness and would be keen to listen at dinner-time, in confidence of course, to the latest m'larky that had happened in her absence.

Such stories were born, passed around in ever increasing circles and then extinguished by the next, even more outrageous claim. It was a time when dictionaries containing some of the more explicit words were limited to the sixth formers and biology focussed on plants and trees, only mentioning humans in the context of bones and major organs. This was our mild rebellion against the backdrop of authority.

On the whole, we conformed with good grace, accepting the necessity for strict rules to instill in us the discipline that would ensure that we abided by another motto, 'Duty before pleasure'.

Acquiring permission slips for every minor deviation from the normal, was one example of this conformity. I still have one, dated April 1968, signed by my form tutor, stating that I was permitted to eat a cough sweet in class.

I did, however, commit one major crime during this era, despite all the good grounding in morals and values, and it went undetected and un-confessed. Only my conscience prompts me to reveal it now. I cannot justify my actions but perhaps I could claim it as a crime of passion because I had fallen in love with another book. This time the author was Jack Schaeffer and my hero was Shane. I borrowed it several times, only returning it to be renewed. I couldn't leave it on the shelf in case someone else lost it or it was collected by the van. I don't think there was a van at that time but the memory of Kit's disappearance still remained raw.

One day, after much soul-searching - so definitely premeditated - I went into the library with a pile of books in my arms, returned Shane to the desk to be removed from my card, watched as it was put back on the shelf, then picked it up again, placed it at the bottom of the pile and walked out past the desk.

The way I sweated and my heart raced that day, taught me that crime wasn't a career option, but I had my book. Then I just had to hide it for the next thirty years or so because I couldn't explain the unstamped ticket inside and

I couldn't remove it without causing damage. Stealing a book is one thing, but I couldn't damage it.

Finally, when I was home-teaching my children, I couldn't keep the secret any longer. I wanted to share the book with them and that meant revealing the seedy story of its origin. I explained that I had no excuse for what I had done and could never condone them following in my criminal footsteps. I emphasised how I had been tormented by years of guilt and fear and would hate them to carry such a burden.

They just laughed and said 'Nah, Mum, we'd just download it now, it's not even illegal.'

Then we all cried because I had suffered so much over the years and taken so long to own up that it had become funny in a tragic sort of way.

I still don't feel that I can vindicate myself but I hope some good has come of it. We read the book together and the girls loved it too, so we studied it as an English project, deconstructing the story, analysing the characters, and then, as a special end of term treat, watching the film version. The telling moment, which proved the excellence of the description in the book, was when Alan Ladd appeared on screen and the girls chorused 'He's not Shane'.

33 Another Year, Another Change

During the second of my two years at High School, we learned of changes in the education system which meant that we would be relocated. Our school and the Grammar School were to be amalgamated. The boys had a relatively new building so we were to move to their site. This was heralded as beneficial to us as they had modern science laboratories, excellent drama and music facilities and purpose built language rooms, but we were never convinced. We had become used to our decaying annexes, which had served us quite well as form rooms. It was a pleasant walk from the art room to the biology room, or the domestic science block, along narrow paths that weaved between areas of garden.

The Grammar School had originally been established due to bequests in the seventeenth and eighteenth centuries, for the purpose of educating boys. We were frequently reminded of this by some of the more obnoxious boys who didn't want to make us feel welcome when we invaded their space in September1969.

We were always a little uneasy in the domain of the benevolent Mr Neale and Mr Wade, after whom this new establishment was named. Because the boys were there first, we felt like interlopers. I'm sure their staff made every effort to help us settle in, but we left behind a lot of our own staff, including Miss Shepherd. Some of these new teachers had never taught girls.

Their headmaster lived in a house in the grounds. Every morning as we walked down the long drive past this house, it appeared to be guarding the entrance.

Some girls thrived in this new environment and met the challenges with enthusiasm, but I was not inspired and became more and more detached from what was happening around me.

The building had windows that didn't leak and doors that closed better against draughts, but it lacked character. All around us were reminders that we had not been in mind when the plans were drawn up. The most striking lack of facilities were those needed to cultivate the next generation of housewives. On 'cookery afternoons' we were collected by a bus belonging to the appropriately named Fenn family, for the nostalgic journey back to our old building.

At the beginning of each lesson we had to calculate cooking times and formulate a written plan to be approved by the teacher, before we even unpacked our ingredients. Then we had to adhere rigidly to this timetable so that our 'meal' was ready to serve at the proposed time or, in reality, nothing was still in the oven when it was time to catch the bus back.

I recall offering to help another girl who was struggling to keep to the schedule. As she beat the mixture for a sandwich cake, she passed me a jug containing the tiniest amount of icing sugar, smiling gratefully, 'If you could just add the water'.

I headed to the nearest sink and turned on the tall tap, directing the jet of water into the jug before calling across to her, 'How much water?' as the tiny scoop of sugar sloshed to the top of the half-pint jug. Cookery was never my best subject.

Sewing was also part of our 'domestic science' curriculum, and entailed another bus ride as the boys' school was not equipped to deliver these skills either. We sewed an apron for Cookery as our first project, followed by a skirt with a zip, and then a blouse, complete with breast pockets and collar. Some of the girls finished all these garments by the end of the year and were rewarded by the chance to parade their creations on the cat-walk at an evening fashion show for parents. I wasn't there, of course; I was still wrestling with the apron.

An unfamiliar lack of vigilance by the teaching staff meant that on such afternoons each school assumed we were at the other, enabling small groups of us to disappear for whole afternoons. We skulked in a little-used cloakroom on the second floor where we whispered in fear of being discovered and perched uncomfortably in the narrow spaces between the hand basins because there was no seating. With hindsight, we would probably have enjoyed the lessons more but we basked in the glory of beating the system, or we would have done if we could have told anyone.

Instead, we scurried out to our buses at the last bell, with a cloth cover over our gondola baskets so no-one noticed that our ingredients were still uncooked, or our hems still unhemmed. Each of us rehearsed excuses about out-of-order cookers and sewing machines, for when we reached home.

Another ploy for missing lessons was a trip to the sick-room. This was nothing like the ones in the books, where grape-carrying form-mates persuaded kindly matrons to let them visit in the night. Here, we had to be sufficiently recovered to catch the bus at three-forty. I recall one hot, humid day when the thought of double games in the afternoon tempted me to the sick-room door after first lesson, but my timing was awry.

Asked how long my stomach cramps normally lasted, I bent double and groaned, 'normally only a couple a' days'.

I was informed briskly, 'You can stay here 'til break'.

In class, my friend and I usually lurked at the back, but

one day, in a fit of ill-judged humour, we chose to sit at the double desk directly in front of the teacher's table. There was just enough space between the two, for her to pass in front of us as she worked her way down the room, chanting French verbs as she went. While she had her back to us, we seized the moment and used our knees to hitch the heavy desk forward so, as she returned, the gap was not there anymore. Her puzzled expression was enough to have the whole class giggling but we didn't laugh for long.

She was not impressed with our effort to lighten the mood. This wasn't a time when humour was appreciated. It was the time when education was a very effective one-way street where knowledge was passed downwards. Respect for authority was still in fashion. Teachers spoke and we listened, and that day we listened to the news that we were up for an 'Order Mark'.

It was about that same time, that I found resolution to a battle which I had fought for many years. At home I had always suffered from an acute paper shortage. Mother was quite happy to buy me wool or donate Granny's left-over scraps, but it's not easy to tell a good story in wool unless tapestry is your talent. She didn't realise the importance of paper to a growing imagination. One birthday I had made such a fuss about it that a number of relations bought me writing sets. I had no-one to write to, the sheets were unlined and the envelopes were only big enough for scribbled notes. I was grateful and they kept me going almost through the next month, but I needed a more regular supply. I was already in trouble for ripping pages out of the back of my exercise books because the front ones then became detached and gave me away.

This was always noticed as each full book had to be signed by a teacher before a new one was issued. I saw an opportunity for another dubious scheme. If I carefully prised open the staples in the centre of a newly issued book I could remove a few pages, replace them with used ones and gain precious sheets for my own use. This didn't work with 'neat' books as the work in them was signed and dated. 'Rough' books were a much easier target and, although the paper was not such good quality, it gave me an adequate canvas onto which I could pour my thoughts. I then realised that no record was being kept as to how often these exchanges took place so, by seeing a different teacher each time, I gradually increased the frequency of my lunchtime swap-shop.

Perhaps out of bravado, rather than necessity, I once placed the entire old book into a newly signed cover, and thereby managed to acquire a whole book of sheets. I didn't feel that I was being greedy. I just needed the security of a stockpile. To wake in the morning with ideas whirling round in my head and no paper, filled me with fear that an inspired idea might evolve, bloom briefly and then whither before I could capture it in writing, bringing back frightening memories of the time when I thought I had to limit my talking in case I ran out of words.

I felt that my bad behaviour had been vindicated in 1970, when I won the only award of my school years: the March Grammar School Old Boys' Association Essay Prize. At least the paper had not been wasted.

As we worked our way up the years, through Lower Removes, Removes and Divisions, and progressed towards 'O' level standard, my grasp of maths became increasingly tenuous. Perhaps 'progressed' is the wrong word.

'Ground to a halt,' was actually how my teacher described it. He refused to believe that logarithms and equations were completely beyond my comprehension. The words with which I was familiar, such as 'long chalk' and 'wide berth' were not on the curriculum and I never learned to tell the difference between my equilateral and my hypotenuse. Eventually, he accepted that I could not be taught. I was sent to the headmaster to face the guilt and shame as he towered over me, exclaiming 'Never, in the history of my teaching, have I had a pupil who did not sit their Maths 'O' level'.

Well, he had now. I was withdrawn from the class and never again had to question why umpteen seemed to have been removed from the place where I had always assumed it lived, after nineteen, before twenty. I no longer faced the trauma of handing in a blank sheet where my homework should have been, waiting in dread for the repercussions. Instead I was allowed to have 'study-time' in the library, giving me the opportunity to fill those ill-gotten sheets of paper with stories of a life beyond the confines of school.

By this time Shakespeare had been brought to our attention and my first experience of a live performance came when we were taken by coach to a theatre in Cambridge to see Romeo and Juliet. We were studying for our English Literature exam and it was thought that it would help us to remember the text better. That was probably only partly successful as I don't recall much of the play, but one scene is etched forever in my mind.

'When 'e said 'Wherefore art thou' 'e looked roight into my eyes,' claimed a girl from Chatteris.

'And mine, and mine,' came back a chorus from the girls of Whittlesey and Coates, Manea and March, united by the magnetism of those beautiful eyes.

We had all fallen in love, and I'm sure I'm not the only one who relives that moment every time I see Ian McShane on screen, still as broodingly handsome as he looked on the stage, illuminated by the spotlight in the darkened theatre, that night when he became the hero of us fen-girls' dreams.

34 It's all in the Distance

When asked how he would describe the Fens to someone who had never been here, my grandson, who had lived his whole eight years in a city, hesitated for only a moment, his eyes scanning the horizon, before replying, 'It's all in the distance'.

I include his quote because I cannot better it. Here is a landscape where the eye is not drawn to a foreground feature but to the vision of width and depth. The changing light and evolving seasons are the artists who draw their picture on this canvas.

During the years that I attended school in March, I crossed the fens twice daily. We always took the same route but every day was a different journey. On summer mornings we headed towards a pale sun that bathed the fields in a buttermilk wash. In winter we were on our way whilst darkness still lingered and I had to be careful not to catch my first glimpse of a new moon through the glass of the bus window. That would have been terribly unlucky. We were sometimes close to reaching school before the first streaks of colour appeared in the sky.

Every year we watched the seasons, each with its own story. In spring we saw the blackness of the soil, hard from winter frosts, broken by the tractors pulling ploughs. The sky was filled with birds, swooping and following, awaiting their opportunity to feed on the worms churned from the dark earth.

Seeds were sown and we watched for the first glimpse of green, attempting to guess what had been planted. It might be a few weeks before we could be sure that we were right. Then we watched the crops grow towards summer.

Sugar beet was hoed, singled and lifted by an army including women, with specially sewn bonnets protecting their faces and necks. As they worked steadily in the cool of the mornings, we looked to see if the rows of plants met by St Swithin's Day, a sure sign that the harvest would be good.

Cabbages grew greener and curlier in their rows, reaching as far as we could see. Velvet fields of barley stirred into a gentle, swaying dance as a breeze caught the ripening ears.

We were not a generation who could escape from school when our labour was required in the fields at harvest time. The age of children working on farms in summer had passed into storybooks, along with the steam engines that Grandfather had driven, pulling a plough across the fields of the fens on winter days when the fair was not travelling.

Farms were getting bigger now, although some were still known as Fen Lots, from a time when lots were drawn to allocate land to villagers.

Horses were no longer a familiar sight and the supporting industries: blacksmiths, wheelwrights, farriers, and saddle-makers were fading into memory. Harvest was now a time for the big machines of Massey Harris and Massey Ferguson. They worked quickly through the ripe fields of barley, oats and wheat, which had taken the place of the traditional flax for clothing, cole seed for oil lamps and hemp for rope. It wasn't long before the familiar smell of burning stubble greeted us, accompanied by the excitement of our bus driving into the smoke as it billowed across the road and emerging triumphant on the other side.

These were the fens as we knew them. We had been born six thousand years too late to see the bog-oaks as living trees, before they fell to their graves in the soft peat. We saw them now as the peat shrank, dragged by tractors and chains from their resting place, piled by the edge of fields, older than the pyramids and still too solid to be sawn. The largest of these recorded was pulled out at Stretham, measuring eighty-two feet.

We were too late to look out on the water which had once covered this area, sometimes supporting life here, sometimes raging with destructive force. We were even a life-time too late to see the wildfowlers with their punts and ice-sledges, the felmongers, and the trappers with wicker fish weirs, although mole trapping and eel catching were still commonplace.

The drainage mills and pumps had done their work and we were surrounded by the fens in their prime, no longer under constant threat of deluge, not yet threatened by the erosion and shrinkage that would be the price of dryness.

We had missed the era when workers would have been seen wearing silk nets over their heads and shoulders to protect them from the biting insects, but life here was still hard. I recall Granny looking upon one woman who had spent her years in the fields and saying 'She ent that old, yer know, it's just 'er skin's bin rizzled.'

Starting out from a garage on Scaldgate, whose name, along with Horsegate, Briggate and Claygate, told of our Norse connections, we left the town whose history goes back to the Domesday Book, yet made us the butt of jokes.

'Yer don't even know 'ow to spell w'ere yer come from,' we were teased.

This was a charge we could not deny because train passengers alight at Whittlesea. Cars drive into Whittlesey. Both signs can be seen vying for authority on Station Road where the road crosses the railway line.

Our bus passed Cemetery Road, site of the only cemetery I have ever seen featured on a Christmas card, pictured above the caption 'Season's Greetings from Whittlesey'. On our left was the school where all my friends from Infants now went, named in honour of Sir Harry Smith, regarded as our local hero for his role in the Battle of Aliwal.

We picked up girls from the village of Eastrea, before chugging on to Coates, where a sign shows geese on the green, bringing to mind the poem which mocks the old law of prosecuting those who steal geese from the common, whilst condoning the theft of the common from the geese.

Our next stop was at Eldernell, site of the Eldernell Miracle, where a shrine was built to commemorate the amazing cure of the bed-ridden Robert Whyt in the 11th century. At one time this area had been part of our own island so we claimed this legend as ours.

We never referred to legends, of course, or tales, myths or fables. We had heard everything first-hand, from someone whose ancestor had been there at the time, or knew someone who had. This made every account an unquestionable truth.

Leaving the villages behind, we travelled on the A605, relatively well maintained for a fen road, though still strewn with pot-holes and ruts. These became increasingly noticeable in winter when frost cracked the surface and the suspension on our old buses creaked and jolted us against each other. I was often trying to write, sometimes finishing my homework, other times attempting to capture in words the scene beyond the window. My efforts were frequently marked with a scrawl as the bus lurched and my pen slewed across the page.

Passing along the oddly named stretches of Goosetree

and Long Gravel, there were signs for Turves, which I believe was associated with the turf industry, and for Burnt House, the origin of which still eludes me. We were now heading down to the old sea-bed and the houses became more isolated, each reached by crossing a bridge over the roadside drains. They often looked as if they were about to collapse and many of them did subside beyond repair. It was common for new ones to be built alongside, suspended on floating rafts. This was a desolate picture in winter when snow could drift from the fields and obscure the narrow grass verge between the edge of the road and the deep drains.

Spring brought its own hazards with the threat of Fenblows, which could lift the surface of a whole field and throw it onto the road, bringing darkness to the daytime sky.

Summer was lovely, despite the sweltering heat inside the buses as the sun poured through the glass and the treeless scene offered no shade. We welcomed the sight of a pair of swans and watched them raising young. They were often the only living creatures in the landscape; although a lady in a dressing-gown, carrying a toddler on her hip, did sometimes appear near one of the houses. They were not the ghosts of a past fen-life, but the wife and son of one of our bus drivers. The child waved to his father as we passed and we all waved back.

As we continued our journey to the end of Long Gravel, a left turn would have taken us to Ring's End, where a Tower House had stood, built for John Morton, Bishop of Ely, overlooking the lake where water from his new leam joined the River Nene on its way to the Wash.

Instead, we turned right towards March, passing another blockhouse, similar to the one that had captured my imagination years earlier, but lacking the charm. This one had large, open entrances and had housed one of the numerous field-guns which had guarded the fens during the war. We picked up the last of our passengers at Westry and headed into the town of March, once the site of a Roman fort and a Roman temple, but better known in the 1960s for its primitive sewers and polluted waters.

We travelled upstairs when the bus was a double-decker and were usually already seated when the driver climbed into his cab outside the garage, out of our view. Each morning we played a game of trying to guess who was driving. We became quite skilled at recognising who took the bends wide and who crashed through the gears.

By the time we reached March the first shops were just beginning to open and one morning I saw the reflection of the bus as we pulled up in traffic outside the shops. I announced, triumphantly 'I was right. It's Peter. I can see him in the shop.'

A second later my friend fled for the stairs in panic as the bus pulled off and she thought we were running away, with the driver really in the shop.

Another drama unfolded before our eyes one icy morning when a car heading in the opposite direction went into the Twenty Foot Drain. Our driver saw it and swung the bus across the road, pulling into the verge on the far side. Jumping from his cab without a word, he ran to assist, leaving us girls sitting in our seats. As other vehicles stopped to help, he returned and we continued our journey to school, arriving late and relishing the opportunity to tell how we had personally been involved in this incident. We talked of our driver being the hero, how he had returned to the bus with soaked clothes after jumping into a raging torrent. By the end of the school day he had been solely responsible for rescuing a whole family from sure death. I don't remember any newspaper coverage or hero's reception. I don't even remember seeing any wet clothes. Perhaps I didn't have the best vantage point but I think most of the story may have been perpetuated and elaborated by those who did, relaying the information to the rest of us. It is true that a car did go into the freezing water that morning and perhaps it is true that he was instrumental in the outcome, if only by catching the attention of other drivers by abandoning a double-decker bus alongside.

The true measure of his worth may lie in the fact that he felt confident to leave us sitting there. He knew that, however curious we were, none of us would attempt to leave the bus. No-one would disrespect his authority. I wonder if the same could be said today?

Each time we reached the school entrance, we mingled with the girls arriving from other parts of the fens.

We were drawn from a far-reaching catchment area and, although there was no fighting or bullying in school as that was not allowed, verbal sparring could become quite heated. There was an element of rivalry between the girls of the different towns, each proud of her own heritage.

Only when challenged by outsiders, did we unite as one tribe of fen folk, with our marked accent and a deep-seated sense of pride in our voice. We came together then to defend our sense of belonging, of being born of islanders who had forged a lifestyle from the harsh realities of their surroundings.

We were all familiar with the historical accounts of King Canute who turned from invader to champion of the fens, and William the Conqueror's thwarted attempts to invade Ely. He had resorted to having to build a causeway to get his men across the water, and been beaten back when the wooden causeway had been set alight by supporters of Hereward the Wake, our fenland hero. We were taught that William only succeeded, finally, when helped to find a way through the swamps and reed beds by a treacherous monk. We disregarded the existence of a traitor in our camp and focussed only on the length of time our ancestors had managed to hold out against this notorious invader. We believed that, had fair play prevailed, they could have held out indefinitely as Ely was so well prepared with stocks of food and access to an endless supply of eels, fish, birds and livestock, and the water surrounding it provided a defence better than any stockade.

Cambridgeshire is the only county with 'bridge' in its name: a clue to the topography of the area where bridges, some still made of wood, span the hundreds of dykes and drains which criss-cross the landscape. Their names don't give much away, or provide useful reference. Angle Bridge crosses a drain at an odd angle.

The traveller might be confused by the sighting of a railway line and how many times the same road snaked across it. A good example of this is just outside Whittlesey, at Three Horseshoes. Another clue in the name.

Some of the names of these hidden places are beautiful. I was always inspired by Sutton in the Isle and intrigued by Old Knarr Fen Drove. Others, such as Pudding Bag Drove, Pode Hole, Runty Fen and Six Mile Bottom, just made us laugh. The meres were now drained but the names lived on in the conversation of the elderly: Ramsey Mere, Ugg Mere, Trundle Mere and, of course, Whittlesey Mere, which is reputed to have covered up to three thousand acres when it was in flood. Drains were often named after their measurements: The Twenty Foot, The Forty Foot and The Hundred Foot, or even more simply, their purpose, such as Catch Water.

We believed that our unique position would have saved us from invasion in wartime. The fens remained largely uncharted, many roads unmade and unmarked.

The towns, villages, or sometimes just a hamlet, might be only five or ten miles apart but seemed foreign even to us, often defeating the stranger who tried to find them.

Some parts of the fens were never drained and even in this twenty-first century, with roads linking all the former islands, winter weather still cuts these links and flooding separates Whittlesey from neighbouring Thorney. The Welney Washes become impassable by road or rail.

Good transport routes were slow in reaching the most isolated areas. As late as the 1970s, diesel was taken by barge to remote pumping stations still not accessible by road.

At weekends and during school holidays, we were unlikely to see friends from other towns. The distance between us seemed far greater then. I do remember the one occasion when I was allowed to invite a friend over for dinner on a Saturday. Her father dropped her off by car and I was so excited. I had never had a guest before. This excitement grew increasingly silly and we were both in a state of uncontrollable giggling by dinner time. We managed the first course behind hands that held back our laughter but just as she took her first mouthful of rice pudding, I made some comment so hilarious that she choked on the rice and spat it back into the dish. Of course, that was even more funny. Mother was not amused. My friend lived for ever in Mother's mind as ''er what spit in the rice pudding'. She was never invited back so maybe it wasn't just the distance between our homes that caused such isolation.

Some pupils lived in places such as Glassmoor Bank, so inaccessible that they had to be collected in a taxi to join the bus. Other girls arrived on buses: from Chatteris, which had once had its own dock and was considered to be the highest point in Fenland; from Wimblington and Benwick, famous for their rector and his musical compositions; from Manea, with its claim to fame as the chosen location for Charles I to build his palace, to be known as Charlemont, once the drainage of the Fens had been achieved; and Stonea, site of Britain's lowest hill fort, just six feet above sea level. Another girl lived in a house which had been built on the edge of a roddon and now leaned backwards at a precarious angle, because hardened roddons do not shrink and sink like the surrounding peat.

We competed with each other, quoting these anecdotes, but this was a time when the importance of history was being usurped by the impact of television fame. As all the buses lined up outside school in their various liveries, we knew we had the trump card. We might be singing 'You never go to 'eaven on a clapped out bus', but were the girls who arrived on a Bristol KSW, previously owned by Hammer Films and having appeared on the screen in the 'On the Buses' series. No history could beat that.

35 Coming Home

When I left school in the summer of 1972 there was no waiting with bated breath for the arrival of my 0 level results. The envelope was delivered and opened along with the rest of the post. I had passed English Language as expected. All the other grades lived up, or rather down, to those predicted. I had failed all other eight subjects. No great fuss was made about it. I don't remember Mother being upset or critical. She never saw any real point in education, beyond learning to cook and keep a clean home. She probably regretted sending me to grammar school where I had wasted my years and opportunities. I had gained an aspiration that only came to fruition much later, after I had my children and she thought I was settled as the next generation of fen-dweller.

She greeted my excited announcement that I was moving to Norfolk to study for a degree with a snort. Her only comment was 'If yer've nothin' better to do wi' yer time'.

She never grasped the concept that education was the key to opportunity if not success. She really couldn't understand anyone wanting to move to Norwich, 'Wi' all them 'ills to climb'.

Father gave me some support, saying, 'So buying you that uniform wasn't a complete waste of money after all', and I was pleased that he lived just long enough to see my graduation certificate hanging on the wall.

A friend pointed out to her that I was the first one in the family to get a degree, adding 'You must be proud'.

'I s'pose I am.'

Her expression said that the thought had never occurred to her.

In these parts, where a mother's success was judged by how many fine, strapping sons she raised, my gaggle of girls and a piece of paper that labelled me a Bachelor of Science, Hons, was not impressive.

My move was made worse by the fact that I took with me a boyfriend of whom she disapproved and her grandchildren, to a Norfolk which she perceived as a foreign land where 'folks talk funny'.

She was proved right about the boyfriend, the relationship didn't last, but I needed to break away, gain new experiences and give my children the opportunity to live lives with less limitations.

This caused a rift that was slow to heal. I visited her in school holidays and the children have lots of letters that they exchanged with her but it was not enough. I wanted to share my experiences with her, show her that it was all for the best, but she was reluctant to look at what she didn't want to see and it was a full two years before I finally persuaded her to visit us, for a day-trip. At this time I was living in a six-bedroomed former vicarage: a beautiful house with a large garden and woodland where the children played and grew their own organic vegetables. She was not impressed.

She muttered 'It's only rented', harking back to her dismay at the time when I had married, and achieved another 'first' in the family: the first to live in a council house.

During these years, the relationship was so strained that it was better to keep conversation light, not venturing into serious discussions. I took the children out of school to give them a better chance of success in an environment that was not governed by tests and league tables. She was mortified that they were not being taught by a proper teacher. Suddenly education was an issue.

I finally passed my driving test without her knowing that I was taking lessons, because I knew her scepticism would destroy my confidence. Only with my licence safely in my possession, did I pluck up the courage to tell her. She said to my daughter, 'I 'ope yer not gettin' in the car wi' 'er drivin', she can't even ride a bike roight'.

I knew I had been right to not expect her approval.

It was much later, and with new-found confidence, that I could look back and see her reasoning. She had always lived life safely, never taking a risk. I was headstrong and made lots of mistakes, never listening to the wisdom of age, only ever learning for myself. She gave me lots of good advice that I wasn't ready to hear and it's only now, as I mow the grass or hang out the washing, treading in her footsteps and those of Granny, that I can feel what they felt and appreciate their need to protect me, to keep me safe as a railway carriage child.

It was only in the last few years of her life that we started to come to terms with our differences. I strove to improve my life. She was content with hers. I craved adventure and met challenges head-on. She clung to her roots and her security. It took a long time for us to realise that it was not our differences that caused discord between us, it was our similarities. We were both headstrong, single-minded daughters of the fens, where generations had only survived because of their dogged determination and immovable faith in what they believed to be right. We were descendants of those who had battled with unshakable stamina against the forces of nature, defying those who thought they could bring a better way of life, resisting the changes that threatened their very existence.

Even as she became physically more vulnerable, she retained all her mental strength, becoming more determined than ever to be seen to be coping. My daughter who lived nearby collected her pension. My son-in-law kept up the garden. Neighbours did shopping, and she maintained, 'I'm alroight as long as I keep me independence'.

She wouldn't allow us to do anything to make her more comfortable as that meant changes. Following a fall she had to allow carers to call daily but she would not let them have a key, insisting 'I've 'eard about them. They come back an' rob yer.'

Eventually she fell again and broke a wrist: ironically as she was trying to get to the door to let in the carers who had not got a key. She was admitted to hospital and told that she could not return to the carriages in their present condition. She had no heating, no hot water and no bathroom. Her protests that she had lived there since she was fifteen and her mother had lived there without such 'paraphernalia' until she died, aged ninety-seven, fell by the wayside. Social Services were not happy with the damp and the company of mice that had taken up residence in the rooms that she no longer used. She was only released from hospital when she agreed to recuperate at the local home for the elderly.

This was a clean, warm place where she had full-time care, but she was desperately unhappy. It broke our hearts to see her lingering in there. She was often tearful, sometimes angry, describing the other residents as 'do-lally or 'alf sharp'. She pleaded with us to take her home but Social Services were sceptical of our ability to care for her.

I had worked for many years in the care-sector and had all the current qualifications, but perhaps they thought I was eccentric too. Whilst I agreed that she would need to accept some changes, I supported her decisions in other areas.

We applied to Warm Front for a grant to put in heating

but the authorities' insistence that she have a wet room installed was pushing her too far. She had never lived in a property with a bathroom, holding fast to her belief that soaking was not good for the skin, and sitting in a bathtub of bubbles wasn't good for anybody. This was an area on which she would not compromise.

As the wrangling dragged on she became even less willing to co-operate. She had lived all her life outside the system, from the time when she attended school if it suited the family and stayed away when it didn't. She had avoided medical intervention unless it was absolutely crucial and took no part in credit, finance or banking, saying 'never a borrower or a lender be'. She took pride in the fact that she had 'never gone t' bed owing anybody a penny'. Now she was being told what she must do in her own home and that was anathema to her philosophy on life where 'if yer don't bother nobody, they don't bother you'.

She even tried to beat the system by agreeing with the social worker that she would sell the property and move back to Ely where she had been born, whilst explaining to us that she wouldn't really sell the carriages. She would just wait 'til it all blows uver'.

She knew that the family would help her reach any compromise with which she was happy.

The professionals who were trying to work with her were as frustrated as we were. The further they tried to push her, the more that old fen grit came to the fore. She withdrew her agreement with Warm Front, refusing them permission to drill small holes to run pipes between the rooms, no longer trusting their assurance that the damage to the carriages would be minimal.

I sought advice from the Showman's Guild and the Council for Travellers to try to ascertain what regulations actually applied to the elderly who didn't travel, but didn't live in a house either. A railway carriage dweller didn't seem to fit into either category. Our rareness made it difficult to find a precedent. We wrote letters and attended meetings but it seemed that no solution was near.

The final showdown came on her eighty-ninth birthday when my son-in-law picked her up for a birthday tea with the family at my daughter's house. We all spent this last birthday with her, singing, sharing a cake and playing cards. At the end of the evening she announced quite calmly that she would not be going back to the home. We tried to explain that she had to go back there until we could legally remove her, but she was having none of it. I rang the care-home and explained. The staff heard her in the background, declaring 'I'm not goin' back there. I shall run away fust'.

Then came the biggest shock of all. We learned that no-one had got the power to take her back against her will. It was only then, after she had spent all those long, unhappy months in the home, that we were finally made aware that it could all have been avoided. She was free and on her way home. She stayed at my daughter's house and I moved in, too. The rest of the family rallied round to support us and we started in earnest to get the carriages ready for her return.

It was November, there was snow on the ground and everywhere was musty after being shut up for a year, but she was able to spend every day there, visit her old neighbours and sit in her armchair by the fire while we worked.

Now that she could see hope again, she became a little more compliant and agreed that storage heaters could be installed if it meant that she would be home sooner. She knew they were more expensive to run but damage limitation was her priority.

We laboured through that winter with her watching and supervising and hindering our progress at every turn. She cried as we pulled out the rotting pantry shelves that her father had put in, and the woodworm-ridden furniture that my father had built. We cried because she cried, and with frustration because she still objected to any change, and we knew we had to put her welfare before that of the carriages.

We worked around her, stripping the twenty six layers of wallpaper from the kitchen with the promise that we would paint it 'yella', the colour she had chosen from the chart. My daughters laughed when they heard the old story about choosing wallpaper and I conceded that now might not be the best time to ask if I could have ballerinas in my bedroom.

When I had left, so long ago now, it had felt like I was in the spring of my life with Grandfather's thirst for adventure pulling me to seize the moment. Looking back now I can see that his character lives on through the generations.

In the years before my youngest daughter went to college to study to be a mechanic, she became fascinated by engines. Seduced by the magic of Martham Carnival, we joined the Waveney Valley and District Preservation Society. With this group of wonderful people, we spent our summers travelling the counties of eastern England, exhibiting her stationary engine and my collection of model buses. From Cambridgeshire to Norfolk, from Suffolk to Lincolnshire, we drove in convoys with caravans and tents.

These old fashioned rallies were a throw-back to the era when Grandfather would have been on the road and I felt his spirit in me. We breathed in the smoke and steam that would have been his environment. We rode on the Gallopers and other rides rescued from the past and painstakingly restored, powered by the vast showman's engines that he had driven.

We spent hours talking to the old-timers who remembered this way of life and, after the public had gone home, we fell asleep to the sound of the fairground music and woke to the camp stirring in the morning haze.

It had felt like the summer was endless. I was free and joyous and exhilarated, but now I was getting to the autumn and, like Grandfather who had his summers of fantasy and returned to the family and carriages for the winter, I knew it was time to go home.

By now I had given up my job in Norfolk and was preparing to move back permanently. This was going to be a life-changing decision and one that I had not taken lightly.

Sometimes, during the long dark days of that first winter, usually when my daughters and I had tackled a marathon task such as knocking off all the old skirting boards or unblocking a disused chimney, we were covered in dust and grime and I would question my sanity, doubting my ability to live up to Mother's expectations.

Our album of photos from that time, show a family of dubious looking characters with black faces and fingernails that never recovered.

By February we had got into a routine of spending the days at the carriages with Mother, taking her back to her warm bedroom at my daughter's house at night. She had also started to go to church again, and to a group for model-railway enthusiasts, who were happy to listen to her stories and to share with her their DVDs and photographs of similar carriages in preservation.

We met some lovely people at that time who volunteered to help with the decorating and donated paint and wallpaper. We were also given a fridge and a freezer, though I wasn't convinced that she would ever go to bed, leaving them plugged in overnight.

My daughters travelled regularly from Norfolk and

Suffolk to help so progress was gathering pace. We were all feeling increasingly positive despite the dirt and the dust, and a constant smell of bonfire smoke in our hair. As soon as she got up in the morning, Mother chivvied us all along, eager to get to the carriages early to 'get in the best o' the day'.

The weather was no deterrent and one day, rather than disappoint her, my daughter drove us safely there and back on treacherous, snow covered roads. Returning at dusk, she carefully pulled into the space outside her house and slid straight into the side of my parked car. The damage was minimal and we all laughed because Mother was there and she found it hilarious.

Then, one night at the end of February, following a pleasant evening of card-playing and a nice supper, she suffered a severe stroke. She was rushed to hospital but we were warned that there was massive bleeding in the brain and little chance that she would survive. She never regained consciousness and we said our goodbyes with despair that we never quite got her home.

After the funeral I went back to the carriages with my girls and we all just stood and wept at the half finished dream: the tins of 'yella' paint that hadn't been opened, the material for new curtains, still unsewn. I found it very difficult to go back then and re-start the work, feeling that the purpose was lost, but the girls held me together, working with me to keep the project going.

There were days that spring, sitting among black sacks of stripped wallpaper and piles of worm eaten wood that crumbled as it was pulled out, when I wondered what I was doing here.

I slept on a mattress in which-ever room had a space, sometimes with a daughter, sometimes alone, always with my camera, recording this journey back to 1887, the colour of the varnished teak, the fragment of upholstery caught on a nail.

Day after day I boiled kettles and trailed buckets of hot, soapy water through the rooms, cleaning out vents that were still filled with soot from the time when these carriages had followed behind a steam locomotive.

A trapdoor into the loft space led to the top of the two rounded carriage roofs. They were covered in a layer of the same soot, filling the drainage channels which reached the length of each carriage, ensuring that rain was carried to the front and back, never spilling over the sides onto the boarding passengers.

Everywhere we looked there were remnants of an earlier life, sometimes irreparably damaged by time and damp.

At other times we unearthed items that were remarkably well preserved. In one of the bedrooms, beneath the dirt and cobwebs, under the six layers of lino, we found a newspaper that had lain beneath our feet, unseen since 1929.

Mother had grown up there without ever seeing these treasures and now I couldn't show them to her. I cried at that loss but I also had moments when I felt like a naughty child again, thinking that she wouldn't have wanted me to disturb them. I could hear her voice scolding me, saying 'Just leave things alone, will yer'.

There were banging, scuttling and shuffling noises. The family heard all these and tried to reassure me that it was only the mice or perhaps the wind in one of the vents that were now uncovered, but I recalled the story told by one of my sons in law. He had been staying at the carriages with my daughter and their baby son. He is a six foot security guard, not prone to bouts of imagination, but he spoke to Granny in the dark passage. They had never met as she had died several years before we knew him, but he described her perfectly: the long white hair and the lace collar of her nightdress.

Now, when they had all gone home at night, I slept with all the lights on and didn't look out of the cover until I knew it was morning.

One night when my little granddaughter was sleeping over, we had just settled on the mattress when we both heard a noise and looked at each other. She turned to the open kitchen door and reassured me, 'It's ok. It's just a bat with square eyes. I can see it flying around.'

We left that night without stopping to pack a bag.

On other nights we heard tapping, growing louder and more persistent, from Granny's bedroom, where she used to tap on the wall with a stick to say she wanted a cup of tea, and knock more loudly until Mother responded.

The noises seemed to be worse when new work was planned. I stood in the kitchen one day, saying to my daughter that I would like to take out the old enamel and wood sink unit, still with the maker's name plate. It had stood there since 1959 and had really seen better days. We were looking towards it when there was such an enormous thud that we felt the carriage shake. Our first thought was that a vehicle had come off the road and crashed into the corner of the carriage behind the sink. We both dived outside but, of course, there was nothing there. I made an immediate decision. The old unit would stay.

As the years have passed, I feel that a compromise has been reached. I have tried to preserve some of the features that would have made it their home and the ghosts no longer haunt my sleep.

I have repainted the outside of the carriage bodies to protect the wood from the weather and changed the colour but a small, oval piece of moulding right at the front remains blue, the colour that Mother chose, the last time she had them painted. Granny's candlesticks sit again on the dressing table. The washing lines that stretched across the kitchen have gone but the big old hooks that held them, remain in the ceiling.

Now we are ten years down the line and peace reigns. Beneath the history of my childhood, I have uncovered an earlier history: the signs warning that it would be dangerous for passengers to put their heads out of the windows, the doors with their third class numbers, and windows saying that the compartment is for smokers.

I have received information and good advice from the Vintage Carriage Trust and the North Norfolk Railway Society. Whittlesey Museum put together a display board of this last remaining railway carriage home in the area, and many local people have come forward with their memories of my family and the carriages.

My intention now is to preserve this history, hoping that my forebears can rest at last, knowing that this unusual structure with its fascinating double life is safe, still nestling in its pretty summer garden and creaking as it braces itself against the fen winds for another winter.

GLOSSARY

'o'ing...hoeing
'ud...would
'um...them
'un...one
a'bin...have been
a'gone...have gone
afore...before
agen...again
Aliwal...battle fought in sand
allus...always
an' all...as well
bassinet...crib
beet...sugar beet
bleddy...bloody
brazzier...bra
britches...pants
bruck...broken
brum...broom
buckshee...free
burners...brickyard worker
bushel...old measure
capers...messing about
casting...to hold draw-hook on carriage
causeway...raised on poles above marshy ground

chaff...left after crop is cut
chitting trays...for starting seeds
cinders...left over from fire
clo'se...clothes
clobber...clothes
club man...collector of payments
cluss...close
copper...to heat water
couplings...link to next carriage
Cremolia...brand of hand cream
cussing...swearing
d'...do
diggers...brickyard workers
dockey-time...eating about 11am
do-lally...simple minded
dolly tub...holds hot water and clothes
drabble...hang in water/damp
drawers...brickyard workers

draw-hook... connects carriages
droves...tracks for driving livestock
ent...isn't/aren't/haven't
fartin'clappers...source of passing wind
fellmongers...dealers in skins and hides
fer...for
fish weirs...trap for fish
fitters...brickyard workers
flat iron...black iron heated on fire
Flettons...bricks
Fly b'night...unreliable
forrad...forward
fourses...eaten at 4pm
frit...frightened
fug...smoke and fumes
fust...first
garb...clothing
GER... Great Eastern Railway
gew...go
gill...old measure
git...get
gizzards...intestines
goin'a ...going to
gotta...got to
gret...great

gunna...going to
headstock...part of carriage underframe
innards...insides
innuff...enough
jack a'lantern...probably rising methane gas
kek...cow parsley
kilns...to fire clay bricks
kittle...give birth
leam...channel cut to carry water
lick and promise...quick wash
lugging...halfcarrying/ half dragging
mangle...to squeeze water from laundry
mek...make
mesen...myself
mistle...fine rain
mo'orbikes...motorbikes
neckerchiefs...tied around neck – cotton
never-never...never pay in full
Newgette's Knocker... Newgate Prison door knocker
nigh on...nearly
no'wt...nothing
o'wt...anything

ol'...old

on the slate...to pay later

orkard...awkward

ornging...nagging for

out and outer...badly behaved child

over Will's mother's...old fen saying

palaver...fuss

picinnini...black child

pie-cot...fancy edging

posher...agitates washing

pruggled...rustled

rig-out...set of clothes

rizzled...shrivelled

roddon...old river bed

rubub...rhubarb

rummy...card game

s'artnoon...this afternoon

screws in joints... painful joints

setters...brickyard workers

short shrift...short measure

shunters...brickyard workers

slaumed...spread thickly

smudgers...brickyard workers

snook...crept secretly

soppin'...dripping

sossin'...playing in water

stays...corsets

stokers...brickyard workers

stove...cooker

stoved...pushed in

suck yer in...get one over you

summat...something

sweating cobbs... perspiring heavily

tall-boy...bedroom furniture

tanner...sixpence

tar paper...cover on signal boxes

tares...weeds

tek...take

th'...the

Tide...brand of wash powder

tie rods...part of carriage underframe

turbaries...where turf is cut

underframe members...supports under carriage

uver...over

varmin...vermin

water wagtail...pied

wet m'whistle...quench
thirst
wi'...with
will a' wisp...probably
rising methane gas
worrit...worry
wuss...worse
yer...your/you

The Mud Walls of Whittlesey

With thanks to The Mud Wall Group
for permission to reproduce this photograph
whittleseymudwallsgroup@gmail.com

OTHER PUBLICATIONS BY THE WHITTLESEY WORDSMITHS

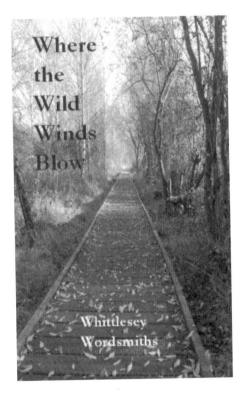

AN ANTHOLOGY OF SHORT STORIES AND POETRY

AVAILABLE NOW ON AMAZON

DUE TO BE PUBLISHED
AUTUMN 2019

A SECOND ANTHOLOGY

FROM OLD FAVOURITES
AND NEW CONTRIBUTORS

ABOUT THE AUTHOR

Wendy was raised in the two railway carriages that are still her home.

She is a freelance writer, editor and publisher of the local U3A magazine and occasional contributor to the Fens Magazine.

In 2017 she set up the Whittlesey Wordsmiths, the local U3A creative writing group

Follow her progress on her writing blog

www.wendywordsmith.com

48330455R00161

Printed in Poland
by Amazon Fulfillment
Poland Sp. z o.o., Wrocław